The
Spiritual
Woman

Also by Lewis Drummond

Love, the Greatest Thing in the World
Spurgeon: Prince of Preachers

Also by Lewis and Betty Drummond

Women of Awakenings:
The Historic Contribution of Women
to Revival Movements

The Spiritual Woman

TEN PRINCIPLES OF SPIRITUALITY AND WOMEN WHO HAVE LIVED THEM

Kay Arthur ❧ Vonette Bright ❧ Jill Briscoe
Evelyn Christenson ❧ Martha Franks
Elisabeth Elliot Gren ❧ Anne Graham Lotz
Henrietta Mears ❧ Jessie Penn-Lewis ❧ Amanda Smith

Lewis & Betty Drummond

kregel
PUBLICATIONS

Grand Rapids, MI 49501

The Spiritual Woman: Ten Principles of Spirituality and Women Who Have Lived Them

Published by Kregel Publications, a division of Kregel, Inc., P.O. Box 2607, Grand Rapids, MI 49501. Kregel Publications provides trusted, biblical publications for Christian growth and service. Your comments and suggestions are valued.

Unless otherwise indicated, quotations of Scripture are taken from the *New American Standard Bible,* © the Lockman Foundation 1960, 1962, 1963, 1968, 1971, 1972, 1973, 1975, 1977. Used by permission.

Text marked KJV is from the King James Version of the Holy Bible.

Text marked NKJV is from The New King James Version. © 1979, 1980, 1982, Thomas Nelson, Inc., Publishers.

Text marked PHLPS is from The New Testament in Modern English (Phillips), trans. J. B. Phillips (New York: Macmillan, 1958).

For more information about Kregel Publications, visit our web site: www.kregel.com

Cover design: Ragont Design
Book design: Frank Gutbrod

Library of Congress Cataloging-in-Publication Data
Drummond, Lewis A.
    The spiritual woman: ten principles of spirituality and women who have lived them / by Lewis and Betty Drummond.
        p.   cm.
    1. Christian women—Biography.
    I. Drummond, Betty.   II. Title.
BR1713.D76   1999   248.8'43—dc 21   99-18858
                                                                        CIP
ISBN 0-8254-2469-0

Printed in the United States of America

1 2 3 4 5 / 03 02 01 00 99

To
Helen Long Fling
Alma Hunt
Marie Mathis (deceased)

———————

With *Heads* full of His Word,
Hearts yielded to His will and mission,
and *Hands* dedicated to bringing all to
a knowledge of God through Christ,
three Spirit-led women
have blessed our lives and challenged
us to love and serve the people
of our country and world

———————

To be spiritually minded
is life and peace.
(Romans 8:6 KJV)

Contents

Foreword

The great need of God's people today is to cultivate a mature spirituality that speaks of, and brings honor to, our Lord Jesus Christ. It seems so many Christian women—and men—"wander in the wilderness" of mediocrity and never "enter the promised land" of true godliness. Consequently, they miss the real meaning of life, the church suffers, and the world does not hear the call of Christ to salvation. If only that scenario could be rectified!

To change that scene is the goal and purpose of this book by Lewis and Betty Drummond. Lewis and Betty have worked with my husband in various settings for many years, and they understand what must be done to develop a genuine spiritual experience of Christ. If Christians will exercise their faith in our Lord along the "steps" set forth in this book, I am confident they will begin to know a new depth and joy in Jesus—and become fruitful Christians.

The unique manner in which Lewis and Betty have presented their work makes for easy and exciting reading. Looking into the lives of contemporary godly women, examining the brief biography of each, and then seeing the spiritual principles and paths each one of these women took in maturing in Christ is quite intriguing. You will find it not only challenging, but very human—these women are real and know God.

Therefore, I most heartily recommend this book to all women, and men also. Read it, take the steps suggested, and find true holiness and maturity in the Lord.

Ruth Bell Graham
Montreat, North Carolina

Introduction

*A*s a new millenium dawns, we are witnessing a surprising interest in spiritual matters. *Time* reports that 54 percent of Americans are searching for some sort of spirituality, and this phenomenon is reflected in all avenues of the media: radio, television, the Internet, books, newspapers, and magazines. Major religious groups have multiplied in the United States to an astounding degree. Even Madison Avenue, "always keenly aware of cultural and social fads, has sought to capitalize on this trend" (*Current Thoughts and Trends*, September 1997, 28). The global dimensions are astounding. A banner story in the daily newspaper of Durban, South Africa, reads, "Mass Move to Spiritual Life." A NBC news item recounts the resurgence of spiritual life in Cuba. The former Soviet Union is ablaze with spiritual interest, and a report from Nairobi, Kenya, tells of a profound revival there. The whole world seems to be on a quest. Granted, a significant amount of current spirituality falls far short of Christian standards, but this prevalent sense of longing could open up doors for the gospel. Certainly it encourages Christian believers to take seriously the biblical admonition to seek a genuine spiritual experience of Christ. After all, as our Lord constantly emphasized, spiritual realities matter most. They are far more real than material concerns. For, as Paul said, earthly things are only temporal; but the spiritual is eternal (2 Cor. 4:18).

Women have often been in the vanguard of the development of Christian spirituality. This does not mean God reserves spirituality for women only. Any true regenerate believer in Jesus Christ faces the necessity—and the privilege—of growing in experience until he or she becomes a mature man or woman of God. But it is fascinating to see how often women have awakened to the reality, responsibility, and rewards of Christian spirituality. We say *Christian* spirituality, for that alone constitutes *true* spirituality. People are looking everywhere for spiritual meaning. They are trying New Age, scientology, Eastern thought, astrology, and parapsychology, but all in vain. Genuine life in the Spirit comes only through Jesus Christ. Such exclusivism may sound arrogant to some, but the fact remains that the Bible—our only authoritative Word from God—declares it to be so. We must seek spirituality through Christ alone.

This book presents examples of twentieth-century women who have made a significant impact in various areas and disciplines of Christian spiritual development. It describes what they discovered about life in the Spirit. Some of these women were actually born in the nineteenth century, but their lives and ministries have extended into the twentieth and are entirely relevant to our demanding day as we move ahead into the twenty-first century. Many are well known and their work extends around the globe. Others may not be as familiar to us, yet their lives exemplify the principles of the spiritual woman and what God would have His children be. Whether famous or unknown, God's hand has rested mightily on each one.

As we look into the lives of these inspiring women of the Spirit, we need to study what they attempted to share, and learn from their experience. The lessons of life that brought them close to God can help us see the principles essential to our own spiritual formation. We shall try to discover the steps they trod and, in doing so, get in step with the Spirit. That is the purpose of this book.

Gratitude must be expressed to all who helped us bring this work to fruition. We thank Ruth Bell Graham, who wrote the foreword. No couple in the twentieth century has meant more to the progress of God's kingdom than the Grahams. Together they have presented the gospel to millions world-wide. We thank Dennis Hillman, publisher of Kregel Publications, who nursed the book to completion. And it is hard to imagine what we would have done without our faithful secretary, Michelle Joiner. She has spent untold hours at the computer and has seen the work through many editings: Thank you, Michelle. To the spiritual women we have presented in these pages, many of whom made a real sacrifice in providing us with biographical material, we express deep appreciation—you are an inspiration. Some of the material in this volume is taken from two of Lewis's previous works: *The Revived Life* and *Love, the Greatest Thing in the World*. It is all presented to you, the reader, that you may be helped in your quest to mature into a genuine spiritual believer in our Lord Jesus Christ.

Our prayer is that we all will truly "grow in the grace and knowledge of our Lord and Savior Jesus Christ" (2 Peter 3:18). If that is accomplished, this labor of love will have been well rewarded. May God lead us all into a dynamic life with Jesus Christ as we strive humbly to grow into His beautiful likeness, for that alone constitutes the essence of true spirituality.

Lewis and Betty Drummond
Birmingham, Alabama

The Spiritual Woman Knows God

MEET JILL BRISCOE
A WOMAN WHO KNOWS GOD

*And this is eternal life, that they
may know Thee, the only true God,
and Jesus Christ whom Thou hast sent.
(John 17:3)*

*L*iverpool, England. A fascinating city and bustling seaport. For years ocean liners from Liverpool plowed through the waves of the Atlantic, carrying emigrants from Britain to America. It was here that the *Titanic* was registered. And down through the years this historic town has produced many notables, including, in recent years, a group of its best-known citizens, the Beatles. Countless other interesting personalities can boast of that leading English city as their hometown. On June 29, 1935, a baby girl was born, a child who would become a woman of destiny. God had in mind to use her significantly and powerfully in His kingdom; her parents named her Jill.

The Early Years

Jill experienced a typical English childhood. She lived in a good home; she went to school; she believed in God—and she was often a selfish little girl, as she later confessed. Still, Jill had no doubts about the realities of the Christian faith in those early years. She said, "I always believed in God, that Jesus Christ was His Son, and that the Bible was true."[1] She would one day learn to live those truths. Her parents, Bill and Peggy Ryder, did not attend church with any regularity, but they were good, hardworking, moral people, and they taught Jill the difference between right and wrong. From her mother and father she absorbed the principles of authority and morality. As a child, living in the family's little row house, she believed that if she did the right thing she was being good, and would make herself and everyone else happy. Doing the wrong thing was being bad. That would make her and everyone around her sad. Jill believed it, yet in her autobiography she asked, "Why, then, did I find myself wanting to be bad instead of good? Why did wrongdoing bring me enjoyment? Why was being 'good' dull and boring?"[2] Jill had many things to make life happy. She had fine friends, a faithful family, and carefree days. Like Eve in the garden, Jill admitted, she enjoyed all of the good things of Eden, yet she wanted to eat of the "forbidden fruit." Why was it so tempting?

School Days

When Jill commenced her education at the Merchant Taylor School for Girls, many of her friends enticed her into eating that "forbidden fruit." They would say they thoroughly enjoyed it and did not die. Why not Jill? She started nibbling, but only in such a way that she would not hurt her parents whom she respected. She told herself that it was just a part of growing up. She would pretend to be good when her folks were around and soon became adept at rationalizing her behavior. In her insightful little book, *There's a Snake in My Garden,* she acknowledged:

> I knew I shouldn't read dirty books, so I didn't. But dirty thoughts were better and could be indulged in behind the smile. I'd been told it was wrong to cheat at exams, but I could dispense with my guilt by arguing that cheating made for better grades, and better grades for happier parents—as long as I wasn't caught! But what if I was? Well, then I could always chloroform my conscience and lie myself out of the situation. Wouldn't that be kinder than telling the truth, which would cause hurt and embarrassment to those I loved?[3]

This cover-up, confusion, and conflict continued in Jill's life from her early school days right through her teenage years. But then came eighteen, and she found herself confused. Her life seemed empty and unfulfilled. There was something—or Someone—missing. That lack left a vacuum in her heart. She had tried all sorts of ways to find fulfillment, but to no avail. She discovered that material things would not fill the emptiness. The reality of that fact came thundering home to her one day when one of her acquaintances, a very wealthy person, committed suicide. She had another friend, sick in the hospital, who blamed all her unhappiness on her health. Jill was a strong young lady. She had good health, she had been brought up in a very happy home, and she knew security. Still, happiness eluded her; still, that vacuum persisted. Where did the answer lie; could there even be an answer? "What did I have to do? Where did I have to go? How good did I need to become, or how bad did I have to be to find—what? In my confusion, I didn't know what I was looking for. Maybe 'it' was waiting for me in another garden, or a new environment."[4] Then, right at that crucial junction and amidst all her confusion, Jill was accepted at a teachers' training college in Cambridge, England. So off she went. Maybe the answer could be found there.

College Life

Jill soon settled into college life. She majored in drama and art, learning the skill of putting on a smile and playing the role of a happy person, even though down deep within, her troubled heart kept her subtly disturbed. Life had become one long "play." When she was not "on stage," she felt alone, frightened, and unsure of herself—especially of people's acceptance of her. She sought their applause, but always wondered if they were *truly* happy with her? When the limelight when out, she felt exhausted, depressed, and totally unfulfilled. Jill did not know God—but the curtain of a spiritual drama was soon to rise on her stage.

Real Life Dawns

*Jill had no true heart experience that would give her
Christ's peace. And there she lay, in the hospital,
flat on her back, utterly confused
and miserable.*

In the midst of all her inner conflict, Jill fell ill with a mysterious stomach ailment and was sent to the Adenbrooks Hospital. For the first time in her life, she had to grapple with the reality of death. She now knew she had to find an answer to all her problems and questions. Jill had always assumed she was a Christian, at least a Christian of some sort. She believed all the things the Bible declared about the life, death, and the resurrection of Christ, but this belief never amounted to more than a mere intellectual knowledge. Jill had no true heart experience that would give her Christ's peace. And there she lay, in the hospital, flat on her back, utterly confused and miserable.

She had tried, really tried. She did not know how to pray. She did not know how to frame the words necessary for salvation. Jill had wanted to be wise, but had ended up conceited and arrogant. She had to admit that she was her own god. But how could she answer her own prayers? She was deeply sick in soul—more than in body. She looked up with her whole heart and cried out to God, "Help! Make me better. Get me out of here! Quick, stop the pain. Are You receiving me?"[5] Jill tried to be absolutely honest before the Lord, but would He hear her prayer?

The Answer

Then, right at that bleak point, the Spirit of God stepped into Jill's life in a powerful way. As she said, "I discovered that when I was flat on my back, there was only one way to look. Up!" As Jill prayed and cried, Janet, a Christian nurse at the hospital, came to her bedside. The providence of God had arranged everything. Janet told Jill the wonderful story of Jesus. She explained, "Jesus came and died on the cross for you, Jill. There He bruised the serpent's head and defeated him, but not before the snake had bruised His heel so that He suffered dreadfully. He rose again triumphant over death and sin and is alive. He wants to come into your life by His Holy Spirit."[6] What did all this mean?

Jill did not have a clue who the Holy Spirit was. Janet's words only conjured up misty pictures of old English churches where she had heard of the Holy Ghost but never the Holy Spirit. When Jill asked who in the world the Holy Spirit was, Janet just laughed. That shocked Jill. Did dedicated Christians laugh? Jill had always visualized them as far too pious for that. But the light was beginning to dawn. Janet painstakingly explained the nature of the Holy Spirit. "The Holy Spirit," she said, "makes it possible for you to possess the very life of Christ." *That melted Jill's heart*. She realized the infinite holiness of God and her own desperate need for forgiveness. Tears streamed down her cheeks as she accepted God's gracious mercy in Christ. Joy filled her very soul. Salvation, forgiveness, and fulfillment overwhelmed her as God's grace flowed into her life. In true repentance, Jill turned her back on the forbidden "fruit and tree of disobedience" and began to walk into a new life of fellowship with Christ. She had come to know this holy God through the Lord Jesus Christ, just as Jesus had said, "If you had known Me, you would have known My Father also" (John 14:7a). That magnificent day would remain forever in her memory.

Discipleship Begins

Jill was most fortunate at this stage in her new Christian life. Jenny (Jill's nickname for Janet) took time to disciple her, to teach her how to walk daily with Christ. She also told other Christian nurses in the hospital of Jill's conversion and urged them to question her about it. Jenny knew how important it was for Jill to share what the Lord had done for her, and as Jill later said, "Jenny was making sure I got plenty of practice giving my testimony!"[7] Of course, Jill could not give this testimony using a lot of theological terms. In those early days she had very little grasp of the Christian faith. All she could say was that Jesus had become her Lord, that she no longer controlled her own life, and that she now meant to live for Him. But that was enough—at least in this early stage of her spiritual life. She knew she had asked Christ into her heart and that He truly had answered her prayer. As she said,

> How did I know? Was it a feeling? No, it was deeper than a feeling, bigger than an emotion; it was an inner conviction. I was convinced with inner certainty that I belonged to Jesus and that he belonged to me. As the Bible says in Romans 8:16, "The Spirit himself testifies with our spirit that we are God's children." It was God's Spirit telling my spirit that he had arrived.[8]

Jill's life had been transformed.

What's Next?

*She realized that in the Scriptures she could find
answers that would help her communicate to others
what God had done for her.*

As she began to regain her health, Jill saw that she would soon have to leave the hospital and face her friends back at college. Now that she had been soundly converted, what would her old college friends think of her? What would they say? How would she answer? She woke up one morning, with these questions still swirling in her mind, to find a new Bible lying on her locker—a gift from Jenny. But the gift was far from ornamental. "Take this seriously," Jenny warned. And Jill did. God's Word became the living Word to her from that hour on. She realized that in the Scriptures she could find answers that would help her communicate to others what God had done for her.

Jill put her new Bible in a prominent place where her college friends, most of whom were not Christians, would see it when they visited her in the hospital. No sooner had she done so than she saw a group of them coming down the hall. Her courage failed. Quickly she covered it with a magazine. As they reached her bed, however, a Christian nurse friend wandered over— sent by Jenny. She picked up the magazine and asked casually, "Can I borrow this for Jenny?" And then the friends saw Jill's Bible. Conversation, once so easy, became awkward. Her visitors began to give each other sidelong glances and soon took their leave. Jill was shaken. She feared losing her friends. But when she told Jenny what had happened, Jenny was unconcerned. "What sort of friends are they," she asked, "if they ditch you because you found God? Anyway," she added, "if you do lose them, God will give you new friends." But Jill did not want new friends; she wanted her old ones. Did becoming a Christian, she wondered, mean that she would have to stop doing all the fun things she used to do with them? "What will I have to give up?" she asked. Jenny mildly replied, "God will only ask you to give up those activities and habits that are going to do you harm. And you will know what those things are. He'll tell you." Jill never forgot that answer. And when she asked how she would know God was speaking to her and how He would instruct her in right and wrong, Jenny answered with spiritual insight: "Here you are in the hospital. You think you have been laid aside by illness, but you haven't. You've been called aside for stillness. So, get your nose in this Bible and start. . . . The Holy Spirit will guide you into all truth. He'll take His Word and make it make sense to you. Start in the New Testament with the gospel of John."[9]

The Disciplines

Jenny aided Jill's spiritual development tremendously. She not only started Jill reading her Bible, but she gave her books that would guide her into Christian maturity as well. The little classics by John R. W. Stott entitled *Becoming a Christian* and *Being a Christian* helped Jill understand what had really taken place in her life. Jenny also impressed on her that she would have to grow in prayer and learn to let Christ speak to her. Jenny, always wise and practical in her mentoring, urged Jill to start with just fifteen minutes a day of Bible reading and prayer. Babes in Christ have to begin with "milk." She also challenged the new "babe" to memorize various verses of the Bible. Jill was off to a good start. So often when people come to Christ, they have to fend for themselves. How grateful Jill felt for Jenny's concern and interest as she was helped to establish a life of devoted discipleship with the Lord Jesus Christ. Under Jenny's guidance Jill began to understand Andrew Murray's admonition, "Let us not be . . . content with the hope that Jesus saves us, while we are careless of having intimate personal acquaintance with Him."[10]

During the remaining days of Jill's stay in the hospital, she read completely through the Old Testament book of Daniel. Prayer took on a genuine aura for her. She began to develop a true fellowship with the Holy Spirit. Before Jill left, Jenny challenged her to try leading some of her college friends to Christ. That was jolt for the new convert. "Me?" asked Jill. "Yes, you," said Jenny.

I was getting my fishing equipment ready!"
A whole new life had begun; she now knew God's will.
Spirit-led women do.

"But how in the world could I ever do that?" Jill retorted. Jenny assured her that the Spirit of God would help her become an effective witness. "But how do I lead them to Christ?" asked Jill. And Jenny had an immediate and simple answer: "Tell them what I told you." With that, she pointed out verses of Scripture that outlined the gospel, and sent her off to witness for Christ. As Jill said, "I was getting my fishing equipment ready!"[11] A whole new life had begun; she now knew God's will. Spirit-led women do.

Back in class after the hospital adventure, Jill was dismayed to discover that she still had to battle her old self—but she had God's Word to guide her now. As she wrote later, "I was not surprised when soon after I was converted I found the verse in the Scriptures that says, 'You desire honesty from the heart, so you can teach me to be wise in my innermost being. Surely, you desire truth in the inner parts, you teach wisdom in the innermost place.'"[12] Through spiritual honesty, she found that Christ does give victory.

As a young believer, Jill said she "inhaled" the biographies of great men and women of God. She read the life stories of Christians like Hudson Taylor, C. T. Studd, Adoniram Judson, William Carey, William and Catherine Booth, Mary Slesser, and Amy Carmichael. These giants of the faith became silent mentors. Above all, she felt a deep gratitude to Jenny, who had spent untold hours discipling her. Forty years later Jill was able to meet Jenny again, and the radiance of Christ still shone on her face. Because of Jenny— humanly speaking—Jill not only came to know God, she continually got to know Him better.

Jill soon learned that many things can impede spiritual development. Busyness often heads the list; it was easy to get so busy doing good things that the most important things never got accomplished. She began to appreciate the principle of prioritizing. As she said, "The art of leaving things undone is a learned art."[13] And so, early on, Jill decided never to let busywork keep her from walking with Christ and leading others to Him. Her motto became, as the Lord Jesus had said: "I do always those things that please Him" (John 8:29 KJV).

Thinking Big

Jill began to plan her first move. Even to this day, she declares, "I constantly ask the Lord to keep me from having a mini-mind-set."[14] She regularly sets before herself a project and determines under God to fulfill it. She confesses that she has an innate tendency to be lazy and the only way to overcome it is by being a task-oriented person. As she says,

> So what in the end can keep me from coming closer to God? I can! . . . What stops Jill Briscoe staying near to God? Jill Briscoe! . . . So whether it's ignorance, busyness, pettiness, laziness, or worldliness, it's our innate selfishness that needs to be hammered to the cross of Christ moment by moment and day by day. Who will take the hammer and fasten "me" to the cross? Someone has! For as in Christ all died—but in Him will all be made alive. There it is! I can reckon myself dead indeed unto sin but alive unto God. That's a mind-set that begins in my head, then captures my heart and finally sets my feet "a-dancing" with delight.[15]

Jill had unearthed the secret of what it means to reckon oneself dead to sin, alive to God and by faith, to walk in victory. That "deeper life" message resonated in her heart.

The Witness

God had laid an old friend on Jill's heart, one who needed a word of Christian witness. Her name was Audrey. Jill called her up and asked if she would come over for coffee that night. Audrey eagerly replied she would be happy to. Jill felt frightened, but she prayed that God would give her just the right words to bring her friend to Christ. Surely God would meet her needs. That evening as they sat with their coffee, Audrey questioned Jill, "What's happened to you? Are you going to a nunnery or something?" Jill writes, "My heart was beating wildly, but I knew that I had to give the best answer I could." And so she read the simple verses of Scripture that Jenny had given her to help others to Jesus. Then she asked whether or not Audrey believed the Bible. "Yes, I do," Audrey replied seriously. And then Jill hesitated. Could she bring herself to ask the big question: "Will you pray with me to accept Christ?" What would Audrey's reaction be? Would she drive her friend away? Finally, she summoned up her courage and asked, "Will you accept Jesus Christ as your Savior and Lord?" Audrey immediately replied, "Yes, oh Jill, yes." They knelt, they prayed, and salvation came. Her first convert. A thrill shot through Jill's heart as she determined to share Christ more and more.

She set herself another task. Visiting back in Liverpool, Jill decided to ask several friends over for a "get-together." Strangely, they all thought Jill had invited them to announce her engagement. What a shock when they found out her true reason! She had brought them together to share her testimony! And share it she did. They all left but one; but that one found Christ that night. Some of Jill's old acquaintances never spoke to her again, but the salvation of one friend surely proved worth it all. God continually deepened Jill's passion for the lost.

Jill, now well on the way to growing into a mature young Christian woman, graduated from college and began teaching in her hometown of Liverpool. She had a class of first-graders in a school there, and soon found she loved the work. She also had ample time to serve the Lord, and, as she discovered, "The mission field is between your own two feet." She realized that if that were true, she even had a ministry with her own pupils. She went to work on the children as best she could and eventually made a deep impression on them. She had the privilege of seeing many of these little ones come to saving faith in Christ. And there were other benefits too. That period gave her "good practice in breaking the Bread of Life small enough for them to digest."

Jill began to give herself to Christian service in the community, moving out into the real world where people needed to hear the gospel of Christ. In particular she became effective in reaching "Teddy Boys," the English version of gang members. She worked at the Chinese Gospel Mission in a depressed part of downtown Liverpool. She found herself preaching from a pulpit in a rowboat to people having picnics on the riverside, and soon was doing open-air preaching about town as well. Her growth in grace increased.

A New Future Opens

In the midst of all her labors, Jill began to realize that she needed a husband to help her keep her good ministry going. Yet, as she had to admit, "a Christian husband seemed as impossible a dream to me as a trip to Mars."[16] She had convinced herself that if she did meet an available Christian man, he would be "short, fat, and ugly." She feared she would be pressured into marrying that type by other well-meaning Christians. This, Jill vowed to herself, she would never do.

During those days Jill received an invitation to attend a conference at Capernwray Hall. Capernwray is a beautiful retreat center in England's Lake District run by the so-called Torchbearers. Major Ian Thomas, a great preacher and man of God, served as the spark and light of the organization. There, to Jill's utter surprise, she met the man whom she said "was to balance me."[17] She describes him in these words:

> Stuart Briscoe was tall, dark, and handsome, so obviously he was a temptation sent by the devil to distract me from following the Lord! Never in all those first days did it occur to me that God could give *me* a man like this. One evening while battling with my vulnerable heart, I read that Jesus sent his disciples out two by two!

Jill prayed that God would give her Stuart if that were His will. It seemed as if the Lord answered, "You surely need someone to take you in tow! Step into my plan for your life, Jill. . . . Say 'thank You!' Let's have a wedding!" And so, as Jill says, "We did."[18] A new life unfolded for this spiritual woman of God.

*Jill soon learned that a wedding lasts only for a day,
but a marriage is for life.*

Jill soon learned that a wedding lasts only for a day, but a marriage is for life. Many adjustments had to be made, but in God's goodness, Jill and Stuart found true happiness. Six months after Jill and Stuart married, it became evident that God had great things in store for the consecrated couple. At the time Stuart worked as a banker and seemed to have a bright future ahead of him in that profession. But it was beginning to conflict seriously with what God was calling him to do. Invitations to speak as a lay preacher began to flood in. A decision had to be made. Jill and Stuart shared a deep burden for young people, especially. Could God be calling them to full-time ministry? How they did pray!

The Call

As Jill and Stuart continued in prayer, it became increasingly evident that full-time service was God's will for them. God impressed upon the couple the admonition of the Lord to Joshua, "Rise up! Why is it that you have fallen on your face?" (Josh. 7:10). Actually, His will became so clear that Jill said they did not even need to pray about it any longer. There was only one response. They made the commitment. Stuart left his banking profession, and they launched out on their newfound ministry.

Jill and Stuart had no idea where God would lead them; all they knew was that the Spirit had called. They claimed the words of the prophet Isaiah when he wrote, "For you will go out with joy, and be led forth with peace; the mountains and the hills will break forth into shouts of joy before you, and all the trees of the field will clap their hands" (Isa. 55:12).

> *Jill and Stuart had no idea where God would lead them; all they knew was that the Spirit had called. They claimed the words of the prophet Isaiah when he wrote, "For you will go out with joy, and be led forth with peace; the mountains and the hills will break forth into shouts of joy before you, and all the trees of the field will clap their hands" (Isa. 55:12).*

The Briscoes' commitment precipitated a struggle. Stuart's father had recently passed away, and his mother was very lonely. Moreover, two different mission agencies had issued invitations to work with them. They did not know which one to choose. They felt assured that God would open the door He wished them to enter, and equally that God would allow them to care for Stuart's mother. But on which door did God have His hand? Finally, Stuart suggested they should put out a "fleece" as Gideon had (Judg. 6:36–40). They prayed that whichever society offered them a house would be God's choice. The night before they had to make their decision, the director of one of the agencies came to their home and spent an evening of fellowship and prayer. Throughout the evening, the issue of a house never came up. Jill and Stuart felt perplexed. Could this be God's way of closing that particular door? But after the agency director left, and as they were getting ready to retire, the telephone rang. The leader of the agency was on the line to apologize for calling at such a late hour, and to say he had foolishly forgotten to mention a rather important detail—*the offer of a house.* That settled it! God had revealed His choice. Jill said, "We laughed for joy." They packed and journeyed eighty miles up the freeway to England's beautiful lake country where their work was slated to begin. Jill and Stuart had a full-time ministry.

A Great Ministry

The Briscoes had the thrill of leading many to Christ. They conducted Bible studies and served the Lord faithfully. And God met their every need. As their work developed they found innovative ways to make the truth of Christ relevant and effective. They trained teenagers to share their faith, calling their teaching program "Operation Andrew"—a good name because Andrew brought his brother to the Lord (John 1:40–41). They began to visit the pubs in town, sharing Christ in that unusual setting. They would sing, testify, speak briefly, give out Bibles and tracts, and then spend time simply chatting with the people. Of course, they were always careful to get permission from the manager first, but they were never refused entry and always received an invitation back. What a unique impact they made! In all this, Jill and Stuart followed the Lord's will, for as He had pointed out, "It is not those who are healthy who need a physician, but those who are sick" (Matt. 9:12).

The Preacher

Stuart became a great preacher of the gospel. As the ministry grew, he served more and more as an itinerant evangelist. His traveling work, however, was very hard on Jill. He would be gone for lengthy periods of time, and Jill began subtly to resent these absences, although she had a difficulty admitting it to herself. She would cram her discontent into a hole in her life and not let it surface. But God spoke to Jill's heart. She acknowledged:

> I was amazed at how hypocritical I could be, pretending all was well yet knowing differently. I watched my senior missionaries and tried to copy their ways. I learned to wave my husband off on a three month tour with just the right evangelical smile. With a false earnestness which apparently all believed, I mouthed my usual platitudes to those who sympathized over our separation.[19]

Finally, she faced up to herself and laid the whole thing before God. Christ met her need in forgiveness and strength. She once more appropriated death to herself and life to the Lord. In resolving this problem she found victory in the cross of our Lord Jesus Christ.

The days passed into weeks, the weeks to months, the months to years. Three lovely children were born to Jill and Stuart: David, Judy, and Peter. "Be fun and be firm" was Jill's philosophy in rearing their offspring. And the children turned out well; today they all serve in Christian ministry. David has become a preacher, graduating from Bethel Seminary in St. Paul, Minnesota. He now serves as associate pastor to his father, Stuart. Judy received her Ph.D. from New York University and has written two excellent books as well as teaching in a seminary. Peter, a graduate of Trinity Divinity School, is senior pastor of a fine Bible fellowship church in Dallas, Texas. Jill wanted the best for her children, and she knew that God's plan and purpose for their lives would be the very best. Using a poem of Amy Carmichael, she would pray:

> Father, hear us, we are praying,
> Hear the words our hearts are saying,
> We are praying for our children.
> Keep them from the powers of evil,
> From the secret, hidden peril,
> Father, hear us for our children.
> From the whirlpool that would suck them,
> From the treacherous quicksand, pluck them,
> Father, hear us for our children.
> From the worldling's hollow gladness,
> From the sting of faithless sadness,
> Father, Father, keep our children
> Through life's troubled waters steer them,
> Through life's bitter battles cheer them,
> Father, Father, be Thou near them.
> Read the language of our longing,
> Read the wordless pleadings thronging,
> Holy Father, for our children.
> And wherever they may bide,
> Lead them Home at eventide.[20]

When Jill heard the first glad announcement that she would be a grandmother—and she was to hear it eight times more—she penned this little poem herself:

> Bent out of shape by this grand title,
> I'd like to kick against life's cycle!
> Unless I see beyond the name
> The miracle of One who came
> To light my life and give me reason
> To welcome this grandmothering season![21]

But now, back to England and the unfolding life of the Briscoes.

An Enlargement of Service

As the children grew older, Jill found herself able to travel a little with her husband. After they graduated from high school, the children accompanied their parents from time to time—a thrill for the whole family. It was good for their spiritual life to see the pressing needs of the world in places like Japan, Singapore, Sri Lanka, Hong Kong, and China. By this time, a worldwide ministry had opened up for Stuart, and the family thoroughly enjoyed traveling and ministering with him. Jill, herself, had become a very effective communicator of the Word of God. This gift meant she had to think out the age-old question of a woman's place in ministry. She was being increasingly asked to address audiences of both men and women, often in the setting of a local church. Jill tells the story in her own words:

> I began to read and study in depth and talk the whole thing out with Stuart for the first time. It wasn't the first time we had discussed the issue of what a woman could or could not do in the context of the church, but it was the first time I had been forced to look at all sides and come to my own conclusions about the matter. It took me all of three years to read and listen, discuss and attend classes on the subject before I became really free about taking those opportunities that were often a first for a woman.
>
> "I don't want to be a 'token' woman, Stuart," I said one day.
>
> "Think of it as being a pioneer instead," suggested my husband.
>
> "Promise you'll tell me if you think I can do what I am being asked, or if I'm only being asked because I'm a woman."
>
> "I promise," Stuart assured me.
>
> Having struggled to pull headship and equality together, I finally came to the conclusion it was a bit like believing in predestination and free will. I couldn't reconcile the two, but in faith I accepted both. Sometimes I acted as an Arminian, and other times I was a good Calvinist. So I applied this approach to the "women's issue"—it seemed to work! I came to believe that the man's headship was given him to make sure the woman was equal. Stuart had certainly exercised his headship in that regard. He had insisted on my equal partnership in all matters.
>
> Where ministry was concerned, if a ruling body of a church or mission invited me to exercise the gifts they recognized and confirmed in me, I was delighted to do so—under their headship and in an attitude of humility and submission. I

went to serve and not to lord it over anyone. If men in the audience questioned how I was using my gifts (and it has been known to happen), I simply told them I was being submissive to the leadership and the support that had been given me, and referred them "upstairs." This usually took care of things!

The Lord certainly has brought me a long, long way. . . . Humorously enough, it has been men who have set me free to exercise gifts some other men say I shouldn't have! When men debate "my gift" nowadays, I ask them to be gentle with me and instead of saying "women can or cannot do this or that," to try putting my name in there and say instead, "Jill can or cannot do this or that." Those who know and love me find that difficult to do! Gifts, I have discovered, are not gendered. I undoubtedly owe the ministry I now exercise worldwide to a husband who believes this with all his heart.

I sometimes wonder how many people would have been helped into the kingdom, encouraged by my writing, or challenged into service if my Stuart had not changed his ideas on women's ministry. I suspect not too many. And I think I would have become bored, frustrated, and angry—and not much use to anyone at all. For this freedom, I praise God and thank Stuart, and all the wonderful men in my life who have so consistently and insistently encouraged me to go for the gold with the gifts that I've got and, what's more, have given me opportunities to do so.[22]

Home was clearly happy for the Briscoes. But then, quite suddenly, there came a most significant changes in their lives.

America Opens Its Doors

One day Stuart burst in with news. "How would you like to be a pastor's wife?" he asked Jill. "A church in America has invited me to be their pastor."[23] Of course, over time they had received many such invitations, but never before had they seriously considered them. The "work of the evangelist" had always consumed Stuart, and Jill had always believed that Stuart's ministry belonged to the world. Was it right that he should consider limiting himself to one church? But the congregation in America persisted with phone calls and correspondence. The church was deeply convinced that the Briscoes should come. Somehow this felt different. "We're going to pray about it!" Stuart said cheerfully, as he set off for another three-month preaching tour. By this time, Stuart and Jill were having to say good-bye for about nine months out of each year. Naturally Jill was excited by the idea of serving one church, simply from the standpoint of having a more normal family life. But they had to know God's will in the matter. God's purpose was all that truly mattered. Jill earnestly prayed, picked up her Bible, and walked out to a lovely English hillside beside a rushing stream. She started reading the gospel of John and pleaded, "Lord, help me to go on reading until I sense your direction." She relates her encounter with God in these words:

> Continuing to read in John 21, I came to the question asked by the Lord, "Do you love me?" That was worth thinking about. Yes, I did love him, even though my love was weak and poor. As Peter answered, so did I, "Lord, you know my heart. I am fond of you!" Then he asked me as he had asked Peter long ago, "Do you truly love me more than these?" More than what? Than Stuart, than my homeland, my children, and my people? More than these? I replied, "You know all things, Lord; I love you a little, and I want to love you more. I would like to think I love you first." I think the Shepherd smiled. Anyway, he gave me my answer: "Keep your love for me the most important thing in your life. 'Seek first his kingdom and his righteousness, and all these things will be given to you as well' (Matt. 6:33). And now you will be shown the right path in this instance."[24]

The decision had been made—to the United States they would go.

In 1970, the Elmbrook Church of Brookfield, Wisconsin, a Milwaukee suburb, formally invited Stuart to become their senior pastor. When Stuart announced to the children that they were moving to America, one of the younger ones bravely declared, "I know all about America because I studied it in school." They knew a little, but hardly everything. Jill recognized that the move to a new culture would be far from easy, but as God had met them at every junction of the road when decision time came, He would certainly do so now. So they packed two suitcases apiece and off to America they went.

A New Country: A New Life

*They realized that where the will of God resides,
that becomes home.*

It was a real transition. The children were startled by much of what they saw as the family made its way to Milwaukee from O'Hare Airport in Chicago. They were astonished to find the taxicabs were bright yellow with words painted on the side. They had been accustomed to traditional black British cabs. Not only that, they noticed the policemen carried guns. This had never been the case in England. When one of the children asked why, Jill face-tiously answered, "In case they meet Al Capone." But these were minor things. When they got to their house their dog, Prince, jumped out and began to run around; he was at home. They realized that where the will of God resides, that becomes home. And, of course, the children were thrilled that their father would now be with them far more than he had ever been before. The family settled in well at Elmbrook. A blessed ministry lay ahead.

The previous pastor of the Elmbrook Church was Bob Hobson, a vibrant Texan. He had become a good friend of the Briscoes. Actually, Stuart had been preaching a series of meetings at the church when Bob Hobson had made the decision to resign his position and join the Capernwray staff. Stuart had urged him not to do so until the meetings concluded. The people would be unable to concentrate, Stuart argued, because the resignation would captivate their attention. Hobson agreed but only, as he said, "As long as you help me find a replacement."[25] And so it came about that the Briscoes moved to America. When the church actually called Stuart and Jill, one of the good members there claimed he had known all along that Stuart would be their next pastor. The arrangement had unfolded in a marvelous fashion under the leadership of the Holy Spirit.

A full-time pastorate for Stuart seemed strange in the light of his effective evangelistic work. But the church not only agreed to have Stuart as their senior pastor, they also encouraged him to pursue his traveling ministry as well. The rest is history—contemporary history. Both Jill and Stuart exercise a service for Christ that has extended around the globe. Their ministry continues to expand. To know and hear Jill Briscoe is to sense her heartbeat for God, for women, and for her family. As she strives to stay close to her Lord's own heart, He has blessed her with wisdom, wit, and disarming honesty. Jill has an active speaking and writing ministry. She has written or coauthored numerous articles and more than forty books, including Bible study guides, devotional material, poetry, and children's books. She serves as executive editor of *Just Between Us,* a magazine for minister's wives and women in ministry. She hosts a television program for women called "Bridges," seen on cable TV in five states. She also advises numerous nonprofit organizations, and serves as director for World Relief and Christianity Today, Inc. She is one busy woman for the Lord.

Lessons Learned

Jill has learned the "secret" of becoming a spirit-led servant of Christ. She has learned the principles of Christian victory and the power of the Holy

Spirit in her life. She lives out those disciplines as she shares God's truth with others. The people who have come to faith in Christ, and the lives of Christians that have been deepened and blessed through her, are countless. Thank God for this spiritual woman who knows the Lord.

Knowing God

Jill truly knows God. What a profound and sublime experience: to know God. When we try to grasp who God truly is, in all His ultimacy and His unfathomable "otherness," we can hardly believe that we can actually come to know Him. The classic *Westminster Shorter Catechism*, in attempting to describe in limited human terms what God is like, gives this wonderful definition: "God is a Spirit, infinite, eternal, and unchangeable in His being, wisdom, power, holiness, justice, power, goodness, and truth." And think, this is the very God who invites us to come and know Him. That is the basis of what spirituality—life!—is all about.

*God has made us so that we need
a constant influx of what keeps us alive,
and the source of that life is God Himself.*

Yes, Jill did come to know God. She became a spiritual woman. But a journey such as hers must never be thought of as the exclusive right of a select few. The Bible clearly tells us that the Father longs for all to gain this knowledge of Him. The matter can be summed up in this way: God has made us so that we need a constant influx of what keeps us alive, and the source of that life is God Himself. That is why we desperately need salvation, for Christ's salvation brings us into a vital, personal relationship with God, the source of life—a life that lasts forever. Jesus said, "This is eternal life, that they may know Thee, the only true God, and Jesus Christ whom Thou hast sent" (John 17:3). Anyone can come to know God and experience life in the marvelous in-depth fashion that our Lord Jesus Christ provides, if they but reach out to Him. It all begins in the wonderful saving grace Jesus Christ so freely gives—just as Jill discovered.

A word of warning: As we launch out on a quest to understand all that knowing God means, we must accept that it will be a long, arduous journey. This is only a big first step. Yet, we plow ahead with a disciplined mind and heart because we know that without salvation we cannot have spirituality. So let us begin.

Spirituality Begins with Salvation

J. I. Packer tells us that there are five principles in coming to know God:

1. God has spoken to man, and the Bible is His Word, given to us to make us wise unto salvation.
2. God is Lord and King over His world; He rules all things for His own glory, displaying His perfections in all that He does, in order that men and angels may worship and adore Him.
3. God is Savior, active in sovereign love through the Lord Jesus Christ to rescue believers from the guilt and power of sin, to adopt them as His children and to bless them accordingly.
4. God is triune; there are within the Godhead three persons, the Father, the Son, and the Holy Spirit; and the work of salvation is one in which all three act together, the Father purposing redemption, the Son securing it, and the Spirit applying it.
5. Godliness means responding to God's revelation in trust and obedience, faith and worship, prayer and praise, submission and service. Life must be seen and lived in the light of God's Word. This, and nothing else, is true religion.[26]

Truly knowing God is far more important than just acquiring information about Him. God reveals Himself through Scripture, experience, and the Holy Spirit so that we may know Him *personally* and *intimately*. Of course, we do need to know truths about God, something of His nature, His characteristics, His grace, His love. But we must *experience* Him if we want to know Him in reality. This is the goal of all theology. It is what thinkers have sought for millennia. God desires that we come to know Him in such a fashion that His life becomes our life—a whole new beginning. Knowing God means walking with Him in the warm relationship of Father and child, a relationship that transcends our limited human minds. But first we must realize our need for salvation.

The Need for Salvation

God alone is the source of all true spirituality. Spirituality follows salvation. Packer points out three characteristics of those who know Christ in salvation. He states that those who know God have great *energy* for Him, they have great *thoughts* of Him, and they have great *boldness* for Him.

Energy

Godly energy can be seen in the lives of significant women in the Bible, and throughout church history. In the Scriptures, women like Deborah possessed incredible energy for God. Deborah actually moved out on the battlefield with her general, Barak, and became the primary figure in the defeat of Israel's enemies. In New Testament days, where would Aquila have been without Priscilla? This great woman of faith was a significant leader in their house church. Countless other wonderful women of God have, through the years, displayed an energetic commitment to the service of their Lord, women such as Amy Carmichael, the Countess of Huntingdon, Susannah Wesley, and a host of others.

Thoughts

Spiritual giants have gigantic thoughts of God. Moses' sister, Miriam, portrayed in the book of Exodus, is a beautiful example of that principle. Her thoughts of God are dramatically expressed in her "Song of Triumph" (Exod. 15:21). And how thrilling it is to read the words of great Christians like Jessie Penn-Lewis, whom we shall meet later in this book. She had such high thoughts of God that her writings remain a constant challenge.

Boldness

And those who know God in the intimacy of His salvation have great boldness for their Lord. Think of Sarah, Rebecca, and Rachel. God was not only the God of Abraham, Isaac, and Jacob; He was the God of their wives as well. And we shall be introduced to several women in this book, women like Martha Franks, Henrietta Mears, and others—all of whom boldly took their stand for Jesus Christ regardless of circumstances. Down through the ages women have laid down their lives for the cause of Christ. Not too many years ago Lottie Moon, in bold self-denial, starved to death, giving her own food to the starving Chinese whom she served as a faithful missionary. Women who know God display a boldness that sets them apart.

It all begins with a recognition of our profound, pervasive personal need for salvation. God's salvation is the primary human need and the foundation of all spiritual greatness.

What makes people become like that: energetic, thoughtful, and bold for God? How can we come to know God in such a manner? It all begins with a recognition of our profound, pervasive, personal need for salvation. God's salvation is the primary human need and the foundation of all spiritual greatness. Why does salvation assume such a central role? It does so because in the final analysis, and at the bottom line of life, sin is what separates us from the God we long to know and the spirituality we wish to experience. Paul made it clear, "*All* have sinned and come short of the glory of God" (Rom. 3:23). We can try to attribute our actions to heredity, environment, and a million other things, but when it comes to an honest assessment of where we all stand, we discover that it is our own sin against God that is the ultimate barrier to life and happiness and spirituality. Sin is a barrier because God is holy and just.

God is holy. One theologian has described Him as the "Holy Other." This means He is righteous, utterly pure and sinless, and on a plane that we erring, sinful human beings can never attain no matter how ardently we may strive for goodness and righteousness. The Bible reminds us, "Our righteousnesses are like filthy rags" (Isa. 64:6 NKJV). At the same time, God is just. Because of this He must deal with our sin and rebellion.

What Is Sin Anyway?

We must have the righteousness of Jesus Himself to be acceptable in God's sight.

God's justice raises an issue: What constitutes the nature of our sin? What have we done to incur God's judgment? Sin can be defined in a number of ways. Some see it as the fulfilling of God-given desires in a manner God never intended for them to be fulfilled. Others understand sin as anything that violates our consciences. Still others see it simply as selfish action. An element of truth can be found in all of these understandings. The Bible itself is explicit on the issue. The Scriptures state that sin is "lawlessnesss" (1 John 3:4). God has established His law in His Word—and in the conscience of every man, woman, boy, and girl as well. We continually "do our own thing," thus breaking His law. In our hearts we know this is true. The Bible also defines sin as "missing the mark." This idea finds its root in the Greek word *hamartia*, "to miss a mark or goal." God has set down His ideal for morals, and righteousness, but strive as we may to attain that goal, we so often "miss the mark." What constitutes this "mark" of righteousness that we continually miss? The answer is Jesus Christ Himself. The Father has revealed His Son as the goal of all righteousness. We must have the righteousness of Jesus Himself to be acceptable in God's sight. And clearly, we regularly fail to hit that perfect target (Rom. 3:23). Therefore, we all stand guilty before God (Rom. 3:12). He is holy and we are sinful. The justice of God demands our judgment. Therein lies the tragedy of human life.

Judgment

The Bible tells us pointedly and graphically that "The wages of sin is death" (Rom. 6:23), death in every sense of the word—physical and spiritual, temporal *and* eternal. We all face a "Payday Someday." The reality of death as the fruit of sin brings to ruination everything that makes life meaningful and fulfilling. This is because it strikes a death blow at our essential relationships.

Let's think for a moment. Life is made up of relationships. We are related to God because He created us and daily sustains us. "In Him we live and move and exist" (Acts 17:28). Our relationship with Him makes up the very essence of our existence. We also live and move in relationship to others. The Bible clearly states, "He hath made of one blood all nations of men for to dwell on the face of the earth" (Acts 17:26 KJV). The creative hand of God has brought us into dynamic relationship with every other person on earth, regardless of race, color, culture, or any other conceivable barrier that would separate us one from another. We all share membership in the one human family. We all spring from Adam. Therefore, we all stand together in life. Whatever affects one, even in a far-flung corner of the world, affects us all. John Donne was right: "No man is an island, entire of itself." And finally, we are related to ourselves. "I" can talk to "me." We have the God-given gift of self-consciousness. A seminary professor once said, "If a dog ever looked into a mirror and said, 'Bow-wow, I am a dog,' he would no longer be a dog." The most advanced anthropoid does not possess this unique characteristic of self-consciousness. Only human beings have been so blessed. These three basic relationships—to God, to others, and to ourselves—make up human life.

The Sting of Sin

It is here, right at these essential points, that sin exerts its damnable power to destroy and bring about death. Sin strikes right at the core of our life's relationships, warping, twisting, and bludgeoning them almost out of existence.

In our relationship with God, the consequence of sin is a constant, nagging consciousness of shame. We stand guilty before God. Our relationship with Him has been severed. We are dead "in trespasses and sins" (Eph. 2:1). No peace; no quiet walk with our Lord. Sin has done its work. And, ultimately, sin causes a final rupture with God in the form of a place Jesus Himself referred to: *Gehenna*, translated in our English Bible as "hell." Unpopular as the idea of hell may be today, it is still and everlastingly real; our Lord Jesus Christ Himself talked about it. The fact must be faced. Sin has destroyed the beautiful relationship we had with God in Eden, and now we stand before holy God in death, desperately separated from His divine life.

Furthermore, sin has impaired our relationship with our neighbors. We can see this in a thousand different ways every day. Turn on the television or read the newspaper and what do we see? Murder, rape, theft, and violence run rampant among us. And that is not mentioning war atrocities, exploitation, poverty, discrimination, and suppression of human rights on a global scale. Sin can even tangle us in its ugly tentacles in our own homes. Animosity, jealousy, ill-will, rebellion, anger, selfishness, and a host of other personal sins can bring death to life's most important interpersonal relationships. Sin creates lovelessness.

This leads to the last manifestation of sin—the impossibility of a full relationship with our own self. We strive for self-oriented goals such as power, prestige, and material gain. These are the things the world applauds, and we are fooled. Worldly goals warp the human personality. They precipitate an "uptight" spirit, frustration, tension, and stress. And all the time we fail to see that our own sinfulness is the underlying dilemma. Though many would like to deny it, *sin is a real problem.* So often we let our hearts deceive us. As the Bible says, "The heart is more deceitful than all else and is desperately sick; who can understand it?" (Jer. 17:9). But we must face reality.

The wages of sin truly is death—death to everything that God intends life to be.

Any Hope?

God gives us a beautiful word in the Scriptures, a word that glows with the glory, grace, and love of the Lord. That word is salvation.

What a terrible dilemma we face. God demands absolute righteousness and here we are, immersed in sin. Can any hope be found? Our Lord shouts a resounding yes. God Himself has provided a solution to our deadly problem. God gives us a beautiful word in the Scriptures, a word that glows with the glory, grace, and love of the Lord. That word is *salvation.* We can be saved from our sins and their penalty. We can be brought to a knowledge and experience of God that completely rectifies and revolutionizes everything. We can be "reborn." Through this wonderful salvation our relationship with God is reestablished. Forgiveness and acceptance flood our life. God sets the righteousness of Christ against our record in heaven and in doing so forgives us for all our unholy wrongdoing, making us pure in His holy sight. What a sublime thought. We can be brought into a new relationship with Him and experience "the peace that passeth understanding" (Phil. 4:7 KJV). Further, we can be brought into a love relationship with our fellow human beings. The Bible says, "The love of God has been poured out within our hearts through the Holy Spirit who was given to us" (Rom. 5:5). God really does enable us to love our neighbor as ourselves. What a wonderful promise —and experience. Finally, we can attain fulfillment within our own selves. Knowing that we are accepted by God, and are in a love relationship with others who accept us, we are in a position to accept ourselves. "I" can live with "me." Our dream of self-realization is fulfilled. Salvation through the grace and love of God is wondrous—and it is available to us all. We can *know* God and experience everything His love has designed for us.

There cannot be even the beginning of true spirituality apart from God's gracious salvation, because without it we cannot know God. It all starts with salvation. We must be forgiven and saved from our sins and their consequences. No sidestepping, no rationalization, no explaining away; we simply must experience God's salvation if we are to know Him and, hence, know life as our Lord intended it to be. But how can this be possible? How can a Holy God ever forgive us, cleanse us, and grant us His great salvation? It is this that Jill Briscoe discovered in the hospital when Jenny told her about Christ. Jill found out. So can we.

Salvation Through Jesus Christ

We have seen and understood our desperate need. There is only one thing we can do. In consequence of this need we must *personally* turn to God Himself, learn of Him, and experience His wonderful salvation in Christ. Are we doing that? Does that constitute our quest? As a Bible scholar once pointed out, "To know God is to sense His dealing with us, and pointing us to His own Son the Lord Jesus Christ." What this means can best be understood by looking at what took place on the day of Pentecost—the Jewish holiday—as recorded in the Acts of the Apostles.

Pentecost was a dynamic day for the first followers of Jesus. Like the burst of a million atomic explosions, GOD CAME:

> When the day of Pentecost had come, they were all together in one place. And suddenly there came from heaven a noise like a violent, rushing wind, and it filled the whole house where they were sitting. And there appeared to them tongues as of fire distributing themselves, and they rested on each one of them. And they were all filled with the Holy Spirit and began to speak with other tongues, as the Spirit was giving them utterance. (Acts 2:1–4)

History was split asunder, and the Spirit of the Living God—the very presence of Holy God—came among us to lead us into the knowledge of Jesus Christ and all He has done to purchase salvation for us.

What a day! What an experience! History was split asunder, and the Spirit of the Living God—the very presence of Holy God—came among us to lead us into the knowledge of Jesus Christ and all He has done to purchase salvation for us. The city of Jerusalem erupted. Thousands gathered. They had to have an answer to the phenomenon.

The Message

The day came to its climax as Peter declared the first full gospel message—the "good news" of Jesus and His salvation. Peter began:

> Men of Israel, listen to these words: Jesus the Nazarene, a man attested to you by God with miracles and wonders and signs which God performed through Him in your midst, just as you yourselves know—this Man, delivered up by the predetermined plan and foreknowledge of God, you nailed to a cross by the hands of godless men and put Him to death. And God raised Him up again, putting an end to the agony of death, since it was impossible for Him to be held in its power. (Acts 2:22–24)

Every word in Simon's sermon is packed to overflowing with truths about God's great act of salvation through His Son Jesus Christ. Eternal, infinite realities were heard for the first time. Look at them:

1. Jesus of Nazareth was *a man*. It is Jesus' humanity that proclaims the Incarnation. Here resides the miracle of miracles. The infinite, ultimate, holy Lord God Almighty, the Maker of heaven and earth, robed Himself in human flesh and became a man. Paul expressed it so beautifully in Philippians 2:5–8: "Have this attitude in yourselves which was also in Christ Jesus, who, although He existed in the form of God, did not regard equality with God a thing to be grasped, but emptied Himself, taking the form of a bond-servant, and being made in the likeness of men. And being found in appearance as a man, He humbled Himself by becoming obedient to the point of death, even death on a cross." The incarnation of the eternal Son of God defies description. To think that such a thing could actually happen is beyond comprehension. But it did. God became man.

2. Jesus lived an exemplary, unparalleled life, "attested by God with miracles and wonders and signs" as Peter said. No one ever lived life as Jesus did. We have never seen one like Him. He performed miracles. His teaching surpassed all others. His sinless, perfect life revealed God Himself. He succeeded where Adam had failed. We should stand in awe of Him; Jesus was the sinless Revealer and Redeemer.

3. But they hung this lovely Man of Galilee on a cross. There He died an agonizing death. How could people have been so heartless and cruel as to take a man like that and nail Him to a tree? And what a horrible, ignoble way it was to die! First Jesus was flogged. A burly legionnaire applied a scourge—a whip of several throngs of leather onto which

were tied jagged bits of metal or bone—time after time, until His back was a mass of torn flesh. Then they crushed the cross-beam of the cross on His shoulders, and the soldiers pushed Him out into the *Via Dolorosa,* the Way of Sorrow. Calvary loomed on the horizon. Even though the Lord was a strong young man, He fell under the weight of the cross, and a legionnaire compelled a man by the name of Simon of Cyrene to carry it for him to Golgotha, the Place of the Skull. Then soldiers flung Jesus down on the cross and drove rugged hand-forged spikes through His wrists. (Contrary to medieval art, crucifixion does not take place by driving nails through the hands. The weight of a man's body cannot be supported by nails that way. In the first century, "hands" in common language, included the wrists.) And finally, the soldiers raised the cross and the Lord hung suspended between heaven and hell.

This gruesome scene went on for some three or four hours when suddenly, from that middle cross, came a bloodcurdling cry, "My God, My God, why hast Thou forsaken Me?" What an utterance! How could this be? The Son of God Himself was crying He had been forsaken by God. Mystery of mysteries!

Death by crucifixion came slowly. The victim continually strained to raise himself. If he slumped his ribcage closed in, and he could not breathe. So he would hold himself until he collapsed; then the agony in his wrists shockingly woke him, and he raised himself again. Up and down, up and down. The Bible tells us the Lord was crucified with two others at approximately nine o'clock in the morning. Dark, ominous clouds rolled off the Mediterranean Sea, blotting out the light of the sun. It was like a million midnights. One could almost sense that demonic forces were dancing around the cross in glee, thinking they had won the victory over God. This gruesome scene went on for some three or four hours when suddenly, from that middle cross, came a bloodcurdling cry, "My God, My God, why hast Thou forsaken Me?" What an utterance! How could this be? The Son of God Himself was crying He had been forsaken by God. Mystery of mysteries! But here we see the real heart and essence of the cross. The physical suffering, horrible as it was, does not reveal the deepest aspect of the story. Through the inscrutable *grace* of God, in that very moment when Jesus cried out, all the sin, rebellion, vileness, and corruption of every human being came down upon the precious broken body of our Lord. In that moment He bore the punishment and judgment of God for all our sins. He did not die for His own sins; He had none. It was for our sins that he suffered and died. He endured the very punishment of *Gehenna*—hell itself—for us. He became our great Substitute. And because of the cross, the righteous and holy God can now forgive and save us. God's full justice has been met. But that does not end the story.

4. As Peter triumphantly declared, "God raised Him up again, putting an end to the agony of death, since it was impossible for Him to be held in its power" (Acts 2:24). What a glorious turn of events! Death did not end it all for our Lord. God raised Him up for our justification (Rom. 4:25). Jesus is alive. He came out of the tomb and now reigns as the King of Kings and Lord of Lords. One cannot but shout as did the angels in glory, "Hallelujah, He is risen." He has conquered death. He is the living Lord who can bring us into an intimate knowledge of God and grant us our greatest needs—the forgiveness of our sins and God's glorious salvation. The entire demand of God's righteousness has been met for us all. The price has been paid. In Christ we become righteous before God. God actually imputes, sets to our account, the righteousness of Jesus Christ. As the Bible says, "He made Him who knew no sin to be sin on our behalf, that we might become the righteousness of God in Him" (2 Cor. 5:21). That constitutes the glorious "secret" of knowing Him.

It's All Grace

What a message of grace! The unfathomable, infinite, undeserved grace and favor of God has procured our salvation through the life, death, and resurrection of our Lord Jesus Christ. Make no mistake; the message is truly a gospel of unmerited favor. Salvation does not come through human effort. God in His infinite wisdom reaches out and in His great love brings us into Christ. Little wonder that John Newton wrote in his great hymn:

> Amazing Grace, how sweet the sound,
> That saved a wretch like me.
> I once was lost but now am found,
> Was blind but now I see.

Grace answers life's essential issues. John Knox, the great Reformer of Scotland, had a dramatic experience in the last hours of his life. As he lay on his deathbed, Satan tempted him to believe that he had merited heaven and eternal blessedness by the faithful discharge of his ministry. But Knox said, "Blessed be God who has enabled me to beat down and quench the fiery dart, by suggesting to me such passages as these: 'What hast thou that thou didst not receive?' 'By the grace of God I am what I am . . . not I, but the grace of God which was with me.'" The great John Knox went on to his reward, not because of his life of dedicated service, but by the grace of God alone through what Jesus had done for him—and for us all. Thus the Bible says, "For by grace you have been saved through faith; and that not of yourselves, it is the gift of God; not as a result of works, that no one should boast" (Eph. 2:8–9). It has been said, rightly, that "Christ is God's Everything."[27] Salvation, knowing God, comes by the grace of our Lord Jesus Christ through faith in Him and His sacrifice for us.

The Riches of Grace

What does the Bible actually mean by "grace"? E. Y. Mullins defines grace with these pungent words:

> Mercy alone . . . does not express the fullness of God's love to the sinful. In the New Testament this love is called grace. Mercy is the withholding of penalty, the pardoning of the transgressor. Grace goes farther and bestows all positive good. Mercy and grace are the negative and positive aspects of love toward the sinful. Mercy takes the bitter cup of penalty and pain from the hand of the guilty and empties it. Grace fills it to the brim with blessings. Mercy spares the object; grace claims it for its own. Mercy rescues from peril; grace imparts a new nature and bestows a new standing. Mercy is God's love devising a way of escape. Grace is the same love devising ways of transforming its object into the divine likeness and enabling it to share the divine blessedness.[28]

That strikes right at the heart of the matter. Grace plumbs the depths of God's love for us as manifested in the Lord Jesus Christ. A. H. Strong elucidates another beautiful aspect of grace when he says:

> Grace is to be regarded . . . not as abrogating law, but as republishing and enforcing it (Rom. 3:31—"we establish the law"). By removing the obstacles to pardon in the mind of God, and by enabling man to obey, grace secures the perfect fulfillment of law (Rom. 8:4—"that the ordinance of the law might be fulfilled in us").[29]

Grace is our only hope. It comes as God's great gift to us, totally unmerited. He just loves us.

Understanding grace we can know God as we trust in Jesus Christ. The Bible says so plainly, "There is salvation in no one else; for there is no other name under heaven that has been given among men, by which we must be saved" (Acts 4:12). Grace is our only hope. It comes as God's great gift to us, totally unmerited. He just loves us.

The Response

This does not mean there need be no human response to the person and work of Jesus Christ in salvation. On the contrary, a human response becomes mandatory. In Acts 2:37, Luke says, "Now when they [those who heard Peter's sermon on the day of Pentecost] heard this, they were pierced to the heart." What pierced them to the heart? It was the truth concerning the life, death, and resurrection of the Lord Jesus Christ or, as Paul put it, the "power of God for salvation" (Rom. 1:16). Then they who heard this message cried out, "Brethren, what shall we do?" (Acts 2:37). Peter immediately replied, "Repent." In the same way Paul later declared to the leaders of the Ephesian church that he was "solemnly testifying to both Jews and Greeks of repentance toward God and faith in our Lord Jesus Christ" (Acts 20:21). To receive salvation and thus come to know God, we must repent and believe the gospel message. But what does that mean?

Repentance

Today the concept of repentance is often minimized when we speak of grace. Yet there can be no question concerning its necessity. No one comes to Jesus Christ unless he or she repents. Remember John the Baptist's words as he stood on the banks of the River Jordan: "Repent, for the kingdom of heaven is at hand" (Matt. 3:2). The Lord Jesus Himself said, "Unless you repent, you will all likewise perish" (Luke 13:3). He explained that the Holy Spirit would convict us of sin (John 16:7–11). But what does it mean to repent? It means to change and to turn—to change our attitude and turn from sin to God. Our mind and will on eternal matters must be transformed. Instead of running from God, we must approach Him in deep regret for our rebelliousness. This entails an entire change of direction. While once we marched in any direction we wanted, serving and satisfying only ourselves—which is the essence of sin—we now "to the rear march" and face God. We step out in God's direction, determined to do as He wishes, to walk, talk, and live in accordance with His purpose for us. Simply put, we surrender to Him. We make the Lord Jesus Christ the actual Lord of our lives. We live to please Him first and foremost. Paul said to the Roman church, "If you will confess with your mouth *Jesus as Lord*" (Rom. 10:9, italics added), then salvation will come. There is no escaping this truth: We must repent and give ourselves utterly and totally to Jesus Christ. Such a decision does not make us less as people— it makes us real people.

Faith

The other side of the coin of salvation is a living faith. Faith is the foundation of favor with the Father. Andrew Murray points out:

> One thing He [God] asks, the one thing that pleases Him, the one thing that secures His blessing is—faith . . . we see that in the greatest variety of circumstances and duties the first of all duties always is—faith in the invisible One. Oh that we might at length learn the lesson: as there is one God, and one redemption, so there is but one way to Him and to it—faith in Him. As absolute and universal and undisputed as is the sole supremacy of God, is to be the supremacy of faith in our heart.[30]

True faith means we put our entire trust in Jesus.
Christ becomes our Savior; he invades our lives,
forgives our sins, and makes us new in Him.

Faith means we cease trusting in ourselves and our good works to curry favor with God. It means we trust God and His grace alone. And let us be clear again, faith is far more than intellectually believing certain truths *about* Jesus. True faith means we put our entire trust *in* Jesus. Christ becomes our Savior; he invades our lives, forgives our sins, and makes us new in Him. Faith becomes a personal encounter with God in Christ. In this encounter we surrender to His will for our lives and utterly cast ourselves on His love and mercy. After all, He is the One who died and rose again for us. Actually, repentance and faith are inseparable. We cannot repent without exercising real faith, nor can we exercise real faith without repenting. In that Divine-human encounter, salvation is wonderfully received. Paul brought it all together when he shared with the Roman church: "Whoever will call upon the name of the Lord will be saved" (Rom. 10:13). In repentance and trust, we simply invite Jesus Christ into our lives to forgive and control us. We cast ourselves upon Him, giving Him all we are or can be, and trust Him to meet our every need. That constitutes biblical faith.

A Total Life Experience

*We cannot come to faith and turn our lives around
by our own ability. God speaks to us and draws us
to Jesus through the Holy Spirit. If we open our whole
heart to Him, He will enable us to exercise true
repentance—and live a life of faith and victory.*

Faith permeates the entire Christian experience. It is central to sanctification as well as salvation, to consecration as well as conversion, to following Christ as well as finding forgiveness through Him. Faith alone pleases God and leads us to fullness of life.

We cannot come to faith and turn our lives around by our own ability. God speaks to us and draws us to Jesus through the Holy Spirit. If we open our whole heart to Him, He will enable us to exercise true repentance—and live a life of faith and victory. And the wonder of it is that in the salvation experience Jesus gives us of His own self. A great Chinese Christian said, "Christianity is Christ. Christianity is not reward, neither is it what Christ gives to me. Christianity is none other than Christ himself. . . . Christianity is not any one thing which Christ gives to me; Christianity is Christ giving himself to me."[31] As the writer of the book of Hebrews put it, "Having been made perfect, He became to all those who obey Him the source of eternal salvation" (Heb. 5:9). God sees us through Jesus. Jesus is our righteousness, our holiness, and our life. Since our own goodness totally misses the mark, the heavenly Father ascribes the righteousness of Christ to us. That becomes our eternal hope. The Bible says, "But to the one who does not work, but believes in Him who justifies the ungodly, his faith is reckoned as righteousness, just as David also speaks of the blessing upon the man to whom God reckons righteousness apart from works" (Rom. 4:5–6). What a salvation! What a life! If you have never made the decision of repentance and faith—or if you are not absolutely sure you have—why not do it right now? Remember how Jill Briscoe found salvation? So can you. God has promised, "Whoever will call on the name of the Lord will be saved"(Rom. 10:13).

The Spiritual Results of Knowing God

An infinite number of heavenly blessings and countless earthly satisfactions emerge out of God's gracious salvation. Our old life with its defeat, depression, and death is replaced with a new life of light and liberty as the children of God. The blessed Holy Spirit beautifully unites us with Jesus Christ. Wonderful!

A New Life *Now*

One night at a youth club coffee bar in a local church, a seminary student was talking with a group of young people. He allowed the "preacher" in him to come out a bit strongly and thundered an old "fire and brimstone" message. Although his message was quite true and very persuasive, when the session ended a young lady spoke up. "Well, I don't know much about heaven and hell," she said quietly, "but I must admit the desire for the one and fear of the other did not move me to become a Christian. What made a deep impression on me, and what brought me to Christ, was when someone told me that Christ could give me a *whole new life* if I trusted Him as my Savior." We must understand, as she did, that Jesus Christ not only deals with the eternal wages of sin, vital as that is, but He also gives us a whole new life. He restores our relationships and fills our life with meaning. Jesus said, "I came that they [all of us] might have life, and might have it abundantly" (John 10:10) and the Bible declares, "If any man is in Christ, he is a new creature; the old things passed away; behold, new things have come" (2 Cor. 5:17). Life is so radically altered that it is made new, taking on the very glow of God. It becomes life *in Christ,* "life on the highest plane." That is knowing God.

Heaven Is Ours

Of, course, God's salvation does offer the blessed eternal dimension; one day we will be in heaven, in the presence of God. And that is what matters most. Heaven is real. The book of Revelation (chaps. 21–22) makes this abundantly clear. In those beautiful chapters we have a vivid, dramatic description of the place where we will live forever. John shares five truths of his vision of heaven.

To begin with he tells us that the "new Jerusalem" (Rev. 21:2), as the name implies, is a new place: "And I saw a new heaven and a new earth; for the first heaven and the first earth passed away, and there is no longer any sea" (Rev. 21:1). This means there will be no war, but only peace; no sin, but only righteousness; no death, but only life.

Next, it will be an incredibly beautiful place. John describes it:

> And he carried me away in the Spirit to a great and high mountain, and showed me the holy city, Jerusalem, coming down out of heaven from God, having the glory of God. Her brilliance was like a very costly stone, as a stone of crystal-clear jasper. It had a great and high wall, with twelve gates, and at the gates twelve angels; and names were written on them, which are those of the twelve tribes of the sons of Israel. (Rev. 21:10–12)

Then, heaven must be seen as an inhabited place. The saints of old and of all times will be there—that includes our friends and loved ones who know

God. Above all, our Lord Jesus Christ resides there for He said, "I go to prepare a place for you. . . . I will come again, and receive you to Myself; that where I am, there you may be also" (John 14:2–3). The "light" of the city is the Lord Jesus Christ Himself and the temple of the city, God's actual Presence.

Further, that city is a comforting place: "He shall wipe away every tear from their eyes; and there shall no longer be any death; there shall no longer be any mourning, or crying, or pain; the first things have passed away" (Rev. 21:4). Think of it—no more tears. Jesus will personally wipe them all away. Get the picture? The fear of death vanishes and we experience the comfort of God's soothing hand.

Finally, the heavenly city is a place prepared for us. When we repent and believe in Jesus, we are promised that one day we will find ourselves in a wonderful mansion for eternity, a mansion our Lord has constructed just for us. As one has put it, "Think of stepping on shore and finding it heaven, of taking hold of a hand and finding it God's hand, of breathing new air and finding it celestial air, of feeling invigorated and finding it eternal life, of passing from storm and tempest to an unbroken calm, of looking up and finding it home." That describes heaven—our home.

Can we have full assurance Christ has saved us?
Yes. God does not leave us in the dark
on this vital issue.

Life at best is short. As the Scriptures put it, "You are just a vapor that appears for a little while and then vanishes away" (James 4:14). We *must be ready*. Eternity hangs in the balance. But how can we *know* we have received this wonderful salvation and thus *know* God? Can we have full assurance that Christ has saved us? Yes. God does not leave us in the dark on this vital issue. The Bible sets forth tests that will give us a definite answer.

The Spiritual Tests of Knowing God

The New Testament book of 1 John abounds with truths intended to give us full assurance that we have received God's salvation. One Bible scholar has entitled this book "The Tests of Life." In this short epistle, John gives five distinct tests to help us see whether or not we truly know God. As John writes, "These things I have written to you who believe in the name of the Son of God, in order that *you may know* that you have eternal life" (1 John 5:13, italics added). If we can give a positive affirmation to each test, we have scriptural assurance, the very promise of God, that we have received His gracious salvation. It is not presumptuous to say—we can know we have been saved. God wants us to know. He wants to dispel any doubts. These tests, therefore, call for careful examination.

Obedience

John first examines our obedience to God. He states:

> By this we know that we have come to know Him, if we keep
> His commandments. The one who says, "I have come to know
> Him," and does not keep His commandments, is a liar, and
> the truth is not in him; but whoever keeps His word, in him
> the love of God has truly been perfected. By this we know
> that we are in Him. (1 John 2:3–5)

*In Christ we have become a new person, and we follow a
new Master. Obedience to Him becomes our basic approach
to life. It is a significant test of our knowledge of God and
our salvation experience.*

John does not mean that we never fail in our obedience to God. We will
sin at times; we have not reached perfection yet. But victory over sin does
become our goal, and one day this goal will be completely realized when
Christ ushers us into His presence. In the meantime, God intends our lives
to exhibit a yieldedness to Him. After all, repentance means making Jesus
Christ our Lord. Lordship spells obedience. We must do the things He says
to do and refrain from those things He forbids. The apostle Paul wrote, "Are
we to continue in sin that grace might increase? *May it never be!*" (Rom. 6:1–2).
In Christ we have become a new person and we follow a new Master. Obedience to Him becomes our basic approach to life. It is a significant test of our
knowledge of God and our salvation experience.

Love

The second test is that of love. The apostle Paul tells us: "Now abide faith,
hope, and love; these three; but the greatest of these is love" (1 Cor. 13:13).
John picks up the same theme in chapter 3 when he states:

> Little children, let us not love with word or with tongue, but
> in deed and truth. We shall know by this that we are of the
> truth, and shall assure our heart before Him. . . . Beloved, let
> us love one another, for love is from God; and everyone who
> loves is born of God and knows God. The one who does not
> love does not know God, for God is love. . . . And we have
> come to know and have believed the love which God has for
> us. God is love, and the one who abides in love abides in
> God, and God abides in him. (1 John 3:18; 4:7–8, 16)

John stressed this principle more strongly than any other test of life. He saw it, as did the apostle Paul, as the *summum bonum,* "the supreme gift," of the Christian experience. If we love one another we are surely born of God. The word that John uses in Greek is *agape.* This word describes a quality of love that far surpasses human love. The human "love words" in New Testament Greek are *philia,* brotherly love, and *eros,* self-oriented love. But *agape* is unique to God and to those who know Him. Paul tells us in Romans 5:5, "The love [agape] of God has been poured out within our hearts through the Holy Spirit who was given to us." Only the regenerate believer in Christ can know this kind of love. *Agape* is utterly self-giving, always seeking, not its own, but the welfare of others. And it can only be experienced through the work of the Holy Spirit as the fruit of love within (Gal. 5:22). Love is an acid test for spirituality. We must ask ourselves, "Is the quality of my love for others of the depth and quality of God's love? Do I love like that?" These questions constitute a probing measure of life in Christ. Genuine believers do exemplify such love.

There is a second half to this test of love. John tells us not to love the world:

> Do not love the world, nor the things in the world. If anyone loves the world, the love of the Father is not in him. For all that is in the world, the lust of the flesh and the lust of the eyes and the boastful pride of life, is not from the Father, but is from the world. And the world is passing away, and also its lusts; but the one who does the will of God abides forever. (1 John 2:15–17)

Our love must not be directed toward temporal, material, secular, humanistic values and priorities. Our Lord said we "cannot serve God and mammon" (Matt. 6:24). Our love must be fixed solely on God and other people. If we are true to our profession, we acquire a new value system and learn to dedicate our time, energy, and resources, on the *agape* love level, to God and our fellows.

Righteousness

The awakened woman, the spiritual woman, the woman who knows God, can live in righteousness.

The third test is related to this abandoning of the love of worldly things. John said: "If you know that He [God] is righteous, you know that everyone also who practices righteousness is born of Him" (1 John 2:29). Our Lord wants His people to live a righteous life. True, we stand positionally righteous, justified, and sanctified in God's sight through our faith in the Lord Jesus Christ. That is why Paul could call the carnal Christians of Corinth "saints." But God intends a pragmatic outworking of that reality in our daily life as well. There are negative and positive aspects to this. On the negative side, we must abstain from that which is unrighteous. We simply do not do those things that displease God. This does not mean we can live in sinless perfection. We know that is unattainable in this life. But a person born of the Spirit of God must not live a life of habitual ungodliness, of practicing sin. On the positive side, our positional righteousness in Christ generates practical godly living. We now hate evil and love good. We cling to our Savior, wanting to live as He lived. Thus John goes on to say, "No one who abides in Him sins; no one who sins has seen Him or knows Him. . . . No one who is born of God practices sin, because His seed abides in him; and he cannot sin, because he is born of God" (1 John 3:6, 9). The awakened woman, the spiritual woman, the woman who knows God, can live in righteousness.

The Spirit

Then John sets forth another crucial test concerning the validity of our salvation experience: "We know . . . that He abides in us, by the Spirit whom He has given us" (1 John 3:24). The Holy Spirit lives and works in and through the lives of all true believers. Paul makes this very obvious when he states, "The Spirit Himself bears witness with our spirit that we are children of God" (Rom. 8:16). An inner, existential sense of the Holy Spirit creates in us a deep and rich assurance. We cannot rely on mere emotionalism to be sure, but the Holy Spirit does bear witness with our spirit that we have come to true faith in the Lord Jesus Christ. And the more objective tests of obedience, love, and walking in righteousness, are reinforced by the Holy Spirit, bringing these realities to our attention and making the promises of the Bible come alive in our life. We need to be conscious of the Spirit's presence, listen to His voice, and experience His peace and assurance.

Jesus

Finally, what we believe about Jesus is a test. John says, "Whoever confesses that Jesus is the Son of God, God abides in him, and he in God" (1 John 4:15). In this passage, John attacks the Gnostics of his day who denied that Jesus, the Son of God, came in the flesh as a real man. This is a theological issue, and good theology is as important as good living. John reinforces that principle by declaring, "We are from God; he who knows God listens to us; he who is not from God does not listen to us. By this we know the spirit of truth and the spirit of error" (1 John 4:6). The question thus becomes—do we believe that Jesus came from heaven as the incarnate Son of God who lived, suffered on the cross, died and rose again for our salvation? Do we believe salvation can be found in none other but Jesus Christ? Do we understand and accept the fact that we must repent of our sins and trust in the Lord Jesus alone if we aspire to know God? Do these great, eternal truths resonate in our minds and in our hearts? Do we believe these truths and have we assimilated them into our own lives? To deny these basic precepts spells death. To embrace them, John tells us, means that we are of God.

A Large Order

Now, these tests may seem a large order. It certainly takes time to examine ourselves by them. Heart-searching honesty and objectivity are difficult. Yet, our eternal well-being hangs in the balance. We give time, effort, and commitment to those things we consider important. There is nothing in all of life more important than having a right relationship with God and knowing the Lord Jesus Christ. These tests should be a top priority. No effort is too great for acquiring the rich assurance that Christ is ours and we are His. Make no mistake, God desires to give us full assurance of salvation and this for a very basic reason: We will never take one step forward in spiritual maturity until we have the assurance of being truly saved. Andrew Murray expressed it all so well when he said:

> The great work of God in heaven, the chief thought and long-ing of His heart is, in His Son, to reach your heart and speak to you. Oh, let it be the great work of your life, and the great longing of your heart, to know this Jesus; as a humble, meek disciple to bow at His feet, and let Him teach you of God and eternal life. Yes, even now, let us bow before Him in the . . . glory . . . the Word (the Bible) has set Him before us. He is the Heir of all that God has. He is its Creator. He is the Upholder too. He is the Outshining of God's glory, and the perfect im-age of His substance. O my Saviour! Anything to know Thee better, and in Thee to have my God speak to me.[32]

Conclusion

We have learned three things. First of all, spirituality is not spiritual unless it is anchored in Jesus Christ. We will never grow spiritually until we know God, and we can only know God through our Lord Jesus Christ. Second, spirituality has its rewards, not only in this life but most assuredly in the life to come. Third, growth in spirituality rests in the assurance of faith. The tests John gave us re-volve around spiritual disciplines that can create such an assurance. Those who know God live a disciplined Christian life. In a word, knowing God lays the foundation for life in its fullest and most meaningful sense.

Can we say with Jill Briscoe, "I know God"? Everything hinges on our response. Remember again, Jesus said, "This is eternal life, that they may know Thee, the only true God, and Jesus Christ whom Thou hast sent" (John 17:3). If we can honestly say, "I know God," then we can begin the journey to a growing and maturing spirituality. A poet put it all together beautifully:

> I had traveled life's way with an easy tread,
> Had followed where comforts and pleasures had led,
> Until one day in a quiet place,
> I met the Master face to face.
> With station and rank and wealth for my goal,
> Much thought for my body but none for my soul,
> I had entered to win in life's mad race,
> When I met the Master face to face,
> I met Him and knew Him and blushed to see,
> That His eyes full of pity were fixed on me,
> I faltered and fell at His feet that day,
> As my castles melted and vanished away.
> Melted and vanished and in their place,
> Not else did I see, but the Master's face.
> I cried aloud, "Oh make me meet,
> To follow the steps of Thy wounded feet."
> My thoughts are now for the souls of men.
> I have lost my life to find it again.
> 'Ere since one day in that quiet place,
> I met the Master face to face.

Have you met Him? Yes? Then let's join hands and begin the journey.

Prayer

Dear God, I do want to set out on that beautiful journey to spirituality. I know it all begins in truly knowing You. By Your strength, enable me to come into such a sweet relationship with You through Christ that I may experience full assurance that I truly know God. Through Jesus our Lord I pray.

10 Questions for Study and Discussion

1. How significant was Jenny's witness to Jill's conversion? What does this mean to us?
2. How important was God's leadership in the lives of Jill and Stuart? How does we find God's leading?
3. What is God like? What are His attributes and characteristics?
4. How do the attributes of God relate to knowing Him?
5. Where does spirituality all begin, and why?
6. What constitutes the content of the story of Jesus?
7. How do we come to know God through Jesus Christ?
8. How does God see us now?
9. What are the fruits of salvation?
10. What are the "tests" of a true salvation experience, and why are they significant?

The Spiritual Woman Submits to God

MEET AMANDA SMITH
A WOMAN WHO SUBMITTED TO GOD

Submit therefore to God.
(James 4:7)

*A*manda Smith knew what living in "submission" meant—her mother and her father were both slaves. Born at Long Green, Maryland, on January 23, 1837, to Mariam and Samuel Berry, Amanda began life in an oppressive system in which she was "owned" by another.

It is safe to assume that Amanda became accustomed to submitting to authority figures as a consequence of her early exposure to slavery. Later, when she came to know Jesus Christ, she was able to turn her knowledge of subjection into the godly quality of righteous submission. Her upbringing contributed as well. Her parents had brought their children up well, making them behave. Moreover, unjustified and terrible as the system was, Amanda said her parents were fortunate enough to have "a good master and mistress,"[1] and they were treated with relative kindness. Through grace, authority in varying forms exerted an early influence on Amanda, preparing her for future service. After her conversion she became known as "the King's daughter." And as a daughter she learned to love and obey her new "King." Thus, the providence of God laid a foundation in her for a life of submission to the revealed will of Jesus Christ. Submission constitutes an essential part of the spiritual woman. We have a great deal to learn from Amanda.

Freedom at Last

Amanda's father labored hard for his owners and, by working extra hours, he was allowed in time to secure the emancipation of his entire household.

Because she was quite young when her father bought his family's freedom, Amanda never directly experienced the adult pressures of submitting to an earthly "master." Yet, she understood discipline from the general ethos of her situation. She also experienced it from her mother and father, but this discipline had a solid Christian ring to it. Both Amanda's parents were devout believers and both had been taught to read. Every Sunday morning after breakfast her father would gather the children around him and share God's Word. The family always asked the Lord's blessings at mealtimes. And before the children jumped into their little beds at night, they invariably spent time in prayer. Amanda said she never went to sleep without saying the Lord's Prayer as she had been taught to do by her mother. All this created a positive atmosphere, and the little girl cherished her freedom and happy home. This background, the legacy of her slave days along with her parents' firm guidance, made a lasting impression that later in life helped her understand total submission to the will of God.

School Days

Amanda started school at the age of eight. Her teacher, Miss Isabel, was the daughter of a Methodist minister, a man called Henry Dull—but Isabel could never be accused of being a "dull" teacher. She conducted the small private school where she taught with graciousness and kindness. It was here that Amanda had her first spelling lesson. This proved to be a limited educational experience, however. Since the school only opened its doors in the summertime, Amanda received no more than six weeks of training at a time. Still, she thrilled at the prospect of learning and told how delighted she felt when she first read the words, "the house, the tree, the dog, the cow."[2] These early school days only lasted about a year in all, and Amanda was unable to attend school again until she turned thirteen years of age. Even then she had to trek five miles with her brother to the schoolhouse. Her mother and father were anxious for their children to be educated and saw to it that they made the daily hike. Amanda studied hard as one of five or six African-American children in the predominately white school. These proved to be happy, productive days for her.

Spiritual Stirrings

Eventually the family moved to Strusburg, Maryland. In that city, while Amanda was attending school, a great old-fashioned revival broke out at the local Allbright Church, with scores of people being converted. These meetings went on for five weeks, and Amanda felt the "awe" that filled them. When the Allbright Church services finally closed, revival services commenced at the Methodist Church. Amanda attended there as well. Though black people were always very welcome to attend, none of them "went forward" for prayer. One night one of the members of the Methodist congregation, Miss Mary Bloser, spoke to the worshipers. Right in the middle of her address, she walked up to Amanda, "a poor colored girl," as Amanda described herself, sitting near the back door, in tears. Mary asked her to go forward and Amanda responded. As she knelt at the altar with Mary's arms about her, she prayed. Amanda confessed that, though she prayed as best she could, it was still a rather ignorant prayer.

> *She quietly confessed, and only then did her heart rest in perfect peace. She made her way home with the childlike resolve, "that I would be the Lord's and live for Him." Her spiritual journey had begun.*

After a time Amanda turned to leave but found that she had difficulty standing. Some nearby folk took hold of her and helped her to her feet. Slowly her strength returned, yet still she felt afraid to take a step. She quietly confessed, and only then did her heart rest in perfect peace. She made her way home with the childlike resolve, "that I would be the Lord's and live for Him."[3] Her spiritual journey had begun.

Happy and bright days followed. Amanda sang and worked and rejoiced in her newfound experience. She joined the church and threw herself into learning more about Christ. She still had not really come to true saving faith in the Lord Jesus, but that would come; she was on a pilgrimage to the cross.

To encourage Amanda as her interest in spiritual things grew, her mother and father joined the church. In spite of this support, her deepening understanding of the religious life did not always prove easy. For a while she got caught up in the arguments of the skeptics. They blinded her until she was unsure if she even believed in the existence of God. She muddled along in that state for some days. As her need deepened it seemed to Amanda that the Lord Jesus was speaking to her in the words of the poet.

> When Jesus saw me from on high,
> Beheld my soul in ruin lie,
> He looked at me with pitying eye,
> And said to me as he passed by,
> "With God you have no union."[4]

God's Great Move

Then, right at that crucial junction, the Spirit of God dramatically stepped in. While visiting with her aunt one day, the young "skeptic" grasped an opportunity to unburden her troubled mind and heart. Amanda recorded the story:

> My aunt was very religiously inclined, naturally. She was much like my mother in spirit. So as we walked along, crossing the long bridge, at that time a mile and a quarter long, we stopped, and were looking off in the water. Aunt said, "How wonderfully God has created everything, the sky, and the great waters, etc."
>
> Then I let out with my biggest gun; I said, "How do you know there is a God?" and went on with just such an air as a poor, blind, ignorant infidel is capable of putting on. My aunt turned and looked at me with a look that went through me like an arrow; then stamping her foot, she said:
>
> "Don't you ever speak to me again. Anybody that had as good a Christian mother as you had, and was raised as you have been, to speak so to me. I don't want to talk to you." And God broke the snare. I felt deliverance from that hour. How many times I have thanked God for my aunt's help. If she had argued with me I don't believe I should ever have got out of that snare of the devil.[5]

After her crisis of belief had been resolved, Amanda set out earnestly, as never before, to know the Lord in truth and reality. Her conversion loomed on the immediate horizon.

Conversion

Soon after this incident Amanda fell suddenly and very seriously ill, so much so that the doctors gave her up for lost. Her own physician said all hope of recovery was gone and she would soon die. Amanda's father came into the sickroom and said to her, "Amanda, my child, you know the doctors say you must die; they can do no more for you, and now, my child, you must pray." But Amanda was so utterly tired she just wanted to sleep, and she drifted off into what was probably a semicomatose state. In that state she had a vision of beautiful angels standing at the foot of her bed speaking to her. Three times they repeated, "Go back, go back, go back." While in this "trance" Amanda seemed to see herself at a great camp meeting (camp meetings were held all over the country at that time) with thousands of people gathered. She herself was sharing the glorious gospel of Jesus Christ with the crowd, standing up with a large Bible, and unfolding the passage, "And I, if I be lifted up from the earth, will draw all men to Myself" (John 12:32).

Amanda was caught up in this vision for some two hours. When she finally awakened, she felt decidedly better. Her father called the doctor in. After examining her, the physician was absolutely astonished; Amanda was on her way to recovery. In a few days she found herself able to sit up, and in a week or ten days, to walk about. Then and there Amanda determined she would once and for all get it settled in her heart and mind that her commitment to Jesus Christ was genuine and real. She must know she had been truly "born again."

A Crisis Moment

She threw herself down and began to pray with all of her heart, "Oh, Lord, have mercy on me! Oh, Lord, have mercy on me! Oh, Lord, save me."

At a "watchnight meeting" in a Baptist church where a traditional revival had started, God gripped her heart. She was sitting near the back door as the preacher invited people to come forward for prayer. Amanda had had no intention of repeating what she had done as a child. Yet suddenly, as she expressed it, "I never did know how, but when I found myself I was down the aisle and halfway up to the altar. All at once it came to me, 'There, now, you have always said you would never go forward to an altar, and there you are going.'"[6] She threw herself down and began to pray with all of her heart,

"Oh, Lord, have mercy on me! Oh, Lord, have mercy on me! Oh, Lord, save me." She cried out until she all but lost her voice. Although praying as fervently as she could, she acknowledged she did not really know how to exercise faith and still peace did not come. But the occasion catapulted her into a time of urgent prayer, day and night, for light and peace.

Amanda would fast and pray, read the Bible and pray some more, constantly seeking the peace of Christ in her life. It seemed as though Satan was deceiving her into thinking that God would never receive her. The Devil would say to her, "You had better give up; God won't hear you, you are such a sinner."[7]

Peace at Last

Then finally one day, it all became blessedly clear. As Amanda expressed it, "Why, the sun has always obeyed God, and kept its place in the heavens, and the moon and stars have always obeyed God, and kept their place in the heavens, the wind has always obeyed God, they all have obeyed."[8] In the throes of such praying, she felt a true understanding of the submission and obedience needed for God to find His way into her heart. On March 17, 1856 (she could date it), while she sat at the kitchen table struggling to pray—and tempted by Satan not to—the Lord told her to pray once more. She cried out, "I will." The Devil tempted her again, urging her to stop. But she cried out once more, "Yes, I will." And, in her own words,

> When I said, "Yes, I will," it seemed to me the emphasis was on the "will" and I felt it from the crown of my head clear through me, "I WILL," and I got on my feet and said, "I will pray once more, and if there is any such thing as salvation, I am determined to have it this afternoon or die."[9]

After Amanda's struggle to submit all to God, the light dawned. As she said:

> I sprang to my feet, all around was light, I was new. I looked at my hands, they looked new; I took hold of myself said, "Why, I am new, I am new all over." I clapped my hands; I ran up out of the cellar, I walked up and down the kitchen floor. Praise the Lord! There seemed to be a halo of light all over me. The change was so real and so thorough that I have often said that if I had been as black as ink or as green as grass or as white as snow, I would not have been frightened.[10]

Amanda felt so happy that she began to sing the grand old hymn:

O how happy are they, who their Saviour obey,
   And have laid up their treasures above;
Tongue can never express the sweet comfort and peace,
   Of a soul in its earliest love.

*The key to it all? She simply said, "I will."
That is what God wanted to hear. She had become
a new woman in Christ.*

At long last Amanda had found peace through absolute submission to God. The key to it all? She simply said, *"I will."* That is what God wanted to hear. She had become a new woman in Christ. That deep surrender to the Lord Jesus brought salvation and peace to her heart. And she was able to carry that commitment throughout her life of service and devotion. Each day presented a fresh opportunity to surrender to God. Though Amanda Smith's life began in the last half of the nineteenth century, her service to Jesus Christ reached well into the twentieth. And what an example of the submissive life this devoted, spiritual Christian has given us. She stands tall in the ranks of godly women who know what genuine spirituality is all about. And it is that spirit which constitutes the point: Submission becomes a lifestyle for the spiritual seeker. True spirituality has its roots in continual and absolute submission to the lordship of Jesus Christ.

An Obedient Life of Service

After Amanda's dramatic experience of submission to the saving grace and absolute lordship of Jesus Christ, her life unfolded in an incredible fashion. God raised up the little ex-slave girl and moved her into a marvelous ministry of sharing the gospel. Doors of service opened in America and then in other parts of the world. She learned, as she herself expressed it, that, "Jesus is a mighty Captain." She found that submission to that Captain brought a spiritual reality into her life that can only be described as remarkable and rewarding. The dynamic presence and leadership of the Holy Spirit had become a vital reality. One chapter in her autobiography is entitled, "Obedience—the Secret of His Presence." This is absolutely correct: Obedience is indeed the secret of experiencing His continual presence. Through it spirituality grows.

Struggles

This does not mean the submissive Christian has no struggles. On the contrary, Amanda discovered that a life of submission means a life of spiritual conflict and warfare. For example, when God began to expand her ministry and service, she felt led to go to England to serve Jesus Christ there.

Amanda's account of the struggle over God's leadership is a fascinating story of obedience. Let us hear it in her own words:

> So that night when I went home and got ready for bed, the thought came to me, "You know that lady told you to pray about going to England." I said, "Yes, that is so." I thought a moment and said to myself: "Go to England! Amanda Smith, the coloured washwoman, go to England! No, I am not going to pray a bit; I have to ask the Lord for so many things that I really need, that I am not going to bother Him with what I don't need. It does well enough for swell people to go, not for me."
>
> So after I had this little talk all to myself, I said my prayers and went to bed. On Tuesday afternoon, I was invited to tea to Brother Parker's. Dr. Parker's brother, a young man, had just come from the Old Country. The young man was telling of his pleasant voyage across the sea. He said that the sea was beautiful and calm as a mill pond.
>
> I listened attentively to all, for I never knew the sea was calm. My idea of the great sea was that it was always rough and tossing. I have learned a great deal about it since then.
>
> Miss Price sat opposite at the table, and as she had crossed several times herself, she said, "There, Mrs. Smith, you see what a pleasant time we could have on board the steamer."
>
> "Yes, but it costs money to go to England, and none but swell folks can go."
>
> "You need not trouble about that," she said, "if you say you will go, I will see to that part."
>
> That was a new version of it. That night when I went home, I knelt down and said, "Lord, if Thou dost want me to go to England, make it very clear. I don't know what I would do there; I don't know anybody, but if Thou dost want me, Lord, I leave it all to Thee." Somehow—I can't explain it—but God made it so clear, and put it in my conscience so real and deep, that I could no more doubt that He wanted me to go to England than I could doubt my own existence. As high as the heavens are above the earth, so are His ways above our ways, and His thoughts above our thoughts.
>
> When I was through at Sands Street, I went down to the Grove, and I was so glad to get there and have a little quiet and rest. I swept and dusted my room and opened the windows, and it was very pleasant. It was the first of April, and,

as I thought it over, "Oh," I said, "after all, I think I can get more rest here than I can by going to England."

Then as I looked out from my window and saw the great ocean and heard the great waves roll in, I trembled. It came to me, "There is Mazie; you can't leave her here alone."

"Yes," I said, "that is so; I guess I won't go." Then a letter came from Miss Price saying, "Let me know by return mail if you will go with me to England. If you will go, all right; if not, I will join a party of ladies who are going."

I sat down to answer the letter and there was such a deep dread came over me as though I ought not to tell her I would not go; I could hardly write my letter.

"Oh," I said, "what is the matter with me?" A whisper came to me: "Don't write her, no."

"But I can't go; I must write." So on I went, and I never wrote a letter with such a dread on me before in my life. I finished it, and took it to the Post Office and threw it into the letter box and was so glad to get it out of my hand. "Now," I said, "I am free." It seemed I was lightened for a little while—no sad feeling in my heart, no burden, everything gone.

"Oh," I said, "how much trouble that letter has given me; that is it."

I made several calls before I went home as I had been away for three months. I did not go home till half past six, so I felt all that sadness is gone. I will have a nice tea and go to bed early. I had been in the house about half-an-hour, I suppose, and my tea was about ready. All of a sudden, as when a gas jet is turned off, an avalanche of darkness seemed to come over me like the horror of darkness that came over Abraham. My heart sank and great dread took possession of me. Every bit of desire for my supper left me. I wanted nothing.

"Oh, Lord," I said, "what is the matter with me? Do help me." Then I said, "I don't mean to sleep tonight till I know what ails me." So I locked the doors and fastened the shutter and turned down my lamp very low. I got on my knees and said, "I am in for it all night, and I must know what the matter is."

I wept bitterly and prayed. Then I thought, "It may be I have grieved the Spirit in some way, in what I said when I called." Then I went, in my thoughts, to each place; and went through all the conversations; but, no condemnation there. Then I went through all my work, every place I had been; no! no condemnation. I prostrated myself full length on the floor and wept and prayed as never before. I said, "Lord, I must know what is the matter with me."

A whisper, "Arise." I rose upon my knees by the chair and said, "Now, Lord, I will be still. Tell me, I pray Thee, what the matter is." After a few moments' stillness, it was as though someone stood at my right side and said distinctly: "You are going about telling people to trust the Lord in the dark; to trust Him when they can't see Him."

"Yes, Lord, I have done so."

"Well, you tell other people to do what you are not willing to do yourself."

"O, Lord," I said, "that is mean. By Thy grace I will not tell anybody to do what I am not willing to do myself. Now, Lord, what is it?" And clear and distinct came these words, "You are afraid to trust the Lord and go to England. You are afraid of the ocean."

My! It took my breath, but I said, "Lord, that is the truth, the real truth."

In a moment, in panorama form, God's goodness seemed to pass before me; His faithfulness in leading me and providing for me in every way, and answering my prayer a thousand times. Now, to think I should be afraid to trust Him and go to England. Oh, such a sense of shame as filled me. I prostrated myself on the floor again; I felt I could never look up again in His dear face and pray. I cried out, "Lord, forgive me, for Jesus' sake; and give me another chance. I will go to England."

Then, I thought, "if I write and tell Miss Price that I will go, she is a stranger, and she may think I am fickle-minded. She won't know how to depend on me, but if the Lord will give me another chance, I will go alone. I pledge Thee, Lord, You may trust me; I will obey." . . .

Lord, obediently I'll go,
Gladly leaving all below,
Only Thou my leader be,
And I still will follow Thee.

Then there came such a flood of light and sweet peace that filled me with joy and gladness. I sang and praised the Lord for I felt He had dealt bountifully with me in great mercy.[11]

Being obedient is not always easy, but the rewards are unfathomable. To be spiritual means to obey the Lord Jesus Christ in all things.

Trials

Amanda's submissive life led her through many trials. She often faced problems of discrimination. The fact that she was both an African-American and a woman prominent in the service of Christ made her a target. On one occasion she had been asked by a Christian white woman to attend a Bible study conducted by a well-known Bible teacher. After the session concluded, another white woman came to her with the caustic question, "Who invited you here?" It took Amanda so off-guard that she could not think of the name of the person who had brought her. The woman waved her hand toward the door telling Amanda to "Pass right out. Pass right out." Amanda was, at least verbally, thrust from the fellowship. It was painful, but over the years she had grown accustomed to such things. Always, her love of God and her submission to Jesus Christ gave her grace to meet unpleasant experiences in the spirit of her Lord. He too had often been rejected by prejudiced people.

God's hand rested mightily on Amanda, and He continued to use her in a powerful way. She developed a close friendship with Mrs. Hannah Whitall Smith and her husband, Robert Pearsal Smith. The Smiths were the driving force behind the well-known Keswick spiritual-life meetings in England. Robert Pearsal Smith appreciated Amanda's dedication and urged her to throw herself into these meetings. Amanda feared racial prejudice and asked if she, as an African-American woman, would be welcomed. Pearsal Smith answered, "Oh, yes, Amanda, there would be no objection to thee going, and I think thee would enjoy the meeting very much. God has wonderfully blessed Hannah [his wife] and scores of ladies of rank have been led to consecrate themselves to the Lord, and have realized great blessing." Amanda went, and God blessed and used her bountifully. She became adept at breaking down prejudices; her submission to Christ overcame great obstacles.

The Keswick movement grew to such significance that its impact was felt worldwide. Probably no single movement in the past hundred years has done more to foster genuine spirituality than it has; the Keswick approach will be outlined later in this book. Certainly Amanda's use of it enabled her to grow spiritually day by day.

Amanda the Evangelist

Her long life and service stand as a monument to what a woman from an unpromising and restricted background can experience when she lives in submission to God.

Amanda became widely known as an adept proclaimer of the gospel. Opportunities to share Christ continued to open to her as she matured in the Spirit. Many came to faith in the Lord through her ministry. Her long life and service stand as a monument to what a woman from an unpromising and restricted background can experience when she lives in submission to God. One of her favorite verses was Hebrews 10:36, "For you have need of endurance, so that when you have done the will of God, you may receive what was promised." Throughout her Christian life she did the will of God— and when God called her home at a good old age she received what was promised. It can be no different for us.

The Key Question

But what does submission to God, to Christ's lordship, really mean? What did Amanda learn about spiritual discipline? This is a crucial question. Paul put it very succinctly when he wrote to the Roman church:

> I urge you therefore, brethren, by the mercies of God, to present your bodies a living and holy sacrifice, acceptable to God, which is your spiritual service of worship. And do not be conformed to this world, but be transformed by the renewing of your mind, that you may prove what the will of God is, that which is good and acceptable and perfect. (Rom. 12:1–2)

The implications of these biblical demands cover a lot of ground; they may even seem a bit overwhelming. To think that God expects daily complete and unswerving submission runs contrary to our fleshly mind. Yet, there it stands: God requires unqualified commitment from His people.

Does God have a right to ask us to surrender our lives to His control? The answer is an emphatic affirmative. There are reasons for this.

Reasons for Submission to God

First of all, God can require our obedience by virtue of His creative hand. The book of Genesis declares, "God created man in His own image, in the image of God He created him; male and female He created them" (Gen. 1:27) and "The Lord God formed man of dust from the ground, and breathed into his nostrils the breath of life; and man became a living being" (Gen. 2:7). God made us what we are. Every man, woman, boy, and girl lives as the result of His mighty creative power. God is the giver of life, and as Creator He has prerogative over the things He has made—and that means each one of us.

When we read the Genesis account, it thrills our heart to realize that God in His unfathomable love brought this wonderful world into being. His power manifested itself in a way that defies understanding, but His love reigned supreme in it all. God created us in love. As the German pastor, Helmut Thielicke, pointed out concerning these early Genesis accounts:

> Their purpose is to show what it means for me and my life that God is there at the beginning and at the end, and that everything that happens in the world—my little life with its cares and its joys, and also the history of the world at large extending from stone-age man to the atomic era—that all this is, so to speak, a discourse enclosed, upheld, and guarded by the breath of God.[12]

This beautiful cosmos in which we find ourselves, designed by the infinite wisdom of God, perfectly manifests His majesty, His glory, and His great grace and love.

How wonderful to contemplate the fact that, though God created the heavens and the earth, the seas, the stars, and all the fantastic foliage and fauna of this world, He reached for something greater in the creation of human beings.

How wonderful to contemplate the fact that, though God created the heavens and the earth, the seas, the stars, and all the fantastic foliage and fauna of this world, He reached for something greater in the creation of human beings. In his essay *In Praise of Mortality*, Thomas Mann wrote, "In the depths of my soul I cherish the surmise that with those words, 'Let there be,' which summoned the cosmos from the night, when life was generated out of inorganic being, it was man who was foreseen."[13] The reformer Martin Luther pointed out:

> "And God said, Let us make man in our own image, after our likeness" (Genesis 1:26). Here Moses speaks in a new way. He does not say, "Let the waters bring forth," or, "Let the earth bring forth, " but, "Let us make man." By these words he tells us of a *(divine)* consultation, or deliberation, which did not occur before the creation of the other creatures. When God desired to make man, He, as it were, took counsel with Himself. This indicates the great difference between man and all other creatures.[14]

Humans are the crown of creation. Nonetheless, we often ask, especially when we find ourselves in distress, "What is the meaning of it all?" During difficult times it is all too easy to see life as a futile journey into nothingness.

One day can seem like the next, a recycling of the "same old thing," drained of any purpose. But in the mind of God, nothing could be further from the truth. God had a goal when He "breathed into our nostrils" and we became "living souls." We exist as His mighty handiwork, the design of His infinite wisdom and love. God does not create in vain. Life has purpose, a wonderful purpose, in God's creative plan. That is reason enough for submission to Him. Fulfilling His intention is what life is all about.

The Goal and Purpose of Creation

If God created us for a purpose which gives meaning to life, obviously it becomes exceedingly important to find out what that purpose is, and then to obey God in fulfilling it.

One would have thought that Adam and Eve, of all people, would have seen God's purpose clearly. But things did not go well for our first parents in the Garden. In the early days life in Eden must have been sheer joy. To live in the presence of God, to enjoy the fruit of His beautiful creation, to see tasks successfully completed each day, to live in harmony with one's spouse and to enjoy walking with God—it must have been bliss. Then tragedy struck. We all know the story of Genesis chapter 3 so well. First came temptation, then the falling into disobedience, and finally the tragic result: death. All the thrill and satisfaction of Eden evaporated in a moment. God's purpose was apparently thwarted. Thrust out of that wonderful spot, Adam and Eve began a life of drudgery and heartache. There seemed no meaning to things anymore. The goal was lost. The truth is, we understand the account so well because we have all lived it. It has been duplicated billions of times since. We sin and die. What an ignoble end to a noble beginning.

Because he has brought us back from "east of Eden"
into the garden of His grace we can fulfill His purpose
and find meaning to life again.

But we must never forget, God created this world out of love. The Lord Almighty determined not to let the failure of Eden be the end of His purposeful, creative act. Even in the expulsion of Adam and Eve from the Garden, the hope of restoration is hinted at. The Bible tells us, "And the Lord God made garments of skin for Adam and his wife, and clothed them" (Gen. 3:21). The God of grace slew animals, shed their blood, and clothed His erring children. The day would come when God in Christ would shed His own blood to reverse the Eden event, restoring to us the bliss of His presence and purpose, and clothing us in the garments of salvation (Isa. 61:10). How gloriously true it is that "God so loved the world, that He gave His only begotten Son, that whoever believes in Him should not perish, but have eternal life"

(John 3:16). Through the Lord Jesus Christ, as the Scriptures tell us, we become "a new *creation*" (2 Cor. 5:17, italics added). God has done for us what we could not do for ourselves. God has re-created us in Jesus Christ. Eden has been restored. Now we can walk with God in "the cool of the day" (Gen. 3:8) and thrill in His presence. Because he has brought us back from "east of Eden" into the garden of His grace we can fulfill His purpose and find meaning to life again. And what is that purpose? *Our purpose is to bring honor and glory to God's name through absolute obedience and submission to Him.* That is the reason God created us, re-created us in Christ, and sustains us in His grace day by day. It was this that Amanda Smith discovered.

Since we are recipients of God's gracious salvation, our absolute obedience and submission to Him should become the natural outcome. He has bought us by the blood of His Son (1 Peter 1:18–19). And if God has done that—which He surely has—then nothing short of complete submission to Him for His glory and praise should be the response. God has the prerogative of our obedience because he created and redeemed us. Do we want to discover God's purpose for our lives? Of course we do. Then we must submit to God.

God's Nature

There is another reason why God expects our submission. God has a right to it simply by virtue of who He is, that is, because of the essence of His divine nature. The great Victorian preacher, Charles Haddon Spurgeon, one day ascended the pulpit and thrilled people as he unfolded the nature of God to them. He said:

> The highest science, the loftiest speculation, the mightiest philosophy, which can ever engage the attention of a child of God, is the name, the nature, the person, the work, the doings, and the existence of the great God whom he calls his Father.
>
> There is something exceedingly improving to the mind in a contemplation of the Divinity. It is a subject so vast, that all our thoughts are lost in its immensity; so deep, that our pride is drowned in its infinity. Other subjects we can compass and grapple with; in them we feel a kind of self-content, and go our way with the thought, "Behold I am wise." But when we come to this master science, finding that our plumbline cannot sound its depth, and that our eagle eye cannot see its height, we turn away with the thought that vain man would be wise, but he is like a wild ass's colt; and with solemn exclamation, "I am but of yesterday, and know nothing." No subject of contemplation will tend more to humble the mind, than thoughts of God. . . .

But while the subject *humbles* the mind, it also expands it. He who often thinks of God, will have a larger mind than the man who simply plods around this narrow globe. . . . The most excellent study for expanding the soul, is the science of Christ, and Him crucified, and the knowledge of the Godhead in the glorious Trinity. Nothing will so enlarge the intellect, nothing so magnify the whole soul of man, as a devout, earnest, continued investigation of the great subject of the Deity. . . . Then go, plunge yourself in the Godhead's deepest sea; be lost in his immensity; and you shall come forth as from a couch of rest, refreshed and invigorated. I know nothing which can so comfort the soul; so calm the swelling billows of sorrow and grief; so speak peace to the winds of trial, as a devout musing upon the subject of the Godhead.[15]

Spurgeon hit the target. When we understand God in His essential being, at least insofar as we can with our limited human knowledge, we are given a graphic reason for submission. Furthermore, this understanding fills life with comfort, joy, strength, meaning, and reality. We need to take the plunge into His immensity and yield to Him. How can we do anything else? He comes to us as the all-powerful, all-knowing, ever-present Creator; and we are mere creatures. He is all in all; and we, because of our sin, are nothing. But when He reaches out and touches us with His grace, manifesting the very essence of His character, only one reaction is legitimate. Thomas, when he saw the resurrected Lord for the first time, fell at Jesus' feet and cried out, "My Lord and my God!" (John 20:28). That is the attitude we must have before the great and holy God of creation and redemption. He is our Lord and we must make Him so in every aspect of our lives. There alone can true spirituality be found. The rewards thereof abound.

The Rewards of Submitting to God

When we rest in the hollow of God's hand, and permit Him to mold and make us into what we ought to be, we are given a life endless in its contribution to a suffering world. There are also certain specific rewards we are given for submitting to God.

A Balanced Life

*In the so-called rat race we often forget
that Jesus said we "cannot serve God and mammon"
[money, material things] (Matt. 6:24).*

To begin with, submission to God's authority gives us balance. Things begins to make sense. Today we are pulled in so many different directions that life can easily get out of kilter. We seek satisfaction in so many ways and it becomes all but impossible to keep things in their proper perspective. We are constantly bombarded with the pitch that we cannot find fulfillment or happiness unless we buy a bigger car, a bigger home, have a bigger bank balance, get a better this, a better that. The pull and demands of our materialistic society all but tear us asunder. In the so-called rat race we often forget that Jesus said we "cannot serve God and mammon" [money, material things] (Matt. 6:24). But as the pressure rises, the Herculean task of resisting seems impossible. We are in danger of falling into serious error in the rush for "the good life."

The demands of the home must be addressed. In this strangely twisted time, with children facing serious problems in school and among their peers, and parents striving to keep some semblance of calm through it all, life at home is sometimes very difficult. Stress and strain can radically warp relationships. The storms of our secular sea have so tossed the fragile ship we call "family life," that it is floundering on the rocks.

Our work is demanding. When the average working parent comes home, there is still so much to be done. Although our jobs may not be as physically strenuous as they once were, the stress of getting ahead, receiving that promotion and striving for "success"—whatever that means—added to our household responsibilities, can fray the nerves almost to the breaking point. Many a home has capsized on the tidal waves of demands.

Society itself brings pressures. "Keeping up with the Joneses," seeing that the children are cared for and educated, maintaining good relationships with friends and family, desperately preparing for retirement, and a million other pulls and tugs not only fray the nerves, but threaten family life and our own sanity.

And the violence in the schools—what next? How can we ever keep all things in balance? Must we go on like this?

> *God, and God alone, provides the secret of a balanced, happy, joyous life. Submission to Christ's lordship brings life into proper perspective.*

The demands multiply until we wonder if there really is any purpose in life at all. The problem, described in these bleak terms, may seem unsolvable. However, there is an answer, a glorious solution. Those who submit themselves to God—permitting Him to work, lead, strengthen, and give direction in decision making—have the answer. God, and God alone, provides the secret of a balanced, happy, joyous life. Submission to Christ's lordship brings life into proper perspective. That is one of the great rewards of being an obedient, spiritual woman of God. In its wake a second blessed reward emerges.

A Real Direction

When we live in the hands of God, life takes on meaningful direction. The unsubmitted life has no goal—at least none that truly matters. But God has a grand, eternal purpose for His people. *The Westminster Shorter Catechism* summarizes the "chief end" of life. It is "to glorify God and to enjoy Him forever." We must bring glory to God by fitting into His divine purpose.

What constitutes the core of God's grand design? The core is His great scheme of world redemption. He means to establish His kingdom on earth as it is in heaven—and He uses His redeemed people in the process. What a privilege! And what a direction that brings to life. Everything we do in His name becomes a great accomplishment because it means kingdom progress. God actually engages in the task with us. Paul said, "For we are God's fellow workers" (1 Cor. 3:9). How wonderful! When we submit to our Lord Jesus Christ we fit into God's ultimate plan. Our goal becomes God's goal, our direction and activities become God's. Our lives are filled with meaning and richness indescribable, and we are satisfied.

A Contributing Life

There is a third reward. If we become submissive to God, we are able to make a contribution to the struggling world. Something deep within us, something ingrained in the very fabric of our being, urges us to make our life a contributing life. A person who is totally engrossed in himself, attempting to find happiness in an utterly self-oriented lifestyle, will ultimately be disappointed. But those who submit to God can make a positive difference in the world—and what satisfaction that brings! Our Lord Jesus Christ said, "For whoever wishes to save his life shall lose it; but whoever loses his life for My sake and the gospel's shall save it" (Mark 8:35). The self-centered life spells spiritual suicide. The obedient life, one completely submitted to Jesus Christ, saves itself and makes an eternal contribution. Knowing our life counts for God and for the well-being of others is a rewarding feeling in itself as well.

Anyone, regardless of situation or circumstance,
can be a contributor to God's grand purpose.
The secret—the open secret—is submission
to God, letting Him do with our lives what He wishes.

But we may say, "My circumstances are such that I cannot really make a contribution." That is self-deception—perhaps even demonic blindness.

Nothing pleases the Devil more than to deceive us into believing that our particular circumstances preclude making contributions to this world. Anyone, regardless of situation or circumstance, can be a contributor to God's grand purpose. The secret—the open secret—is submission to God, letting Him do with our lives what He wishes. God will let no moment pass if that moment is submitted to Him. He will use the smallest act for good and for kingdom progress. God has said: "For I know the plans that I have for you . . . plans for welfare and not for calamity to give you a future and a hope. Then you will call upon Me and come and pray to Me, and I will listen to you. And you will seek Me and find Me, when you search for Me with all your heart" (Jer. 29:11–13). What a wonderful promise! So we are thrust back again to the promise of great rewards if we live in submission to God. The obedient life makes its contribution. And that, in turn, makes life worth living.

Eternity

Finally, the submissive life reaps eternal rewards. The day will dawn when we shall stand before God, and rewards will be measured out commensurate to our life of submission. Remember what Jesus said, "And whoever in the name of a disciple gives to one of these little ones even a cup of cold water to drink, truly I say to you he shall not lose his reward" (Matt. 10:42). Every action in Christ's name has its everlasting compensation—even the smallest acts. So often we think to receive great rewards we must do something "big." Little menial tasks, we surmise, bring menial rewards. Not true. What makes religious headlines on earth may not be of any importance in heaven. We are not judged on the basis of how "important" our service to Christ seems in the eyes of other people; we are rewarded on the basis of our faithfulness. That is why Jesus said, "Many who are first will be last; and the last, first" (Matt. 19:30). What a surprise when we stand before the Lord and He hands out stars for our crown. We will not be rewarded according to the nature of the task God has given us to do; stars will be received simply because we were obedient to whatever that task may have been Someone who appears important now may receive little reward, while some obscure but faithful Christian might receive much. The "first" will come from the ranks of the obedient, submissive, and faithful servants of Christ.

Again, let it be understood that perfect surrender to the will of God does not necessarily mean there will be no trials or troubles. There may well be more. But God will fill the surrendered heart with faith so that victory can be achieved in life's extremities. As Andrew Murray put it:

> Faith has a twofold victory. In one case, it conquers the enemy or the difficulty by securing its removal or destruction. In the other, there is no deliverance from the trouble, and yet

faith conquers in the power it receives to endure, and to prove that its spirit is superior to all that men or devils can do. The triumphs of faith are often seen as remarkably in those who obtain no deliverance from the threatened evil, as in those who do. After the mention of the heroes whose faith was rewarded with success, we have here the mention of those who, in the midst of suffering that was not removed, proved that their faith lifted them up above all the pains with which earth could threaten them. They were tortured, not accepting their deliverance when offered them at the price of their faithfulness, that they might obtain a better resurrection. Spiritual and eternal realities were by faith so clear and near that they reckoned not the "sufferings of this present time to be compared with the glory which shall be revealed to us" (Rom. 8:18).[16]

In this passage, we are reminded of the centrality of faith. So look up! God does have a reason and purpose in it all. He will see you through—and deeply bless you in the process, difficult as it may seem at the moment.

We submit to God on our quest for spirituality, not to feel better, but because it is His will and we love Him.

The rewards that Jesus gives for submission, especially for submission during trying times, will last for eternity. That crown will never tarnish; those stars will shine with the brilliance of God's praise forever. Remember, Paul said, "For I consider that the sufferings of this present time are not worthy to be compared with the glory that is to be revealed to us" (Rom. 8:18). The submissive heart reaps a bountiful harvest forever. A word of caution though: It is quite easy to fall into the trap of what could be called "selfish spirituality." We may find ourselves submitting to God, serving Christ, and pursuing the spiritual disciplines simply because it makes us "feel good." Or we might find ourselves going after the things of the Spirit just because we do not want to feel guilty or uneasy. Such an approach inevitably leads to bondage. It is an attempt to keep the law, rather than experience the liberty of the Spirit wherein true joy is found. This understanding of spirituality obviously still has its roots in the old "self-life." No—we submit to God on our quest for spirituality, not to feel better, but *because it is His will* and we love Him. Of course, if we do fail our Lord, if we sin and feel guilt as a natural consequence, we must put things right and then go forward for Christ's honor, having learned our lesson. The principle remains. Self is out; the Spirit is in.

The Scriptures clearly present all the rules, regulations, and principles for living life in spiritual submission to the lordship of Jesus Christ. These require a hard look.

The Rules and Regulations of Submission to God

To discover and live out the will of God, we need to understand and follow certain "rules" of submission. They can help us to acquire a grasp of God's will and plan for daily living. Before we look at them, however, we must be clear that commitment to Christ is a *free choice* on our part. Such rules of submission are not to be understood in any legal sense, as if we have no choice in the matter. True, God wants submission, and that on the solid ground of His divine prerogatives. True also, great rewards come from such surrender. Yet, the decision to give our all to Jesus Christ as Lord is a free one. God will never force us against our will. We are not under the *law,* but under *grace* (Rom. 6:14). God created us in His image, and that means the freedom of grace—He honors our right to choose. Paul saw this principle and expressed it in a beautiful autobiographical passage in Romans, "But I have written very boldly to you on some points, so as to remind you again, because of the grace that was given me from God, to be a minister of Christ Jesus" (Rom. 15:15–16).

The Lord deeply desires that we submit to His will, but He wants us to do so voluntarily. He will not force us. He longs to see us submit out of our love for Him. That becomes the honored motive.

Two key concepts emerge from Paul's statement: *grace* and *ministry.* Simply put, God grants His grace to enable us to submit to His purpose in ministering. To minister means "to volunteer." Paul volunteered by the grace of God to give his life totally to his Lord and His service. The prophet Isaiah exhibited that same spirit when, after hearing God's gracious call, he responded, "Here am I, send me!" (Isa. 6:8). The Lord deeply desires that we submit to His will, but He wants us to do so voluntarily. He will not force us. He longs to see us submit out of our love for Him. That becomes the honored motive. As Paul said, "The love of Christ controls us" (2 Cor. 5:14). When we do decide out of love to follow Christ at all cost, His grace becomes sufficient. Then certain rules or principles can give substance and guidance to our decision. Let us look at some of these rules.

The Role of the Bible

To begin with, we must submit to the Scriptures. We will have much to say concerning Bible study and its place in spirituality later; let it simply be said here that we must learn to obey the Word of God. The Bible reveals our real selves to us. Through it we can begin to get our lives in line with God's will. Hebrews 4:12 declares, "For the word of God is living and active and sharper than any two-edged sword, and piercing as far as the division of soul and spirit, of both joints and marrow, and able to judge the thoughts and intentions of the heart." The Bible is a brilliant mirror, and its light penetrates into the deepest recesses of our personhood. As the psalmist said, "Thy word I have treasured in my heart, that I may not sin against Thee" (Ps. 119:11). Nothing reveals our inner nature to ourselves with such penetrating honesty as does the Bible. If we aspire to know ourselves in the light of God's will, we must seek out personal truths there.

There is another reason for coming to grips with the Word of God if we aspire to submit to Christ. As we have seen—especially in the life of Amanda Smith—a life of submission manifests itself in service to our Lord. Service is certainly God's will. Our Lord has given us the primary tool for effective service, namely, His Word. Paul put it this way to Timothy: "Preach the word; be ready in season and out of season; reprove, rebuke, exhort, with great patience and instruction" (2 Tim. 4:2). Though Paul was speaking specifically to the ministry of preaching, the principle remains the same for all service. We serve our Lord best when we share with others the truth of His precious Word. All Christian ministry revolves around the Scriptures.

> *Every test and temptation the Devil brought,*
> *Jesus rebuffed with Scripture*
> *(see Matt. 4:1–11). We can do no less.*

Furthermore, obeying the Scriptures becomes essential for spiritual warfare. We may not always be aware of it, but we are engaged in a real spiritual battle. The world, the flesh, and the Devil war against the people of God. We cannot escape the onslaught, and we can be defeated if we do not understand God's way of being a conqueror in Christ. But God has shown us the way to be victorious. The Bible has promised: "In all these things we overwhelmingly conquer through Him who loved us" (Rom. 8:37). To be a victor we must know the Scriptures. The Bible gives us discernment. It is the "sword of the Spirit" (Eph. 6:17). We recall how Jesus defeated Satan immediately following His baptism. Every test and temptation the Devil brought, Jesus rebuffed with Scripture (see Matt. 4:1–11). We can do no less. How shall we be successfully submissive to God if we do not obey Him with knowledge, wisdom and insight? We must know and obey the Scriptures.

The Role of the Spirit

Coupled with the objective witness of the Holy Scriptures is the inner subjective witness of the Holy Spirit. We must always submit to the Holy

Spirit. He dwells in every believer, making the believer's body the temple of God (1 Cor. 6:19). We must obey the inner promptings of the Holy Spirit so that we can gain greater insight into our situation and know the purposes of God. Recall Amanda's experience of Him in her decision to travel to England. The Spirit also takes the truths of the Holy Scriptures, makes them understandable, and impresses them on our hearts and minds. Failing to act according to these prompting hampers true spirituality. We must listen to the Holy Spirit as He speaks through the Scriptures, through circumstances, and even through other people. Then, when we discern the will of God, we must obey. This principle applies to every aspect of life. The Spirit of God becomes the guiding hand in our witness for Christ (Acts 1:8), in our prayer life (Rom. 8:26–27), in our effective service for our Lord (1 Cor. 2:4), and in our development in holy living (John 17:17).

Other "Authorities"

We must obey the "authorities." Who are these "authorities"? The basic authority is Jesus Christ Himself. But there are others, church leaders for example, who in submission to Christ we ought to obey. The writer of Hebrews wrote, "Obey your leaders, and submit to them; for they keep watch over your souls, as those who will give an account. Let them do this with joy and not with grief, for this would be unprofitable for you" (Heb. 13:17). This does not mean these leaders are "little Caesars." No, they are servants themselves. But God Himself has instituted their position in the life of the local church. Therefore, they should be followed as they direct Christians into a deeper walk with Christ. Obeying those whom the Holy Spirit has gifted and given us as leaders is tantamount to being submissive to God's plan for the local church.

The Home

We must learn to submit at home. Paul sets out very clearly the authoritative structure of the godly family. In what New Testament scholars call the *Haustafel*, as recorded in Ephesians 5:21–6:9 and Colossians 3:18–25, we find the principles of how the Christ-centered home should be ordered. And it all begins with submission. Paul says in Ephesians 5:21: "Be subject to one another in the fear of Christ." That principle is the foundation; the rest of the passage outlines the exact role and position of "authority" for each family member. Following God's design for the home brings about harmony and peace.

The Governmental Leaders

The Bible says clearly that we should submit to government authorities. Again we look to Paul for guidance in this important area. In instructing

Timothy, the apostle said,

> First of all, then, I urge that entreaties and prayers, petitions and thanksgivings, be made on behalf of all men, for kings and all who are in authority, in order that we may lead a tranquil and quiet life in all godliness and dignity. This is good and acceptable in the sight of God our Savior. (1 Tim. 2:1–3)

We may answer, "Yes, but our government authorities are not doing the right things. They are not godly leaders." We must recall that Paul wrote these words to Timothy in the first century under Roman rule. The caesars of his day were not only godless tyrants, they persecuted Christians to the point of death. Tradition tells us that Paul himself was beheaded by the Roman emperor, Nero. Yet, Paul said we should not only pray for leaders, but we should submit to them. He wrote,

> Let every person be in subjection to the governing authorities. For there is no authority except from God, and those which exist are established by God. Therefore he who resists authority has opposed the ordinance of God; and they who have opposed will receive condemnation upon themselves. For rulers are not a cause of fear for good behavior, but for evil. Do you want to have no fear of authority? Do what is good, and you will have praise from the same; for it is a minister of God to you for good. But if you do what is evil, be afraid; for it does not bear the sword for nothing; for it is a minister of God, an avenger who brings wrath upon the one who practices evil. Wherefore it is necessary to be in subjection, not only because of wrath, but also for conscience' sake. For because of this you also pay taxes, for rulers are servants of God, devoting themselves to this very thing. Render to all what is due them: tax to whom tax is due; custom to whom custom; fear to whom fear; honor to whom honor. (Rom. 13:1–7)

A Word of Prophecy

Finally, there are times when we must submit to the "word" from others. The Bible speaks of the gift of prophecy. On some occasions and in some circumstances we may hear a prophetic word of authority from the Lord through other people. This may be a personal word of encouragement and direction from a Christian friend, or a necessary rebuke. And certainly we should always listen well to preachers expounding God's truth. Preaching is God's primary source of prophecy. When someone speaks or preaches in the Spirit, and from the Word of God, we would do well to take note. We have much to learn from others as they, for our good, speak an authoritative word to us.

The Motive

The chief end of humanity is "to glorify God and enjoy Him forever." We obey God for His praise and honor.

The final basic rule and principle of submission is that we must obey God because it glorifies Him. We said earlier that the chief end of humanity is "to glorify God and enjoy Him forever." We obey God for His praise and honor. Paul rightly said: "Whether, then, you eat or drink or whatever you do, do all to the glory of God" (1 Cor. 10:31). Every aspect of life, every conscious effort and decision, the totality of our being, must be directed to the glory of God—*soli deo gloria*. When we realize who He is, what He has done in creating this marvelous universe and giving us life, the incredible manifestation of His grace in the life, death, and resurrection of Jesus, and His purpose in kingdom progress, how can we but give Him all glory, honor, and praise? When we see Him, we will have no difficulty doing that. But we need to be diligent in this discipline now, until that grand hour arrives.

Glory for Us

Not only are we to give glory to God, but one day we will actually share in that glory. The Corinthians were told, "For momentary, light affliction is producing for us an eternal weight of *glory* far beyond all comparison" (2 Cor. 4:17, italics added). The very idea that we shall be partakers in the eternal glory of God Himself is a sobering but joyous thought. Paul prayed for the Ephesian church, "I pray that the eyes of your heart may be enlightened, so that you may know what is the hope of His calling, what are the riches of the *glory* of His inheritance in the saints" (Eph. 1:18). We have an inheritance of His glory waiting for us. Thus we do well to heed the words of Simon Peter when he said, "Grow in the grace and knowledge of our Lord and Savior Jesus Christ. To Him be the glory, both now and to the day of eternity. Amen" (2 Peter 3:18). As we grow in the grace and knowledge of our Lord Jesus Christ, submitting to Him day by day, we become increasingly able to give God due glory, the glory we shall one day experience.

Not Easy

Of course, it is never easy to live in complete submission the way our Lord expects us to but,

The surrender becomes . . . possible when the soul sees how truly and entirely Jesus, the Mediator of the new covenant, has undertaken for all, and engages to put His own delight in God's law into the heart, to give the will and the strength to live in all God's will. That faith gives the courage to place oneself before Christ and to say—Lord, here am I, ready to be led by Thee in the new and living way of death to my will, and a life in God's will alone: I give up all to Thee.[17]

Faith and grace bring victory.

Conclusion

We obey our Lord by putting our entire trust in Him and His grace for the power to submit to His will. We obey Him through the Scriptures, by the inner witness of the Holy Spirit, and by the authorities that we encounter. We do so because it brings praise and honor to Him. These are the "rules." They are not rigid laws that we must obey or be "doomed and damned"; they are simply the principles through which our Lord Jesus Christ receives glory to Himself by our submission to His will. And it is this submission which generates spirituality.

A fitting close to this step is the testimony of a faithful black African who gave his life as a martyr for Jesus Christ. Before his death he wrote:

> I'm part of the fellowship of the unashamed. I have the Holy Spirit's power. The die has been cast. I have stepped over the line. The decision has been made. . . . I'm a disciple of His. I won't look back, let up, slow down, back away, or be still. My past is redeemed, my present makes sense, my future is secure. I'm finished and done with low living, sight walking, smooth knees, colorless dreams, tamed visions, worldly talking, cheap giving and dwarfed goals.
>
> I no longer need preeminence, prosperity, position, promotions, plaudits, or popularity. I don't have to be right, first, tops, recognized, praised, regarded or rewarded. I now live by faith, lean on His presence, walk by patience, am uplifted by prayer and I labor with power.
>
> My face is set, my gait is fast, my goal is Heaven, my road is narrow, my way rough, my companions are few, my Guide reliable, my mission clear. I cannot be bought, compromised, detoured, lured away, turned back, deluded or delayed. I will not flinch in the face of sacrifice, hesitate in the presence of

the enemy, pander at the pool of popularity, or meander in the maze of mediocrity.

I won't give up, shut up, let up, until I have stayed up, stored up, prayed up, paid up, preached up for the cause of Christ. I am a disciple of Jesus. I must go till He comes, give till I drop, preach till all know, and work till He stops me. And, when He comes for His own, He will have no problems recognizing me . . . my banner will be clear!

That's submission; that's spirituality!

Prayer

Dear Lord, You truly are Lord. I realize that means You deeply desire to be the Lord of my life. May I, therefore, have Your strength and grace to submit honestly and deeply to Your divine will each day, in each decision. I do desire—really desire—to be submissive to Your lordship. In Jesus' name. Amen.

10 Questions for Study and Discussion

1. How significant was Amanda Smith's social background for her ability to submit to God? Do the same principles apply to us today? How?
2. How did Amanda's spirit affect her life of submissive service? What can we learn from that?
3. Why should we submit to God? Is it proper to do so?
4. How do God's goal and purpose in creation impact our lives?
5. What are the rewards for submitting to God? Which ones are more important?
6. What are the essential attributes of God and how do they relate to submission?
7. How can submission to our Lord give direction to life?
8. What role do the Bible and the Holy Spirit play in helping us to live the submissive life?
9. What "rules" guide us in discerning God's will, and how do we apply them?
10. What is the "secret" for finding the ability to submit to God?

The Spiritual Woman Overflows with God

MEET ANNE GRAHAM LOTZ
A WOMAN WHO OVERFLOWS WITH GOD

Filled up to all the fullness of God.
(Ephesians 3:19)

$\mathcal{A}$ msterdam in 1983 witnessed an evangelism conference that made history. Evangelists traveled to the Netherlands from all over the world, even from as far off as Nagaland in northeast India, to share in fellowship and inspiration. The Billy Graham Evangelistic Association had launched the affair, and everyone had a high level of spiritual anticipation. Bringing Christ to the whole world constituted the challenge of the conference. It became a marvelous experience for the several thousand who participated. Certainly this proved to be the case for one evangelist from Africa; the conference also gave him a new perspective. After attending the conference for several days he remarked to a fellow delegate:

> I want God to speak to me. I have earnestly prayed that God would speak to me and show me something, tell me something, impress me with something that would profoundly impact my life that I might win others to Jesus. I've been here for days praying for that. I've been here for nine days, and still God hasn't spoken to me. But today, the tenth day, as I earnestly prayed and sought the mind and heart of the Lord, God spoke to me in a powerful way. And I just can't believe it; it was through a sister.

A "sister?" Who was this woman?

Some years earlier a similar conference had taken place in Raleigh, North Carolina. Some five or six hundred men and women had assembled. All enjoyed a time of rich spiritual blessing. The Bible was faithfully taught and lives were deeply challenged. Many of those who attended were never the same again. Who presented the challenge? Who so powerfully shared God's Word? That same "sister." At the time, one man questioned whether or not the Lord could use a woman in a teaching role, especially to men. Nonetheless, that "sister" had taught with the unction of the Holy Spirit upon her. Everyone was deeply touched. When there was a break in the service, and a question period began, the skeptic who himself had been moved mightily by the Spirit said in dazed amazement, "A woman can't do what you just did." That "sister" certainly had an unusual gift.

We move next to South Africa. The same woman had just finished teaching God's Word for three solid hours and now was being interviewed live on national television. Well into the session, after asking the usual questions, the interviewer commented that "Many believe a woman cannot teach men as well as women." The "sister" answered simply, "A man or a woman cannot speak on their own, but God certainly can."

This woman, used with such power by the Spirit of God despite her detractors, is someone we should meet.

The Beginnings

It all began April 1, 1948, in a little town in North Carolina. Montreat boasts a small college and a beautiful view of the Smoky Mountains. In that idyllic setting God placed one of the most significant Christian families of the twentieth century. On that April day and in that place Anne was born, the second daughter of evangelist Billy Graham and his devoted wife Ruth. Like her parents, she was destined to become a servant of God.

Anne grew up in a wonderful Christian family. The future will record her father as one of the most anointed evangelists the church has ever seen. Anne also had the blessing of a godly and wise mother whose life reads like a saga of spiritual power. This wonderful legacy and blessed home life became Anne's heritage.

One might assume that Anne would naturally have gifts and abilities to serve the Lord. But there have been many great evangelists, preachers, and Christian leaders whose children have never made a mark on Christian history. Sadly, some have even been detrimental to the kingdom of God. Birth into a well-regarded Christian family does not assure a life of fruitful service. Yet God profoundly touched this particular woman in a significant way.

The Parents

Little needs to be said about Anne's parents; their life story is well known. Billy has preached to more people than any single person in the history of the church. And Ruth has stood by his side, lending strength. Millions have come to faith in Jesus Christ, Christian lives have been revitalized, marriages have been turned around, and institutions have been restructured to the glory of Christ, all through Billy's ministry. Billy himself says that when he gets to heaven, he intends to ask the Lord one question: "Why me?" It does seem incredible that God should reach down to make a North Carolina dairy farmer's boy into such a world-transforming figure. God also reached out to the Far East and picked a medical missionary's daughter to be his companion in service. Such is His providence and grace.

Mother Ruth

Ruth Bell Graham's biography is as fascinating. Ruth was brought up in China, where her father, Dr. L. Nelson Bell, served as a missionary doctor. From the start Ruth understood the need for winning the lost to faith in Jesus Christ and ministering to people's needs. As a child she was educated on the mission field in China and Korea. Later she traveled to America to enter Wheaton College, west of Chicago. Ruth fully intended, after she graduated, to return to Asia and give her life to missionary work in Tibet. But God had other plans. At Wheaton, she met a lanky young preacher who loved the Lord—and baseball!—and they fell in love. His name was Billy. They soon married and settled down in Western Springs, Illinois, where Billy became pastor of a small Baptist church. After a pastorate of some two or three years there, he set out on the evangelist trail with the Youth for Christ organization. Billy had a short stint as president of Northwestern Schools in Minneapolis, Minnesota, but still kept up his itinerant evangelist ministry. Then came 1949, and the first great Los Angeles crusade. The rest is history. Ruth never made it to Tibet, except that her support, prayers, love, her constant devotion to Christ, to her husband, and to her growing family was a worldwide universal influence that only eternity will be able to record.

Early Years

Anne is one of five children. The oldest is Gigi, and Anne's younger sister is Ruth, affectionately called "Bunny." Her two brothers are Franklin and Ned. Billy and Ruth did a good job rearing the children, however rocky the road seemed at times. Every one of the five now exercises a deep devotion to Jesus Christ, and each has developed a unique ministry of his or her own. Out of the five, no one would have guessed that Anne would develop an incredible worldwide ministry. Like many middle children, Anne was a retiring little girl. She had a sweet and sensitive heart, though, and through the faithful instruction of her mother and others, she continually grew in awareness of her need of the Lord Jesus Christ.

Salvation Comes

*Ruth shared the gospel with her little daughter,
and though, as Anne said, she did not understand
every sentence, she clearly heard God's voice. At her
mother's knees, she bowed down, tears in her eyes,
and surrendered her life totally to Jesus Christ.*

Anne confesses that she cannot remember exactly how old she was when she accepted Christ. She does remember that the Holy Spirit brought the gospel home to her in an unusual way. Many years before Anne's birth, Cecil B. DeMille had produced a silent movie entitled *King of Kings*, the story of the life of Christ. Though it was in black and white and had subtitles—hardly the kind of thing that would attract the modern moviegoer of today—it had become a classic, and was shown around the world for many years. Anne had the opportunity to watch it one Easter, while still a young girl. The presentation struck her heart. In the film itself no one played the part of Jesus.

The Lord was simply represented as a bright light. As the crucifixion drama unfolded, the "Light" slowly went out. When that gripping moment came, Anne began to sob. Young as she was, she had grasped that Jesus had died for her. Right there, Mother Ruth stepped in, understanding that Anne had fallen under conviction of her childlike sins and had become conscious of her need of the Savior. Ruth shared the gospel with her little daughter, and though, as Anne said, she did not understand every sentence, she clearly heard God's voice. At her mother's knees, she bowed down, tears in her eyes, and surrendered her life totally to Jesus Christ. She turned from her sins to the Savior and asked the Lord Jesus Christ to come into her heart. That became the moment. God not only saved a precious little soul for eternity, He began to prepare a life for fruitful ministry to His glory.

As Anne grew up, in many respects she was just a typical schoolgirl, in spite being known as "Billy Graham's daughter." She developed a unique personality of her own over the years though still her timid, quiet spirit was her most dominant feature. In her late teens, she met another "P.K."—preacher's kid—who loved the Lord.

Meet Danny

Danny Lotz, like Anne, had the blessing of being brought up in a wonderful Christian home. Unlike Anne, though, he was a "Yankee," not a Southerner. His father had been pastor of a Baptist church in the New York area for many years. Reverend Lotz was a great old man of God, and he had been careful to instill in his children the love of Jesus Christ. Danny had a vital faith in the Lord Jesus.

Since he was always active in sports, it seemed quite natural that, in time, Danny would come to lead a chapter of the Christian Athletes in North Carolina. This organization encourages men and women to grow in Christ, sharing their testimony in the context of their sports life. Danny has an older brother, John, who served as assistant athletic director at the University of North Carolina. Another older brother, Sam, an executive with Dow Chemical, died in the mid-1980s. Danny's younger brother, Denton, exercises a far-flung ministry as the General Secretary of the Baptist World Alliance. He travels the world, inspiring and challenging Baptist leadership to commitment and world evangelization. He often addresses government officials when there is persecution, pleading that Christians be given freedom to express their faith without fear of reprisal. Obviously, Danny came from a wonderful family with a godly father and mother whose influence, though they are now both gone, continues in their children.

When Danny met Anne, it was love at first sight. Although Danny was a bit older than Anne, their love had heaven's blessings, and they soon married. They settled in Raleigh, North Carolina, where Danny began his dental practice and Anne became a homemaker. Three wonderful children arrived through the years—two lovely daughters, Rachel-Ruth and Morrow, and a dedicated son, Jonathan. All three of the children eventually graduated from Baylor University in Texas and now carry on an effective life of ministry and service for the Lord Jesus Christ. The Graham and Lotz legacy continues.

A Fresh Challenge

The Holy Spirit revealed: "I know your deeds. Behold, I have put before you an open door which no one can shut, because you have a little power, and have kept My Word, and have not denied My name" (Rev. 3:8). Anne took that Bible verse as God's promise.

In 1974, Anne knew God had spoken to her. From the Scriptures, the Holy Spirit revealed: "I know your deeds. Behold, I have put before you an open door which no one can shut, because you have a little power, and have kept My Word, and have not denied My name" (Rev. 3:8). Anne took that Bible verse as God's promise. It became her call to share His truth. In a Baptist church in Raleigh, where Danny served as a deacon, Anne began to teach a small group of women. She felt absolutely terrified as she faced the task. Her timidity had never entirely left her. But as she said, she felt far more terrified not to teach, because she knew God had called her to that ministry and had given her His wonderful promise. Later Anne received a second promise that helped calm her fears. She read in Malachi 3:10 that God would "pour out for you a blessing until it overflows." So, in quiet biblical fashion, she launched out into a Bible teaching ministry that ultimately has become worldwide in scope.

The Bible Study Fellowship

Anne built her group around the Bible Study Fellowship program. This effective curriculum provides women with the opportunity for an in-depth searching of God's Word. The program serves as a supplement to traditional Sunday school. It meets during the week and is designed just for women. As Anne began this teaching ministry, God put His hand on her work in the Raleigh church. In an incredibly short time, five hundred women were meeting every week to study the Bible. The Bible Study Fellowship program maintains strict discipline. If you miss a stated number of sessions without a legitimate excuse, you are excused from the study. This may seem rather legalistic, but because the absolute limit for each group has been set at five hundred, there can be a number of women waiting to enroll. It was certainly so in Anne's case. Five hundred women filled up the meeting hall and a long waiting list quickly developed.

And so Anne's ministry began. But what about the long waiting list? Was it right that women should be refused admittance if they were so eager to be taught? Anne solved the problem by starting a second group. That new class soon filled up to its capacity of five hundred, and then a third, a fourth, and a fifth, until finally there were six groups meeting with five hundred in each group. Still the waiting list continued to expand. The growth was absolutely phenomenal. As the groups grew in number Anne grew in teaching ability and in her own spiritual life. She saw it all as God's call. Though she has now dropped out of that particular program and given it to others, the eleven classes still carry on in Raleigh. The Lord has kept His promises.

A Second Call

After she had worked for twelve years in the Bible Study Fellowship, Anne had something of a "second call." She read in Deuteronomy:

> The LORD our God spoke to us at Horeb, saying, "You have stayed long enough at this mountain. Turn and set your journey, and go to the hill country of the Amorites, and to all their neighbors in the Arabah, in the hill country and in the lowland and in the Negev and by the seacoast, the land of the Canaanites, and Lebanon, as far as the great river, the river Euphrates. See, I have placed the land before you; go in and possess the land which the LORD swore to give to your fathers, to Abraham, to Isaac, and to Jacob, to them and their descendants after them." (Deut. 1:6–8)

Through this passage Anne felt she now was to go into all the world. In a sense, the rest of her life has unfolded in that context. On April 1, 1988 (which Anne can specifically point to, as it was her fortieth birthday), God confirmed this call through a pungent passage in Acts 26:

> But arise, and stand on your feet; for this purpose I have appeared to you, to appoint you a minister and a witness not only to the things which you have seen, but also to the things in which I will appear to you; delivering you from the Jewish people and from the Gentiles, to whom I am sending you, to open their eyes so that they may turn from darkness to light and from the dominion of Satan to God, in order that they may receive forgiveness of sins and an inheritance among those who have been sanctified by faith in Me. (Acts 26:16–18)

There could be no escaping God's demand—Anne had to respond.

Launching Out

Anne resigned her position in the Bible Study Fellowship and stepped out into ministry, ready to share God's truth wherever and however the Holy Spirit would lead her. God began to open doors. In her very first Bible conference Anne spoke to a gathering of pastors, evangelists, and church leaders. They were all men, and although there were only eight hundred, Anne said it seemed like thousands. Again, she was frightened to death. When she got up to speak, something happened that hardly encouraged her. The men were seated around tables. Some of them actually stood up and turned their chairs around so they were sitting with their backs to her. But she claimed the wonderful promise that God had given to Jeremiah:

> Now the word of the LORD came to me saying, "Before I formed you in the womb I knew you, and before you were born I consecrated you; I have appointed you a prophet to the nations." Then I said, "Alas, Lord God! Behold, I do not know how to speak, because I am a youth." But the LORD said to me, "Do not say, 'I am a youth,' because everywhere I send you, you shall go, and all that I command you, you shall speak. Do not be afraid of them, for I am with you to deliver you," declares the LORD. Then the LORD stretched out His hand and touched my mouth, and the LORD said to me, "Behold, I have put My words in your mouth." (Jer. 1:4–9)

It seemed as though the Lord had said to her,
"Anne, you are accountable to Me, not to the audience.
I'll decide who the audience is; you just be obedient to Me."

So in faith, Anne spoke and God blessed her in a marvelous fashion. It seemed as though the Lord had said to her, "Anne, you are accountable to Me, not to the audience. I'll decide who the audience is; you just be obedient to Me." That settled the matter.

The Secret!

People have been amazed that this simple girl from North Carolina can communicate the Holy Scriptures with such force. How does one account for this? There are several reasons for Anne's effectiveness. First of all, it is the Word of God that she teaches, and the Bible has its own innate power. The Scriptures are God's truth, inspired by the Holy Spirit, and they are authoritative in all matters. Anne faithfully elucidates the Bible; she does not speculate. She has full confidence in the truthfulness and authority of the Word, and she communicates this confidence. God honors that.

Second, in all of Anne's teaching, one thing is paramount: the glorious gospel of Jesus Christ. Here is an outline of one of her teaching sessions on the Resurrection where the centrality of Christ and the Good News are clearly evident:

I.   **What confirms the Resurrection?**
  A.   Jesus was literally buried. The visible enemies of Jesus put guards on the tomb and sealed it. There was no human way Jesus could get out other than by resurrection.
  B.   Satan kept destroying the seed promised to Adam and Eve in the Garden of Eden, but God always reserved a remnant. He would surely preserve the life of Jesus.
  C.   The soldiers never would have permitted the body of Jesus to be stolen because their very lives depended on it, yet the tomb was empty.
  D.   What the guards actually saw and confessed confirms the Resurrection. They had to be bribed to keep quiet.
  E.   The disciples' spirit confirms the Resurrection. They had not expected it at all and were overjoyed when they saw the risen Lord.

II.   **Confronted with the Resurrection**
  Our response must be one of faith. In the final analysis, though many human factors confirm the Resurrection, it can only really be accepted by faith. Through faith we meet the risen Christ.

III.   **The command to share the story of the Resurrection**
  A.   The whole church is commanded to tell the world about the resurrected Lord.
  B.   Because the evangelistic call is for the whole church it comes to women as well. Women must share the wonderful story of the life, death, and resurrection of Jesus Christ with others.

Christ Is All

This basic outline of Anne's message on the Resurrection shows the centrality of Jesus Christ in her teaching. She clearly and faithfully shares what the theologians call the *kerygma*, the gospel. That explosive Greek word literally means "the proclamation"; and as Paul said, "In the wisdom of God the world through its wisdom did not come to know God, God was well-pleased through the foolishness of the message preached [*kerygma*] to save those who believe" (1 Cor. 1:21). The world may call God's truth "foolishness," but the message of Christ proclaimed stands as the wisdom and power of God. Paul declared in Romans, "I am not ashamed of the gospel, for it is the power of God for salvation to everyone who believes" (Rom. 1:16). If there has ever been a teacher of the Word of God, faithful to the full gospel it has been Anne. Power resides in the Word, and Anne shares that Word.

The Spirit's Power

ℐ am a woman under compulsion. I am locked in by the evidence of giving a verbal expression of what I know, what I've seen, what I've heard, what I've experienced by faith, what He has said to me through His Word."

But there must be more than just the communication of the "letter" to see true spiritual life imparted. As Paul said, "The letter kills, but the Spirit gives life" (2 Cor. 3:6). Anne walks in the Spirit. As she herself said in an interview in *Ladies Home Journal* magazine: "Spending time, every day, by myself, reading Scripture, praying, talking with Him. That's the core of my life, the heartbeat, from which everything else stems."[1] These authors have heard many people speak in many different settings, but it must be said, never have we heard anyone speak with any more genuine spiritual unction than Anne. She is a very dear friend, but that is not why we feel so blessed by her ministry. She has the genuine anointing of God on her life. Anne walks with the Lord in the honesty and integrity of her heart, thus the Holy Spirit fills her and uses her in a powerful way. She says that her authority comes from God and her service must always be a characterized by four spiritual virtues:

1. *Credibility:* Anne has a testimony attested to by everyone who knows her. She is credible because of her consecration to Jesus Christ.
2. *Integrity:* There can be no question about Anne's absolute honesty and integrity in all of her relationships, and above all, in her relationship to God and to His Word.
3. *Divine Authority:* She speaks with authority because she teaches the authoritative Word.
4. *Absolute Obedience to Christ:* Anne walks in submission to the Lord Jesus Christ. She fulfills the great commandment of love by reaching out to others with the hand of Christian compassion.

Anne exemplifies these spiritual virtues in a beautiful way, and this unquestionably accounts for her powerful ministry. She possesses the touch of the Spirit because she feels called by God to the work. As she says, "I am a woman under compulsion. I am locked in by the evidence of giving a verbal expression of what I know, what I've seen, what I've heard, what I've experienced by faith, what He has said to me through His Word." By her own confession she feels, as did Jeremiah, that the Lord speaks to her in the words, "'For I know the plans that I have for you,' declares the LORD, 'plans for welfare and not for calamity to give you a future and a hope'" (Jer. 29:11). Summing up, she says, "I am seeking to be obedient." That always brings spiritual power.

Prayer the Key

*Anne exemplifies in a beautiful way the simple
principle that little prayer means
little power, and much prayer means much power.*

Above all, Anne is a great woman of prayer. Few people know this, but Anne spends hours before God in fervent prayer and intercession. Billy Graham has shared his deep admiration for the prayer life of his beloved daughter. He has such confidence in her that she has become something of a counselor to him. Anne exemplifies in a beautiful way the simple principle that little prayer means little power, and much prayer means much power.

Small wonder, therefore, in the light of these spiritual qualities, that this woman of God speaks with authority. She overflows with God. Anne has become a Spirit-filled evangelist in her own right. She has brought many to a faith in the Lord Jesus Christ. For some, however, there is a problem.

The Problem

For some, the question of whether women should teach God's Word to men is a real issue. Many—especially men—have questioned Anne's right to speak. Anne herself is well aware of what Paul said in 1 Timothy 2:12, "I do not allow a woman to teach or exercise authority over a man, but to remain quiet." Since Anne believes the Word of God she wants to be faithful to this verse. She has prayed over the matter and studied the verse tenaciously. Finally she has come to the realization that the verse lays primary emphasis on *authority*. A woman must not usurp authority in the ministry of Christ. She would never accept a senior pastor's position, for example. Anne speaks from no authoritative position, except the authority of God's Word and in this she speaks not *from* authority, but *under* authority. She lives and serves under the authority of her husband, her pastor, or whomever the male leader may be in any given situation. This principle came home to these authors very clearly on one occasion when Anne spoke at the seminary where we served as president and president's wife. She stood up to speak and said, "I am here today to speak under the authority of President Drummond and also under the authority of the student leader of this group." It was a real manifestation of her unassuming, yet powerful giftedness. And how she blessed us all.

Furthermore, we know the apostle Paul would never contradict himself. What he said in the Timothy passage must be understood in the light of everything else he wrote. Paul clearly put his stamp of approval on women ministering in certain circumstances. For example, he seemed quite happy that Priscilla led the gifted preacher Apollos into a clearer understanding of the gospel. Also, Priscilla served in the church that met in their home, apparently in a leadership role. Paul wrote to the Romans, "I commend to you our sister Phoebe, who is a servant of the church which is at Cenchrea" (Rom. 16:1). Paul must have approved of women ministering under proper authority. Throughout the Bible we can see that God has used women in powerful ways, women such as Miriam, Deborah, Esther in the Old Testament, and Priscilla, Dorcas, Phoebe, and others who faithfully served Christ and the early church in the New Testament. Moreover, in his sermon on the Day of Pentecost, quoting the prophet Joel, Peter preached:

> "And it shall be in the last days," God says, "That I will pour forth of My Spirit upon all mankind; and your sons and your daughters shall prophesy, and your young men shall see visions, and your old men shall dream dreams; even upon My bondslaves, both men and women, I will in those days pour forth of My Spirit." (Acts 2:17–18)

Notice, God pours out His Spirit on daughters as well as sons. They both prophesy and declare God's truth. And later in Acts we read, "Now this man [Philip] had four virgin daughters who were prophetesses" (Acts 21:9). In the light of these biblical realities, and with Anne's humble spirit, it seems difficult not to affirm her and other women in their service for Christ.

Subservient to the Bible

In Billy Graham's autobiography, he tells of hearing Anne speak on one occasion: "I felt that our daughter Anne Graham Lotz was speaking directly to me when she told the huge assembly, 'It is not only your words, it is your life which is the evangelistic message to the world.' That thought haunts me."

Anne's spirit and approach make it obvious that she keeps herself in line with the Scriptures, and God's hand rests mightily upon her. She goes from strength to strength. In Billy Graham's autobiography, he tells of hearing Anne speak on one occasion: "I felt that our daughter Anne Graham Lotz was speaking directly to me when she told the huge assembly, 'It is not only your words, it is your life which is the evangelistic message to the world.' That thought haunts me."[2] Anne is God's servant. He speaks through her. So the issue is not whether a woman can be used in the ministry; rather, the question becomes, has God called her and is she obedient to all God reveals about ministry in the Scriptures? And again in Anne's own words, "I am seeking to be obedient." That obedience makes for spiritual greatness. Anne is a woman overflowing with God.

A Broad-Based Ministry

Anne has taught on every continent and to every conceivable kind of gathering. Her father has called her "an excellent Bible teacher and author." She writes books, speaks to multitudes, and faithfully serves Christ. Her first work, *The Vision of His Glory*, won the Gold Medallion Award of the Evangelical Christian Publishers' Association in 1997. Her book, *God's Story*, won the award in 1998.

*Her life overflowed with God when she became,
as Paul put it, "filled with the Holy Spirit" (Eph. 5:18).*

Anne discovered that her ability to live a life pleasing to her Lord did not come about by mere human effort. Nor did it come about because she was the daughter of a world-famous evangelist. Her life overflowed with God when she became, as Paul put it, "filled with the Holy Spirit" (Eph. 5:18). The Holy Spirit had animated the life of our Lord—and He could make her ministry glow with divine life as well.

Jesus' Promise

Our Lord Jesus Christ gave His people a promise, a promise that should become our "Magnificent Obsession." He said, "He who believes in Me, as the Scripture said, 'From his innermost being shall flow rivers of living water'" (John 7:38). Then John explained: "This He [Jesus] spoke of the Spirit, whom those who believed in Him were to receive" (v. 39). Jesus declared that life can be like a fountain overflowing with the presence of God. Anne Graham Lotz certainly exemplifies that kind of spirituality for us. We can examine the experience of many great Christians and discover a similar pattern. But what is the essence of the overflowing life? How can it be realized? A brief journey through the Scriptures will make it clearer.

The Overflowing Life

Some have argued that the Holy Spirit invades Christians subsequent to salvation in a second great experience. This misses the scriptural mark. The Bible explicitly states that every believer possesses and is possessed by the Spirit of God. Every true Christian experiences His wonderful working. Many scriptural passages point to that truth:

> Peter said to them, "Repent, and let each of you be baptized in the name of Jesus Christ for the forgiveness of your sins; and you shall receive the gift of the Holy Spirit." (Acts 2:38)

> God . . . gave us the Spirit in our hearts. (2 Cor. 1:22)

> Having . . . believed, you were sealed in Him with the Holy Spirit of promise. (Eph. 1:13)

> You also are being built together into a dwelling of God in the Spirit. (Eph. 2:22)

> God . . . gives His Holy Spirit to you. (1 Thess. 4:8)

The biblical passages on this theme seem all but endless. One of the wonderful facts about our Christian faith and our developing spirituality is that, as believers, we too can possess the Spirit of God within us.

The Person of the Holy Spirit

The Holy Spirit always seeks our best and addresses us on a person-to-person basis. And because He is God, we need to hear His voice and follow Him.

Who is this Holy Spirit? To begin with, the Spirit of God is a personality, one of the Divine Trinity. He possesses the attributes and characteristics of God the Father and God the Son. He must never be seen as a mere influence or principle of good. To make this unmistakably clear, the Bible ascribes four specific characteristics to the Holy Spirit. The first is *willpower*, the ability to make decisions and act. The Scriptures declare that the "Spirit works all these things . . . *as He wills*" (1 Cor. 12:11, italics added). Second, the Bible ascribes *personal knowledge* to the Holy Spirit. Paul told the Corinthians, "For who among men knows the thoughts of a man except the spirit of the man, which is in him? Even so the thoughts of God no one knows except the Spirit of God" (1 Cor. 2:11). Because He is the Divine Spirit, not only is he knowledgeable but

He contains all knowledge. Third, as implied in the previous attribute, He possesses a *mind*. Romans 8:27 reads, "He who searches the hearts knows what the mind of the Spirit is." Finally, the Holy Spirit *loves*. Again we read in Romans, "Now, I urge you, brethren, by our Lord Jesus Christ and by the love of the Spirit, to strive together with me in your prayers to God for me" (15:30). Because He loves, the Spirit can be grieved by our disobedience. Therefore, the Scriptures admonish us, "Do not grieve the Holy Spirit of God, by whom you were sealed for the day of redemption" (Eph. 4:30). Resistance might be no more than a subtle quenching of the Spirit; but it still grieves Him. Thus Paul said, "Do not quench the Spirit" (1 Thess. 5:19). The Holy Spirit always seeks our best and addresses us on a person-to-person basis. And because He is God, we need to hear His voice and follow Him. He dwells within us to do His wonderful, multifaceted work in creating the overflowing life.

The Inner Work of the Holy Spirit

The moving of the Holy Spirit in our lives creates a panorama, and what a beautiful picture it can become. His inner work, as His name indicates, begins in creating holiness in the believer. Of course when we come to faith in Jesus Christ, we are immediately "sanctified"—that is, made holy in God's sight. This constitutes our "grace position" in Christ. However, God wants to create in our everyday lives the holiness that we already have in Christ. We are sanctified in Christ, and at the same time we are being daily sanctified by the Spirit, paradoxical as that may sound. The Spirit works within us to form Christ there.

Of course, the "law of sin and death" (Rom. 8:2) still operates in us. In this life we must always contend with the old self. However, the Spirit of God, in His practical sanctifying work, sets us free from the downward pull into sin. Paul said, "The law of the Spirit of life in Christ Jesus sets us free from the law of sin and death" (Rom. 8:2). The new law of the indwelling Spirit gives us victory; hence as our spiritual life deepens and we become more holy, more Christlike day by day.

Truth

*Sensitivity to the Holy Spirit is the only way
to keep ourselves from moral error and from
being sidetracked in life.*

The Spirit of God brings us to truth. Jesus made this clear when He said, "When He, the Spirit of truth, comes, He will guide you into all the truth; for He will not speak on His own initiative, but whatever He hears, He will speak; and He will disclose to you what is to come" (John 16:13). Paul reiterated the principle when he wrote, "'Things which eye has not seen and ear has not heard. . . . To us God revealed them through the Spirit; for the Spirit searches all things, even the depths of God" (1 Cor. 2:9–10). The Holy Spirit reveals truth in three ways.

First, He gives us assurance of our salvation. "The Spirit Himself bears witness with our spirit that we are children of God" (Rom. 8:16).

Second, the Holy Spirit interprets the Word of God to our hearts and minds when we read the Bible. He is the Author of Scripture; He alone knows its full meaning. How important, therefore, that we give ourselves to His instruction and influence as we study it. The Holy Spirit alone can enable us to understand the Word of God and, by His power, live according to it.

Third, the Holy Spirit keeps us from moral error. As we have already seen, we live in a day when we are pulled in every direction imaginable. If it is not the printed page, it's television; if it is not television, it's the radio—constantly urging us to believe this, believe that, believe the other thing. What is truth? What counts in life? Where can reality be found? What is right and wrong? Sensitivity to the Holy Spirit is the only way to keep ourselves from moral error and from being sidetracked in life. He alone is our sure Guide.

Direction for Life

The Holy Spirit not only leads us into truth, He constantly shows us the path we should follow. He grants us the wisdom to make right decisions in our relationships, our vocational goals, our family life, and in every area of our daily existence. What interests us interests Him. How gracious of our Lord to have such a personal concern in the smallest details of our life. One of the best indicators that we truly belong to God is that "All who are being led by the Spirit of God, these are sons of God" (Rom. 8:14). The Holy Spirit is called the *paracletos*: "One who comes by our side" (John 16:7). He draws close to lead us into a life of purpose. Actually, the Holy Spirit comes to us—and lives in us—to do countless wonderful things. He aids us in our difficulties; He gives us His comfort in sorrow and trial; He directs us into all that God has for us to do; He empowers us in Christ's service; He becomes our Friend and Counselor in every situation we face. Who could ask for more!

Prayer

The Holy Spirit aids us in prayer. We cannot pray properly without Him. Paul stressed this when he said: "The Spirit also helps our weakness; for we do not know how to pray as we should, but the Spirit Himself intercedes for us with groanings too deep for words; and He who searches the hearts knows what the mind of the Spirit is, because He intercedes for the saints according to the will of God" (Rom. 8:26–27).

The gracious Holy Spirit comes along as the "Professor"
in the school of prayer. He knows all things, including
the mind and will of God, and thus makes our prayer life
pleasing to the Father. Through the Spirit our prayers
take on the aura of Christ.

We really do not know how to pray as we ought, nor do we know what to pray for that will be in keeping with the will of God. But the gracious Holy Spirit comes along as the "Professor" in the school of prayer. He knows all things, including the mind and will of God, and thus makes our prayer life pleasing to the Father. Through the Spirit our prayers take on the aura of Christ.

Service

The Holy Spirit alone makes our service and witness for Christ active and effective. He can be properly called the "Great Empowerer." If the Holy Spirit does not act in a dynamic way, our work will be of little effect. The Lord said, "Apart from Me you can do nothing" (John 15:5). We would be wise to remember the words of our Lord Jesus just before His ascension: "You shall receive power when the Holy Spirit has come upon you; and you shall be My witnesses both in Jerusalem, and in all Judea and Samaria, and even to the remotest part of the earth" (Acts 1:8). This same truth is expressed in Acts 4:31: "When they [the disciples] had prayed, the place where they had gathered together was shaken, and they were all filled with the Holy Spirit, and began to speak the word of God with boldness." Service that really impacts the world will always come from the Spirit as He leads, empowers, and blesses God's work through us. He turns our service into a testimony to Christ's glory.

The Final Goal

To summarize: the Holy Spirit works within us, effecting salvation, sanctification, and service (Gal. 4:19). He does this in three ways: (1) He shows us our sin and leads us to repentance; (2) He produces in us the beautiful "fruit of the Spirit," (Gal. 5:22); (3) He lives through us, making our lives holy and prompting us to effective service. The Holy Spirit is called "the Spirit of Christ"; therefore, as He has increasing control and dominance in our life, He forms us into an embodiment of Jesus Christ. And so we overflow with the presence of the Lord Jesus to the glory of God. Amazing grace!

But how do we relate to Him? What does the Bible say about the Christian's reaction to the indwelling Spirit of God?

The Spirit-Filled Life

The Bible uses many metaphors for the Holy Spirit's relationship with the believer. The Bible says:

> We are *born* of the Spirit. (John 3:8)
> We are *indwelt* by the Spirit. (Rom. 8:9)
> We are *baptized* in the Spirit. (1 Cor. 12:13)
> We are *filled* with the Spirit. (Eph. 5:18)

Paul presents the admonition as a continual experience, and he employs the imperative voice. We must be filled with the Spirit every day.

The last description on the list—"filled with the Spirit"—is the one we are, at present, most interested in. The Bible employs this and similar expressions time and time again. Perhaps the clearest use of it can be found in Paul's oft-quoted admonition to the Ephesian church when he urged, "Do not get drunk with wine, for that is dissipation, but be filled with the Spirit" (Eph. 5:18). The grammar Paul uses is instructive. He presents the admonition as a continual experience, and he employs the imperative voice. We must be filled with the Spirit every day. But why does the Bible place such stress on this sort of continual experience?

Christlikeness

We will never be truly Christlike until we overflow with the Spirit's "rivers of living water." If we have restricted the Holy Spirit to a small area of our life, we will be like our Lord only in that area. Anne Lotz saw this clearly. She gave herself fully to the Spirit's control. That lies at the root of her overflowing life. We must pray that we might be "filled up to all the fullness of God" (Eph. 3:19). The Spirit-filled life, the Christlike life, and the overflowing life are synonymous.

Spiritual Growth

Our Lord also made it clear that the fullness of the Holy Spirit becomes essential for spiritual growth and maturity. We must abide in Christ; only then do we bear fruit (John 15:1–5); and abiding in Christ and living the Spirit-filled life are one and the same. Have we set our spiritual sight on becoming mature Christians? Is our goal fixed on being the sort of disciple the Bible envisages for us? Then we must move into the fullness of God by the Holy Spirit.

Empowerment

One of the great tragedies of the day is that many churches—and individual Christians—are inept at influencing the community in any significant way for Christ.

Furthermore, it should now go without saying, if our Christian service has any lasting impact, that work must be empowered by the Holy Spirit. One of the great tragedies of the day is that many churches—and individual Christians—are inept at influencing the community in any significant way for Christ. How different from the early church! How different from the church in other parts of the world today! How incredibly different from the times when God pours out His Spirit in *great revival power!* One illustration makes this obvious.

Real Revival: A Picture of Power

The Hebrides form a windswept archipelago off the northwest coast of Scotland. Icy storms blow off the North Atlantic, making the islands a chilling and bleak place to live. In 1949, however, the spiritual climate was even more dismal than the weather. Churches were virtually empty on a Sunday morning. Hardly a soul had serious thoughts about God. And then, two Spirit-filled women of prayer decided to do something about it. They took it upon themselves to intercede for their needy community, asking the Spirit of God to move in a powerful way. The women were sisters and both in their eighties when they began to cry out to God for revival. They prayed continually, sacrificially, and fervently. Probably the townsfolk, if they had known—or cared—would have scoffed and said, "What can two old women do?" Little did they know the power of prayer when the Holy Spirit generates the burden. The sisters prayed and prayed until finally they received the impression that an evangelist from Scotland, Duncan Campbell, should come and preach to them. They suggested this to their pastor, and being a true man of God, he perceived that their idea was inspired by the Holy Spirit. He invited Campbell to the Hebrides to preach in his church.

When Campbell received the invitation he was in the midst of a busy schedule of evangelistic meetings on the mainland of Scotland. He wrote back saying he would not be able to come unless he had a cancellation. Imagine his utter amazement when, for one reason or another, and within a matter of days, every single engagement was canceled. He began to realize that the Spirit of God was urging him to go to the Hebrides and minister there. So he packed his bags and sailed across the small body of water, ready to share the things of Christ with the secular people of the Hebrides. He knew, however, that he would need many others to help him there.

At the same time the sisters were praying, a small handful of men on the Isle of Lewis in the Hebridean group had been longing for spiritual awakening. They too had felt a deep concern for the spiritual condition of their town and had begun to meet several nights a week in an old barn outside their village, there praying fervently that God would revive His work (Ps. 85:6). This went on for some months until finally, in the midst of the prayer meeting, one of the younger men stood up and said, "Men, this is futile. Could it be, that we, who are most concerned for a true spiritual awakening, are the very ones standing in its path? God has laid upon my heart a passage of Scripture." He then read from the twenty-fourth Psalm:

> Who may ascend into the hill of the LORD? And who may stand in His holy place? He who has clean hands and a pure heart, who has not lifted up his soul to falsehood, and has not sworn deceitfully. He shall receive a blessing from the LORD and righteousness from the God of his salvation. (vv. 3–5)

No sooner had the young man uttered those words from the Bible, than the Holy Spirit fell upon the group in incredible power. They were smitten to the dirt floor of the barn under deep conviction of their own personal sins—though they were the most dedicated Christians in the area. They poured out their hearts in confession and soon found God's wonderful forgiveness. Once they had got all their sins "confessed up to date," as Bertha Smith, the great missionary of the Shantung Revival used to say, the Holy Spirit again came upon the men and raised them up in choruses of praise to God. Their voices seemed to ascend to heaven itself.

When the men were at last able to contain themselves, they discovered it was now the early hours of the morning; it was time to make their way back home. When they arrived at their little village, however, they discovered that the lights were on in most of the houses and a large group of townsfolk had gathered at the local police station. They thought some tragedy had occurred. When they inquired they discovered, to their astonishment, that the very moment the Spirit of God had fallen on them in the barn, the same pervasive Holy Spirit had fallen on the entire town, waking people out of their sleep, and bringing them under conviction of their sins. They had been so disturbed that they had dressed and gathered together, hoping someone could tell them how they might find the salvation of Jesus Christ and have their sins forgiven. Before dawn finally broke on that blessed morning, many had come to Christ. And it was these people who eventually joined hands with Duncan Campbell, providing the help he so badly needed in his ministry. Revival spread through the entire Hebridean Islands—and it all began with the prayers of the two Spirit-filled women.

The Way to Fullness

All these marvelous truths concerning the importance—yes, the necessity—of the Spirit-touched life demonstrate the experience of Christ's fullness. We have seen that to be filled with the Spirit we must walk daily in the abiding presence of our Lord. What then makes up the pathway to such a life? Several things need to be said first.

Pentecost Principles

Jesus fulfilled His promise on the Day of Pentecost. Luke wrote: "And when the day of Pentecost had come, they were all together in one place. And suddenly there came from heaven a noise like a violent, rushing wind. . . . And they were all filled with the Holy Spirit" (Acts 2:1–4). Pentecost reveals certain vital principles concerning evangelistic methods. Further, tremendous truths about prayer and waiting on God emerge. That wonderful day also demonstrates much about the doctrine of the church. For present purposes, however, we will confine ourselves to two issues.

First, on the Day of Pentecost the "Age of the Spirit" burst on the scene of human history. Since that hour, whoever puts their faith in Jesus Christ as Lord and Savior will immediately receive the gift of the Spirit. This is why Paul told the Corinthians that their bodies were the temple of God (1 Cor. 6:19).

Second, the early believers not only received the Holy Spirit for the first time, they also were filled with God's power. As the *American Commentary* points out, these first faithful followers had "a reception from the Spirit of extraordinary powers, in addition to sanctifying grace." In a word, they received the Spirit and were filled with the Spirit simultaneously. That should always be the pattern for new converts.

Pentecost was unique. That divine moment became God's signal hour to pour out His Spirit on all flesh (Acts 2:17).

At the same time this particular passage should not be pushed too far. Pentecost was unique. That divine moment became God's signal hour to pour out His Spirit on all flesh (Acts 2:17). It was a singular event in the life of the church and can no more be repeated than the crucifixion or the resurrection. At the same time, the passage surely implies that a Christian should have real experience of the Holy Spirit rather than merely knowing that Christ lives in his or her life. Our Lord wants His people to be conscious of the Holy Spirit's infilling. Pentecost forcefully projects that truth. Why not present to new converts the full message of the gospel as it relates to the Holy Spirit? If believers are ever open to all God has for His people, the moment of conversion is certainly the time. Genuine New Testament evangelism demands such an approach. We must help new believers to receive Christ as their Savior, but also we must point them to the Spirit's fullness. Evangelism of this depth could solve many of the problems new Christians have in subsequent spiritual growth.

The Example of Jesus

Our Lord clearly exemplified the Spirit-filled life. Jesus lived out His entire ministry in the anointing of the Holy Spirit. His baptism demonstrated that fact (Luke 3:21–22). All He said and did was directed by and permeated with the Holy Spirit's presence and power. John put it this way: "For the one whom God sent speaks authentic words of God—and there can be no measuring of the Spirit given to him" (John 3:34 PHLPS). Jesus always walked in the fullness of the Holy Spirit (Luke 4:1). If Christ stands as our example in all things, and surely He does, then we should attempt to emulate Him in His relationship to the Spirit of God.

Space forbids delving into numerous other New Testament passages that teach the same essential truth. The Bible abounds in examples regarding the importance of the Spirit-filled life (for example, Luke 1:15, 41, 67; Acts 6:3; 7:55; 8:17; 9:17; 10:44, 46; 11:15–16, 24). The overwhelming weight of the Word of God fully supports the idea that being filled with the Holy Spirit is a valid, vital experience for true spirituality. If we take the Bible seriously we cannot sidestep the fact that the Spirit-filled walk is God's intention for all His people. That is how we relate properly to the third person of the Trinity.

Unfortunately, even a casual look at contemporary Christianity demonstrates that considerable confusion persists on the subject. Before going any further it might be beneficial to deal with some current misconceptions. So many false ideas have emerged that even sincere Christians have been put off. It is important not to miss the truth because others have perverted the plain biblical teaching on the Spirit. So we will begin by graciously, but honestly, attempting to clear away some of the weeds that have sprung up in the beautiful garden of spiritual reality.

Some Necessary Corrections

The first thing to be uprooted is the idea that when people receive the Spirit's fullness they enter a state of sinless perfection. This "experience" is often called a "second work of grace." The exponents of this approach describe an event, similar to the conversion experience, that takes believers into an orbit of perfection such that they will never sin again. It is obviously impossible to square this with the Bible. To believe we can live faultlessly is simple self-deception (1 John 1:8); to say we never can sin is actually to call God a liar (1 John 1:10). We must wait for heaven for that level of perfection.

The "Gift"

Second, some teach that the fullness of the Spirit must be accompanied by a certain "gift of the Spirit." Usually the gift insisted on is the gift of tongues: *glossolalia*. An illustration may help here. One night a layman friend called at our home. He had brought along a fellow layman whom we had never met. As we talked together, this new acquaintance asked us if we had ever been filled with the Holy Spirit. As unassumingly as possible, we shared our view. Then he asked, "Well, have you ever experienced the infilling of the Spirit with tongues?" "No," we replied, "God has not seen fit to bestow that particular gift." He then said, "But you *should* seek the Spirit with tongues."

One can appreciate the man's zeal and be grateful for his concern that all Christians become Spirit-filled believers. He failed, however, to understand what Paul forthrightly declared to the Corinthian believers. Paul told them in unequivocal terms that God gives specific gifts, "as He wills" (1 Cor. 12:11). After all, in bestowing His gifts the Holy Spirit creates a body, unified and diversified. It would be a rather strange body if all had the gift of tongues. The body would be no more than one big tongue, not a normal body at all. In a later step we shall look at the doctrine of the gifts of the Spirit in considerable detail. In the meantime it is enough to say that there is certainly a legitimate gift of tongues (1 Cor. 14:1–5), but it is not the litmus test as to whether or not one is Spirit-filled.

Emotions

In the third place, some say that being filled with the Holy Spirit must always be an emotional experience. That growth of underbrush needs to be uprooted. Of course, being filled with all the fullness of God can certainly be emotional at times. Religious emotions are not wrong in themselves. They can be God-given and a source of true blessing. But to insist that being Spirit-filled must invariably manifest itself in great emotional upheaval misses the mark. That approach can degenerate into mere human emotionalism for its own sake. As unique individuals, we all react differently to various situations. For example, some have a very moving, emotional reaction at conversion. Others do not. It is wrong to insist on certain emotional responses to the gospel. The same principle applies to the Spirit-filled life. Let the emotions be as they will. A changed and fruitful ministering life becomes the test of reality.

Automatic Filling

A fourth false idea declares that the more one subdues "self," the more God *automatically* fills one with His Spirit. This approach can subtly sidetrack the Christian principle of faith. Faith and commitment matter most in claiming the infilling. It may be possible to yield to God and exercise faith unconsciously, but such an experience is rare. Conscious commitment and faith generally play a role. What finally matters is obedience to God's will and truly seeking the Spirit's fullness. The Bible says God gives the Holy Spirit to those who obey him (Acts 5:32), and who ask (Luke 11:13).

Self-Centeredness

Our search for the Spirit's fullness can also be perverted by self-centeredness. Remember our caution in step 2 of this book on "selfish spirituality." The blessings of our Lord must never be sought for any self-oriented end. For example, God never grants the Spirit's fullness that we may be thought of as "first-class Christians" while seeing others as inferior. We must not seek power in God's service so that self will be honored. Only God's glory matters. Moreover, the Spirit should not be desired so that we can retreat from reality, merely feel good, and live in some antiseptic ethereal spiritual realm. We need to come to grips with the blood, sweat, and tears of this world. God wants to be real to us, but not for our own indulgence. *The glory and service of Jesus Christ is the only legitimate goal in striving for God's fullness.*

Biblical Terminology

Before passing to the more positive presentation of the principle of the Spirit-filled life, it would be well to pause for a moment and put our terminology on a biblical basis. Error in nomenclature can bring about error in thought, if not in actions.

The Christian lifestyle has been called the "infilling of the Spirit," the "baptism in the Spirit," the "second blessing," and the "second work of grace." Such terms as *second blessing* and *second work of grace* are inappropriate. Neither these words nor the concept they imply can be found anywhere in the Bible. Being filled with the Spirit is far more than a "second blessing." Paul's admonition to the Ephesians in 5:18 urges us to be: *"continually* filled with the Spirit." Never does the Bible present the filling as a once-and-for-all experience. Life, dominated by the Spirit, is a daily blessing.

Baptism

The terms *infilling* and *baptism* are scriptural, however. Can a distinction be drawn between the two? At times they appear to come together in the Bible. In the bulk of scriptural references, however, something of a delineation can be drawn. The term *baptism by the Spirit* usually refers to the primary experience of being baptized by the Spirit into the body of Christ at the time of conversion (for example, Matt. 3:11; Acts 1:5; 1 Cor. 12:13), although this should no doubt be a time of filling with the Spirit as well. The expression *filled with the Spirit* normally describes the experience of those who already know Christ, that is, those already "baptized" with the Spirit. By continually filling the believer with the Spirit, God equips His people for service, ministry, and godly, fruitful living (for example, Acts 4:8, 31; 6:5; 7:55). We should guard against being legalistic, but it seems best to follow the general scriptural pattern to avoid confusion.

Michael Green, an excellent New Testament teacher, summed it up well in his fine volume, *I Believe in the Holy Spirit*. He wrote:

> While baptism in the Spirit is the initial experience of Christ brought about by the Spirit in response to repentance, faith and baptism, the fullness of the Holy Spirit is intended to be the continual state of the Christian. It is not a plateau onto which you are ushered by some second stage in initiation, a plateau which separates you from other Christians who have not had the same experience. The New Testament gives no support to that view whatsoever. In plain language, we are meant to be progressively filled with the Spirit of our Saviour Jesus Christ.[3]

The Real Meaning

The Holy Spirit who lives in the believer wells up and overflows to quench the thirst of needy lives. Christians should be a constant fountain of God's marvelous blessings.

The positive side of the truth can now be presented. What does it actually mean to be filled with the Holy Spirit, and how do we experience it? How can we live the overflowing life? The Bible makes it clear that the way to do this is to stay close to Christ. We need to be continually dependent on Him, constantly coming to Him as to a full fountain, thirsting for His best, trusting Him to fill us to overflowing with His Spirit. This gets to the heart of what Jesus meant when He said, "If any man is thirsty, let him come to Me and drink" (John 7:38). The Holy Spirit who lives in the believer wells up and overflows to quench the thirst of needy lives. Christians should be a constant fountain of God's marvelous blessings.

Anointings

Furthermore, there are times when God gives us special touches to fulfill some specific service or ministry. These experiences have been called "anointings." Anointing can be seen in such instances as Samuel anointing David so that his role as king of Israel would be fulfilled adequately (1 Sam. 16:13), or the anointing Jesus received for His messianic task (Acts 10:38).

Anointing implies a special outpouring for a definite undertaking. Situations arise in which God may choose to use us in an unusual way. That becomes the hour for a special anointing. Most of us have seen this aspect of the Spirit's work in action when, for example, someone shares God's word with great power. It can also happen in a simple witnessing encounter. We should earnestly pray for these special anointings. But again, we must not be too definite in our terminology. The Bible also occasionally describes this phenomenon as being "filled with the Spirit," for example in Acts 4:8, when Peter addresses the leaders of Israel.

A Summary

The experience of the fullness of the Holy Spirit can be summarized: As we "walk in the light as He is in the light," continually cleansed by Christ's blood and yielded to God's authority, we come to Him daily for the infilling of His Holy Spirit. Through this filling we find that life overflows with divine power and presence, making service effective and Christ-honoring. God uses this vital aspect of spiritual living to make us what Christ would have us to be.

To Be Filled with the Spirit

The final question is: How does one become—and stay—filled with the Holy Spirit? A few simple principles should answer this fundamental question. Together they form spiritual exercises that we can engage in regularly. These exercises should not be seen as a rigid formula for spiritual living. They are simply guidelines, or disciplines, to experience God's fullness.

Consciousness of Need

We must begin by becoming conscious of our need. If we are satisfied with our present spiritual state, little progress can be made. The Lord Jesus Christ said, "Blessed are those who hunger and thirst for righteousness, for they shall be satisfied" (Matt. 5:6).

Many things should move us to see this need. Tragic situations over the world cry out for help in Christ's name. We cannot begin to meet those demands in our own strength; we must have God's power. Our desperate society cries out for revival, but we require the infilling of the Holy Spirit to awaken others. Furthermore, we yearn for the fullness of God simply because of who He is and all He has done for us. The psalmist expresses the heart of the earnest Christian: "As the deer pants for the water brooks, so my soul pants for Thee, O God. My soul thirsts for God, for the living God" (Ps. 42:1–2). We must acknowledge our need, and if we have no real hunger for God or what He has for seeking believers, we should ask Him to create such a desire.

Confession of Sin

After God has created something of a genuine hunger and thirst in us for His best, and after we have become conscious of our need, we must confess and forsake all our known sins. It is absolutely necessary to turn from them in repentance and make restitution as necessary (Matt. 5:23–24). We then can claim the biblical promise, "If we confess our sins, He is faithful and righteous to forgive us our sins and to cleanse us from all unrighteousness" (1 John 1:9). And we must strive to say with Paul, "I also do my best to maintain always a blameless conscience both before God and before men" (Acts 24:16).

Commitment of Life

We must surrender the throne of our heart to Christ's control. In the final analysis, we always face one basic issue: Will I control my own life or will I truly make Jesus the Lord of all? We are forced to decide. Remember, the Holy Spirit comes to "those who obey him" (Acts 5:32). Christ must be Lord. Andrew Murray expresses it so well:

> Christ is my Leader; I must cling to Him, I must follow Him, in His leading. Christ is my High Priest; I must let Him lift me into God's presence. Christ is the living Son of God, our life; I must live Him. I am His house; I can only know Him as Son in His house as I yield myself to His indwelling.[4]

And again:

> The distinguishing mark of the earthly life of our High Priest (Jesus); the source of His heavenly glory and His eternal salvation; the power of His atonement of our disobedience; the opening of the living way in which we are to follow Him our Leader; the inner disposition and spirit of the life He bestows:—*of all this, the secret is obedience.*[5]

Many Christians seem unwilling to make such a commitment. Why? Perhaps we feel that such a decision will make us less than real people. To give up ourselves to another—even God—appears to destroy something of our essential freedom and personhood. Yet nothing could be further from the truth. The Devil's deception lies behind that feeling. The fact is, we only become a real people when we yield to Jesus Christ. We become truly "free" only as the Son of God sets us free (John 8:36).

We also may fear that God will ask some terrible thing of us if we yield ourselves to His control. Never forget, however, that God is our loving Father.

Understanding and compassion characterize our Lord. He only wants the best for His children. His will always brings fulfillment and meaning to life.

We may even fear that we will not be capable of keeping such a commitment. But Jesus, our High Priest, enables us by faith to live in obedience. As we yield, He strengthens. As we submit, His power becomes ours, and it is enough.

We rarely find it easy to yield ourselves to Jesus Christ—even realizing all these truths. But God will help us even here. For example, one day a man came to a minister of the gospel and said that he wanted to be filled with the Holy Spirit. Yet he could not bring himself to yield to the absolute lordship of Jesus Christ. The minister asked, "Are you willing for God to make you willing, and will you pray for that?" The man replied, "Yes, I'm willing to do that." So the man of God pointed the inquirer to 1 John 5:14–15: "This is the confidence which we have before Him, that, if we ask anything according to His will, He hears us. And if we know that He hears us in whatever we ask, we know that we have the requests which we have asked from Him." Obviously, God wants His children yielded, thus the prayer would surely be answered. So they prayed that God would make the seeker willing to yield himself to the lordship of Christ. As they shared in mutual prayer, claiming God's promise that He would hear, the power of Christ entered the inquirer's life, and he found that he could willingly present himself without reservation to God and seek the fullness of the Spirit.

Perhaps most of us need to begin there. Such a sincere prayer will surely be divinely honored. The Father will hear and enable us to make a commitment to Jesus Christ as the Lord of our lives in the fullest sense.

Claiming the Spirit

After coming to a consciousness of our need, confessing our sins, and committing control of our lives to Christ, we claim the fullness of the Spirit. Jesus said, "If you then, being evil, know how to give good gifts to your children, how much more shall your heavenly Father give the Holy Spirit to those who ask Him?" (Luke 11:13). On this wonderful promise, the great man of revival, Jonathan Edwards, said:

> From which words of Christ, we may also observe, that there is no blessing we have so great encouragement to pray for, as the Spirit of God. The words imply that our heavenly Father is especially ready to bestow his Holy Spirit on them that ask him. The more excellent the nature of any benefit is, which we stand in need of, the more ready God is to bestow it, in answer to prayer.[6]

God deeply desires His hungry-hearted children to ask Him for this gift of the Spirit's fullness. The term "ask" that Jesus used in the Luke passage quoted above actually means "continually ask." Thus we must ask both in the crisis moment and on a regular basis.

Contentment with Him

Finally, having asked, we now by faith simply *accept* the gift and thank God for His goodness. We need not necessarily pray long and agonizingly. We accept salvation by faith and do not ask for any sign or particular feeling that God has genuinely saved us; likewise we claim by faith the infilling of the Holy Spirit and rest content. If we have "paid the price," in faith we trust God will hear.

So simple, yet so profound! We can walk in God's presence and experience His fullness in our lives. Then blessings abound.

The Blessings of the Spirit-Filled Life

There are three summary points on the inner work of God's Spirit. First, the Lord becomes consciously real to us. The closeness and intimacy of Christ's presence produces peace and "joy inexpressible and full of glory" (1 Peter 1:8). Of course, He always stands by our side, whether we realize it or not. But when we walk in the fullness of the Spirit, Jesus manifests Himself in a most gracious manner. Trials, testings, temptations, and trouble will occur. We might find ourselves locked in spiritual warfare as never before. God may even seem "hidden." When those days do come, faith is the answer. Regardless of our situation or feelings, the Lord Jesus stands with us and imparts His power. We rest on His promises *by faith*. When Christ abides in us in all His fullness, fellowship with our Lord becomes the glorious result.

> *To think we actually rest in God's hands*
> *and that He abides in us, to lead, strengthen,*
> *direct, and use us — it is overwhelming.*
> *But it is true.*

Second, the reality of the Spirit's leadership and power for living and service becomes ours. This has already been amply stressed, but the blessing—the glory—of it warrants a continual prayer of praise to God for His grace of the Spirit. To think we actually rest in God's hands and that He abides in us, to lead, strengthen, direct, and use us— it is overwhelming. But it is true.

Finally, the Spirit-filled life generates and sanctifies the spiritual, awakened life. Paul expressed it this way: "If we live by the Spirit, let us also walk by the Spirit" (Gal. 5:25). That puts the capstone on the blessed life.

Conclusion

So there we have it; true spirituality means living an overflowing life, overflowing in the Spirit's wonderful work. The Holy Spirit fills us with holiness and godliness. May we, like Anne, become "filled with all the fullness of God."

Prayer

Heavenly Father, You have promised us the fullness of Your Holy Spirit. I long to be filled with all You are. I give myself to You and claim Your promise; Lord, fill me with the Spirit. And Father, now keep me close to You and use me for Your glory. Through Christ I pray and claim the answer to this earnest prayer.

10 Questions for Study and Discussion

1. What was the importance of Anne Graham Lotz's background in her life of service? Did her godly home become essential for her usefulness? What does that mean to us?
2. How do we account for Anne's ability to overcome her early timidity? Does something of that timidity help her today? Why?
3. How should we seek the "Magnificent Obsession" of God's overflowing life?
4. What is the source of the overflowing life?
5. Why do so many professed believers seem bereft of the overflowing life? What is the problem?
6. What does the Holy Spirit accomplish in His indwelling work?
7. What is the relationship between the Holy Spirit and effective service? And godly living?
8. What role does faith play in the Spirit's fullness?
9. How are we filled with the Spirit *every* day? What are we to do if we fail to walk one day in His fullness?
10. What constitutes the ultimate goal of the Spirit-filled life?

The Spiritual Woman Abides in God

MEET JESSIE PENN-LEWIS
A WOMAN WHO ABIDED IN GOD

Abide in Me.
(John 15:4)

$\mathcal{J}$t was said of Jessie Penn-Lewis that she was "a Christian lady, whom the King delighted to honor."[1] She lived sixty-six years of trial and testing, but few people have been used so effectively by God. Her story is like a bright ray of sunlight to the depressed and defeated. Jessie Penn-Lewis's understanding of life can be best related in her own words: "From the hour the Spirit of God whispered 'Crucified' to me, I also saw clearly the principle of *death with Christ* as the basis for *the full working of God through the believer*."[2] That terse statement sums up her victorious Christian outlook.

Jessie Jones came into the world on February 28, 1861. Though a significant portion of her ministry took place in the nineteenth century, she had the joy of reaching the pinnacle of her service to Christ during the great Welsh Revival of 1904 to 1906. Still, she was essentially a Victorian lass. The oldest of eight children, she had five younger brothers and two younger sisters. She was born into a wonderful family, and, as she put it, into "religious surroundings, in the lap of Calvinistic Methodism." Her grandfather, the Reverend Samuel Jones, was a well-known pastor in the Welsh Methodist Church. Jessie's father worked in an engineering firm in the little town of Neath, in South Wales. This churchgoing, hardworking, and productive family provided Jessie with a marvelous background which she could draw on in her service for Christ.

A Happy Home

God made Jessie's home a happy one. It was always open to ministers of all denominations, and always, as the Scriptures urge, "Given to hospitality" (Rom. 12:13). Jessie's parents were not strict denominationalists; they worshiped as Methodists, to be sure, but they lived on good terms with the local Anglican rector as well. Jessie, as a child, attended the Sunday school of St. David's Anglican Church in Neath, later joining the choir.

> $\mathcal{J}$essie remained physically frail, struggling against recurring illnesses all through life. As one biographer expressed it, "No true understanding of Jessie Penn-Lewis can be reached without remembering this handicap."

Jessie was a precocious child. She walked by nine months, and at the age of four she could read her Bible. She would readily pick up a storybook, devour it, and then describe every character in it. Unfortunately, Jessie was also a sickly child, and the family doctor prohibited any kind of pressure or stress being put on her. Because of this she was unable to receive any formal education until she was eight, when her parents began to send her to a boarding school for periods of three months at a time. The off months she spent in farmhouses in the mountains where she could regain her strength.

Jessie remained physically frail, struggling against recurring illnesses all her life. As one biographer expressed it, "No true understanding of Jessie Penn-Lewis can be reached without remembering this handicap."[3] At one point, when Jessie was ten, she seemed to gain a little strength. She entered a boarding school in Swansea, where the school leaders took special precautions concerning her health. All this was to no avail. Before long she was forced to return home, where her mother could take care of her. There Jessie became an ardent reader. The house was filled with so many books it looked like a library. Her father was a great admirer of the classics, and he made sure Jessie could always put her hands on the best literature.

Beginning Service—and Sadness

Jessie took an interest in a crusade her mother had been involved in at this time—the temperance movement. Her parents were strict disciplinarians who saw the consumption of alcoholic beverages as taboo. The temperance advocates in those days called themselves the "Templars," and they banded together in "lodges." Young Jessie's commitment to the movement so impressed her mother's lodge that, at the age of fourteen, she became honorary secretary, and she served in that capacity for two years.

Then tragedy struck the family. In the prime of his life and at the pinnacle of his profession, Jessie's godly father passed away. It was a hard time. In those days, precious little social help could be found when a family lost their breadwinner, and the Jones family had so many mouths to feed. As Jessie wrote, "My mother was left with eight children; I was the eldest, being sixteen, while the youngest was only three months old." And so the struggle began. Jessie had inherited a solid background of tenacity and courage from her parents. She knew what it meant to walk in integrity, and even in her teenage years she had developed an unusual capacity for sacrificial love. She set to work. With her help, and with the blessing of God, the family survived those difficult days. Our Lord does provide (Phil. 4:19). Jessie lived out her teenage years realizing that truth.

> *Jessie had inherited a solid background of tenacity
> and courage from her parents. She knew
> what it meant to walk in integrity, and even in her
> teenage years she had developed an unusual
> capacity for sacrificial love.*

Marriage

When she was only nineteen Jessie met William Penn-Lewis—and fell in love. The couple soon married. William had been warned by friends that he was marrying someone who might be an invalid for life. This in no way deterred him. Jessie herself said the marriage could only be described as a "genuine love match." It looked as though a rewarding life lay before them, though possibly a difficult one because of Jessie's ill-health. William became the auditor's clerk for the county of Sussex in the south of England. That meant the newlyweds would have to move to Brighton, the beautiful resort town on the English Channel. They hoped the better seaside climate would relieve some of Jessie's health problems.

Being brought up in church, Jessie had regularly heard the gospel. The Calvinistic Methodists faithfully declared the Good News of Christ. Not only that, a revival had swept through Wales about the time of her birth leaving in its wake a deep religious fervor in many of the congregations. In those dynamic days Charles Haddon Spurgeon was reaching the apex of his ministry along with other great British preachers. Christian literature, with an emphasis on the new birth, abounded everywhere. But, strange as it may seem, Jessie still had not come to know Christ in a true saving relationship.

Converted at Last

Some eighteen months into her marriage with William, Jessie began to feel ill at ease concerning her faith in Christ. Though she knew all of the right words and had imbibed many a sermon, still something was missing. She felt disturbed about the Lord's second coming. Subtly, but very clearly, she realized she was not ready to meet Him. Jessie began to seek Christ with all her heart.

God always embraces the earnest, seeking sinner. The Bible says, "Those who diligently seek me will find me" (Prov. 8:17). Conversion was coming:

> My conversion occurred without the aid of any human instrument, but the day—New Year's Day, 1882—and the hour are imprinted on my mind. Only a deep desire to know that I was a child of God; a taking of my too-little-read Bible from the shelf; a turning over of the leaves, and my eye falling on the words, *"The Lord hath laid upon Him the iniquity of us all"*; again a casual turn of the sacred pages and the word, *"He that believeth hath eternal life."* A quick facing out whether I *did* believe that God had laid my sins upon the Lamb of God on the cross; a pause for wonderment that it really said that I had eternal life if I simply believed God's Word; a quick cry of, "Lord I *do* believe"—and one more soul had passed from

death to life, a trophy of the grace of God and the love of Him who died. The Spirit of God instantly bore witness with my spirit that I was a child of God, and deep peace filled my soul.[4]

Jessie's journey to spirituality had begun.

The Victory Sought

As Jessie began to mature in her spiritual life, she became conscious of the power of sin. She struggled to overcome temptation, and was particularly disturbed by "one besetting sin"—it seems everybody has one. While this effort occupied Jessie's heart and mind, her husband William received an appointment to become Borough Accountant of Richmond, Surrey, on the western edge of London. This move proved providential. Settling in Richmond, Jessie and William made their way to Holy Trinity Church and came under the powerful ministry of the Reverend Evan H. Hopkins. Hopkins was a well-known personality in the Keswick Conventions, the spiritual life conference movement briefly mentioned earlier. Actually, he has been called the theologian of the early Keswick Conventions. As Jessie sat under his ministry, God created in her heart a deep hunger for victory in her life.

One day, while Jessie was visiting in the pastor's home, Mrs. Hopkins asked her directly: "Are you a Christian?" Jessie, of course, replied that she was. But then Mrs. Hopkins asked a second probing question, "Do you know the way of victory over sin?" Jessie had to admit that she did not; she was still in the throes of spiritual warfare. But, oh, how she longed to be an overcomer.

At 8:00 A.M. on February 28, 1884, on a half-sheet of notepaper, Jessie wrote,

> Lord Jesus, on this my 23rd birthday I do again yield my whole self unto Thee, soul and spirit, life, time, hands, feet, eyes, lips, voice, money, intellect, will, heart, love, health, thoughts and desires. All that I have, all that I am, all that I may be is Thine, wholly, absolutely and unreservedly. And I do believe that Thou dost take me, and that Thou wilt work in me to *will* and to *do* Thy good pleasure. Lord, use me in whatever way it seemeth good to Thee, keep my eyes fixed on Thee, ready to obey even Thy glance. Thou art my King, my Saviour, and my Guide. Take not Thy Holy Presence from me, but day by day draw me nearer, until that glorious time when I shall see Thee face to face, and faith be lost in sight. Amen.

Jessie got her first glimpse into the "secret" of Christian victory. She discovered that it began in surrender. Full surrender to Christ would unlock God's fathomlessly rich treasure-house. Under the Hopkinses, the Keswick message exerted its influence on Jessie's earnest quest. She longed for it to be said of her, as was said of the great Puritan Richard Sibbs, "Heaven was in him before he was in heaven."

The Keswick Movement

Through submission to the Lord and identification
with Christ in His death and resurrection, holiness
and sanctification can be realized.

The teachings of the Keswick Movement, so influential in the Hopkins's ministry, have been used by God powerfully for many years around the world. These teachings advocate Christian victory over sin and temptation through surrender to Christ in the *entire* Christian experience, not merely in conversion alone. Keswick teaches that through submission to the Lord and identification with Christ in His death and resurrection, holiness and sanctification can be realized. The movement has blessed countless people down through the hundred-plus years of its ministry, and through its ideas Jessie certainly got a good solid start.

William Finds Christ

During this enlightening time for Jessie, William came to genuine faith in the Lord Jesus Christ. He had a wonderful conversion experience and immediately set his hand to serving His newfound Lord. He became an effective speaker, especially in open-air meetings, and he began to witness for Christ through a mission in Richmond. Now Jessie and William, hand in hand, could go forward and mature into great servants of Christ.

Fullness

After Jessie's full commitment to Christ's lordship, her next step was to learn the vast difference between working for God and allowing God to work through her.

Jessie gave herself sacrificially before the light of the Spirit dawned on her. She was the librarian and a committee member of a Rescue Home for girls, and she conducted Bible class there every Sunday afternoon. As Jessie evaluated the class, she realized that the spiritual fruit being reaped did not measure up to all the energy she was expending on it. Still, in spite of bouts of pleurisy and lung infection, she gritted her teeth and pressed on. Later she had to confess that much of her service really was no more than "consecrated self," as she expressed it. She wrote, "I could not but own that I did not know the Holy Spirit in the *fullness* of His power." It took Jessie some time—and struggle—to understand her need of the Holy Spirit's strength, and that, as Jesus said, "Apart from Me you can do nothing" (John 15:5).

While Jessie struggled with illness and her earnest attempts to serve Christ, a book written by Andrew Murray, *The Spirit of Christ*, fell into her hands. She devoured it. Murray wrote on the theme of permitting God to work *in* and *through* the surrendered believer in the power of the Holy Spirit. With Murray's emphasis on the inner work of the Spirit, Jessie began to realize that it was not what she did, but what God did in and through her that mattered. As Jessie read, she said, "It seemed so deep, and almost beyond comprehension, but I do so long to know more of it. I seem to know so little—may He teach me!" God created a passion in Jessie's heart to experience the outpouring, unction, and fullness of the Holy Spirit in her life. The next leap in the Spirit was about to be taken. She began to cry out to God for His fullness. God always meets the needs and the cries of the open, yielded heart—and Jessie certainly had that kind of heart. Ten days later, Jessie's diary records these beautiful words:

> I came on the words "To others it comes as a deep, quiet, but clearer insight into the fullness of the Spirit of Christ as being theirs, and a faith that feels confident that His sufficiency is equal to every emergency." These words fairly "lit up" to me, and I saw that this had been my experience lately. I have never seen His power as I see it now. . . . Has not Jesus been teaching me knowledge, love, and obedience these last years; and have I not been entering into the fellowship of His death this winter as never before? Have I not been seeing the hopelessness of the flesh and feeling keenly its utter insufficiency?[5]

A great step forward had been taken—but God had even more to come.

Although Jessie had experienced this move of the Holy Spirit in her life, she still had to conquer her besetting sin: her hasty spirit. This weakness plagued her yet and, although Jessie's physical exhaustion must have fueled it, she felt that could be no excuse for behavior that did not exemplify the Lord Jesus Christ. And there was more. Jessie was very self-conscious around people and ill at ease about her Christian service. These problems, she realized, though not gross sins of the flesh, were sins of the human spirit. Jessie longed for victory over them. There was more work to do

More Work

At this time, Jessie received an invitation to become the honorary secretary of the Richmond YWCA. She hesitated to take the position because of her health. When she consulted with her doctor he was categorical that she should not take on such a task. Jessie was convinced that she would, in any case, live only a short time in light of her serious lung condition. So she told her doctor that she would rather "die doing something for God," than do nothing and live a few days longer. She accepted the position and enthusiastically went to work with all the strength she could muster.

A Lesson Still to Learn—and Learned

Although Jessie had experienced a true surrender to Christ and the fullness of the Spirit, she needed a deeper touch and anointing of God. What she really lacked was a "breaking." That alone would make her a victorious spiritual woman. And God did the work. Jessie said, "He began to break me and there came to me the terrible revelation that every bit of this activity, this energy, this indomitable perseverance, was *myself* after all, though it was hidden under the name 'consecration.'"[6] The difference between consecrated activity and brokenness before God is vast indeed. Before God uses a person mightily, a breaking must come. As the psalmist said, "The sacrifices of God are a broken spirit; a broken and a contrite heart, O God, Thou wilt not despise" (Ps. 51:17). And that breaking is a lifelong process. Jessie began to learn that the "self-life" must be put to death and exchanged for the "Christ-life." As Paul said, "Not I, but Christ" (see Gal. 2:20). Simply put, Jessie "died." The final step to spirituality lay before her—and she would take it.

This did not mean that testing times cease. Jessie began asking herself why she was seeking all God had for her. Did she want it for the Lord's glory alone, or so she would be considered a great spiritual servant? She wondered whether she had simply consecrated her "self," or if she was truly yielded, broken, and daily seeking God's best? Through such testings, the road to victory began to open for this woman of God.

The Clue

In the setting of all Jessie's questioning a word came home to her that struck deep in her soul: CRUCIFIED. Suddenly she realized, as she put it, "Calvary precedes Pentecost. Death with Christ precedes the fullness of the Holy Spirit."[7] This truth, this core of the Keswick message was what the Hopkinses had been trying to get over to Jessie for months. Then, one morning in March of 1892, the very glory of the Lord broke in on her receptive spirit. God manifested Himself. The step was taken, and God blessed her. She later listed what that experience had been like:

1. It was sudden, and when I was not specially thinking about the matter.
2. I knew in my spirit that He had come.
3. My Bible became like a living thing and was flooded with light.

4. Christ suddenly became to me a real Person; I could not explain how I knew, but He became real to me.
5. When I went to my Bible class, I found myself able to speak with liberty of utterance, with the conviction of the Spirit at the back of it, until souls were convicted of sin on every side.
6. There was power in prayer, so that it seemed I only needed to ask and have.
7. My spirit took its way to God, freed from every fetter that held to anything on earth.[8]

Jessie Penn-Lewis had learned to identify with Christ in His death and resurrection, and now Christ could live His life completely through her (Rom. 6:1–14). At last, the biblical message Evan Hopkins had been preaching got through.

The Meaning

What does it mean to be identified with Christ in His death and resurrection? Stephen Olford expressed it beautifully in his book *Not I, But Christ:*

> "I have been crucified with Christ" (Gal. 2:20). These words mean that our old self was crucified with Christ "so that the body of sin might be rendered powerless, that we should no longer be slaves to sin—because anyone who has died has been freed from sin" (Rom. 6:6–7 NIV). Observe that *this crucifixion with Christ is a past event.* We "have been crucified with Christ" (Gal. 2:20). The verb is in the perfect tense, indicating a completed action. This teaches us that the judicial (or positional) crucifixion of our sinful flesh took place some two thousand years ago—which is more easily understood when we remember that God judges the human race through one of two representatives: Adam or Christ. When Adam sinned, the human race sinned in him; when Jesus Christ came to redeem sinful people by His death, the human race died in Him. In Colossians 3:3 Paul writes, "you died" (past tense), denoting that our death dates from the death of Christ. The apostle goes on to tell us that when Christ died, *"He died to sin once"* (Rom. 6:10). This is something more than His death *for sins* (plural). The penalty of our sins was fully dealt with by our Lord Jesus Christ, as was the power of *sin.*
>
> Because we are united with Christ in His death, we share in the release from the dominion of sin. We are no longer under law, but under grace (Rom. 6:14). To the glory of God,

all the objectives and ends of Christ's crucifixion were accomplished judicially in us! God's law can make no claim on our sinful flesh that has not been dealt with in Jesus Christ—because of our union with Him in His death.

Perhaps an illustration will help. Capt. Reginald Wallis wrote many books on the victorious life and made a tremendous impact on my life. He tells of an incident during the American Civil War when men were drawn by lot to join the army. A man named Wyatt was called up to fight for the South. He was the sole breadwinner for his very large family. Realizing this hardship, another young man named Pratt volunteered to go instead. He was accepted and drafted to the front, *bearing the name and number of Wyatt.*

Eventually Pratt was killed in battle, and having died as the substitute and in the name of the other man, the full name of Wyatt was recorded as killed in action. At a later date Wyatt was again called up for service, but at the recruiting office he calmly stated that *he had died already.* When the entry was researched, it was discovered that although the real Wyatt was alive and well, he was *dead in the eyes of the authorities* because he was identified with his substitute. Therefore, he went free.[9]

In the same way, when Jesus died, I died and, therefore, I am free. That is my positional status in the Lord Jesus Christ. As a result, God isn't going to expect my death since His Son was my substitute. This is the liberating truth of *identification* with Christ.[10]

We will look into these blessed realities more deeply in a moment. They precipitate victory for us all.

The Rest of Faith

Now Jessie could rest by faith in Christ, appropriating His victory and power. At last, she could say "God is doing great things for me."[11] Jessie's work went on, and God poured out His power and victory on it. She began to bless people across Great Britain and her influence exploded in every direction. She became involved in a local mission, and she reached out through the Rescue Home to needy people. The YWCA was especially blessed by her efforts. There she organized the "Ready Band," a group of girls who gave themselves to any kind of Christian service. Yearly attendance at various YWCA classes increased from sixty-nine hundred to nearly thirteen thousand during the three years following her deepening experience. In describing the

YWCA work in those days a biographer said, "It seemed as if every member became a worker." And God provided for all of these extended ministries. Jessie adopted the philosophy that if God did not financially support the work, she would take it as an indication that He was through with that particular area and she would launch out into another Spirit-led ministry. God was accomplishing a marvelous work through His "crucified"—and "resurrected"—servant.

The Ministry Expands

Jessie's ministry began to take on a widespread significance. She traveled all over England, and then began to touch other parts of the world. For example, Miss Soltau, director of the Missionary Training Home of the China Inland Mission (now Overseas Missionary Fellowship), asked Jessie to bring a devotional talk during a Good Friday meeting at Mildmay. Jessie gave a fine message, and the Mission printed the heart of her presentation to send to the missionaries in China. It was then republished under the title "The Pathway to Life in God." The first edition soon sold out, and within five years, thirty-two thousand had been printed. That one little booklet has blessed Christian workers all over the world and still continues to inspire people. It was the start of a tremendous writing ministry for Jessie.

A New Move—More Ministry

*My life is not my own. I can do nothing else but
be obedient to the heavenly vision—since God has chosen
the foolish things of the world to confound the wise,
here am I, raised from the grave to be His instrument!"*

As the nineteenth century began to round out, Jessie's husband was appointed Treasurer of the Corporation of Leicester. Another change loomed before them. Would this mean Jessie's growing ministry would be curtailed? Within a month of their moving to Leicester, Jessie received her first call to overseas ministry. But would her health allow her to travel so far from home? It would be a strain, but Jessie felt led of God to go, and she responded with these words, "My life is not my own. I can do nothing else but be obedient to the heavenly vision—since God has chosen the foolish things of the world to confound the wise, here am I, raised from the grave to be His instrument!"[12]

Jessie first visited Sweden. This was her initial experience speaking through an interpreter, and it was difficult for her. She had to admit, "It was with much fear and trembling" (see 1 Cor. 2:3).[13] But God blessed her and she rose to the occasion. The following year she went to Russia, and through the bitter cold of January and February, she ministered to great effect in St.

Petersburg and Moscow. A Russian Christian responded with these words:

> Twenty years have we waited for you! God sent a messenger twenty years ago to tell us of *Christ for us,* and one or two others come now and then with the same message; but now God has sent another revelation: *Christ in you.* Twenty years have we been babes, but now it shall be *no more!* We are so, so happy![14]

Returning to England Jessie was asked to speak in Doncaster, Brighton, Richmond, and Finsbury. Then in late summer, she traveled to Switzerland, and later went as far as South Africa.

And everywhere she went she communicated the message, that for victory and effective Spirit-filled service, it is essential to identify with the death and resurrection of Jesus.

More Travels and Writing

As a new year dawned, Europe once again beckoned. From Russia, to Finland, to Denmark, back to Finland, and then to Denmark again Jessie traveled, letting God teach His wonderful message through her. In Russia, she ran into a problem, however. People attended her conferences in vast numbers. Many of them were "sectarians," that is, they were not members of the Russian Orthodox Church. In Russia at that time, the Orthodox authorities persecuted Baptists, Methodists, and other so-called "sectarians." Fines were imposed on them, their property was confiscated, and often they were imprisoned and exiled. It was the czar's religion or nothing. As a consequence, the ecclesiastical authorities took a dim view of Jessie.

After her Russian experience, Jessie Penn-Lewis wrote a book entitled *Conflict in the Heavenlies,* a collection of messages she had delivered on spiritual warfare. This became something of a classic. It went through various title changes and editions and finally culminated in her renowned volume, *War on the Saints,* written in collaboration with Evan Roberts, God's man in the Welsh Revival. *War on the Saints* remains the definitive book on biblical demonology and satanic warfare written to date.

*The cross always remained her central theme.
And for good reason: The cross brings lost people to an
awareness of their sin and the need of salvation.*

Jessie was always concerned that her primary message be the atoning death of Christ. She wrote another book under the title *The Message of the Cross* and later rewrote it as *The Cross of Calvary and Its Message.* She drew on the apostle Paul when he said, "May it never be that I should boast, except in the cross of our Lord Jesus Christ" (Gal. 6:14). The cross always remained her central theme. And for good reason: The cross brings lost people to an awareness of their sin and the need of salvation. Moreover, true believers are identified with Jesus Christ as they share in His cross and resurrection. The cross rests at the center of the entire Christian experience. As someone has said, there has always been a cross in the heart of God. Little wonder that Oswald Chambers, author of the famous daily devotional book *My Utmost for His Highest*, wrote to Jessie and said, "Your *Cross of Calvary* is preeminently of God."[15]

The living Christ truly became Jessie's Victor. Being identified with Him in life and death, the cross and the empty tomb, Jessie lived by faith, and achieved the conquering, spiritual life. God honored her significantly.

Health Trials

She spoke with genuine authority, not only opening up the Scriptures but applying them to home relationships and showing the way into a life that in itself was a witness to God's grace and power.

Despite Jessie's giant spiritual steps forward things were never easy for her. Her ill-health proved a constant burden. At times she broke down completely and was forced to stop her work. During these difficult days she would travel to Eastbourne on the Channel coast and, in the care of friends, try to regain her strength. Constant separations due to illness and speaking complicated her family life too. But the loving relationship between Jessie and her husband saw them through all difficulties. God was faithful.

As might be expected, Jessie attended the Keswick Convention year after year and spoke to the women's meetings on many occasions. It was said of her that "she spoke with genuine authority, not only opening up the Scriptures but applying them to home relationships and showing the way into a life that in itself was a witness to God's grace and power."[16]

To America

Jessie also traveled to the United States and Canada and had a wonderful ministry there. She spoke at the Moody Bible Institute in Chicago during its annual Worker's Conference. Then she traveled east by train to Northfield, Massachusetts, the birthplace of the great evangelist D. L. Moody. She spoke twice in the Moody chapel, where for many years the evangelist had conducted Bible conferences. Then on she went to New York City, where she spoke in the church of A. B. Simpson, one of the great men of God in the early twentieth century. She also spoke in the Reformed Episcopal Church of the Atonement in New York City, as well as the Harlem branch of the YWCA. And she managed to see Niagara Falls as well!

The Welsh Revival of 1904

At the turn of the twentieth century a tremendous revival broke out in Wales. The early stirrings of the Holy Spirit took place at the Welsh Llandrindod Convention. These conferences were the Welsh counterpart of the Keswick Convention in England and had been instigated largely through Jessie's influence. Six ministers were deeply touched at the first Llandrindod Convention, and, as a result, they agreed to meet once a month for a full day of prayer. Faithful prayer always forms the foundation of true revival. Then, at the 1904 Llandrindod Convention, as the Spirit of God moved, people decided to gather together for a midnight prayer meeting. They consecrated themselves totally to the Lord—and great things began to happen. Jessie expressed it like this, "We have prayed for revival. Let us give thanks! The 'cloud the size of a man's hand' about which the Rev. Seth Joshua wrote in October is now increasing. God is sweeping the southern hills and valleys of Wales with an old-time revival."[17] Under the leadership of Evan Roberts, R. B. Jones, and a host of others, the revival spread over the land.

Writings on the Revival

Jessie herself wrote an account of this great Welsh Revival in a little book entitled *The Awakening in Wales*. She contributed weekly to *The Life of Faith*, an evangelical publication, and she also wrote for *The Christian*, a periodical that had grown out of the Moody evangelistic meetings in Britain. In both of these periodicals she continued to report the marvelous things that God was accomplishing.

During genuine spiritual awakenings, Satan will often attempt to counterfeit true experiences and divert people from what the Lord is doing. In *War on the Saints*, which Jessie finished around this time, she attempted to expose satanic counterfeits of the Spirit's work. Some have argued that Jessie's super-sensitivity to demonic deviations, deviations that did to some extent manifest themselves during the Welsh Revival, inhibited the movement. Such could hardly have been the case. In attempting to keep the revival pure and biblical, Jessie wrote well.

Wales saw wonderful days as spiritual awakening swept the nation. On one occasion these authors had the privilege of talking with a dear old lady who could remember the marvelous experiences of the Welsh Revival. Down through the years she had remained a radiant Christian. Those converted in such deep movements of God, for the better part, persist in their Christian commitment to the end.

Labors and Loss

As the "labors more abundant" increased, so did a dark cloud of acute personal trial. Failing health began to plague Jessie's dear husband William. His physician insisted he take three months of complete rest. This did little to alleviate William's physical deterioration. His illness forced him to resign his position as city treasurer and retire. Jessie and William moved to the Surrey Hills some sixty miles south of London, hoping William would be able to regain his health there. The Hills boasted the best climate in the country. But it was all to no avail. On March 24, 1925, William Penn-Lewis went to be with his Lord. He was buried in the Friends Burial Ground in Reigate, Surrey. In a simple little service, led by the great F. B. Meyer, loved ones and friends laid him to rest. It seemed appropriate that William should be interred in a Quaker meeting house burial ground, as he was a direct descendant of William Penn, the Quaker colonizer of Pennsylvania. Jessie grieved but found the comfort of Christ.

Last Days

The time was rapidly approaching for Jessie's own homegoing as well. Two years after the death of her husband, Jessie's health began seriously to decline. She had always been frail, but now with the bereavement and the weight of loneliness, it looked like God was ready to call her to Himself. She bore up well by the grace of Christ. She had reached sixty-six years of age, and the journey had been long. It seems most fitting that her final trip was to Wales and the Llandrindod Convention. After this she returned to London exhausted. A few days later, on August 15, 1927, she quietly slipped into the arms of the Savior whom she had known, served, and loved so well. She was buried beside her husband in the little cemetery at Reigate. A giant had gone home— but what a legacy she had left. Her writings, her lingering testimony, and the memory of her life still proclaim that same message. There is victory in Christ.

The Path to Victory for All

What is the essence of a life of victory? The answer: abiding daily in the Lord Jesus Christ and claiming as one's own all that He is. As our Lord Jesus Christ Himself said:

> I am the true vine, and My Father is the vinedresser. Every branch in Me that does not bear fruit, He takes away; and every branch that bears fruit, He prunes it, that it may bear more fruit. You are already clean because of the word which I have spoken to you. Abide in Me, and I in you. As the branch cannot bear fruit of itself, unless it abides in the vine, so neither can you, unless you abide in Me. I am the vine, you are

the branches; he who abides in Me, and I in him, he bears much fruit; for apart from Me you can do nothing. If anyone does not abide in Me, he is thrown away as a branch, and dries up; and they gather them, and cast them into the fire, and they are burned. If you abide in Me, and My words abide in you, ask whatever you wish, and it shall be done for you. By this is My Father glorified, that you bear much fruit, and so prove to be My disciples. (John 15:1–8)

This passage, spoken by our Lord at the crucial time just before His crucifixion, strikes right at the heart of the matter. The spiritual woman abides in Christ. It is that straightforward. But much more is implied. Jessie Penn-Lewis learned the principle—and we can also.

The Meaning of Abiding

Abiding in Christ means being in "fellowship" with Him. Fellowship is a wonderful kind of intimacy. If we had lived in the first-century Roman world and had spoken Greek, the original language of the New Testament, we would see immediately the scope of the word *koinonia* that we translate "fellowship." Joseph Henry Thayer, in *A Greek-English Lexicon*, defines *koinonia* as,

> The thing in which one shares . . . i.e. in the benefits of Christ's death . . . in the Body of Christ or the church . . . to obtain fellowship in the dignity and blessings of the Son of God . . . (becoming a) partaker in common of the same mind of God and Christ . . . and of the blessings arising therefore.[18]

Quite clearly this scholarly definition portrays a rich experience. Through *koinonia* we walk in intimate union with the Lord Jesus Christ. We share in His life so that all He is in His divine personhood becomes a precious reality to us.

The Joy of It All

*God loves us. He did not create us as He created
the inanimate objects of the universe. He formed us
as objects of His love, with whom He could
have fellowship.*

Fellowship allows us the sheer joy of being close to Christ. John expressed it this way: "What we have seen and heard we proclaim to you also, that you also may have fellowship with us; and indeed our fellowship is with the

Father, and with His Son Jesus Christ. And these things we write, so that our joy may be made complete" (1 John 1:3–4). Think: The all-knowing, all-powerful God actually invites us, people like us, into His intimate fellowship! How can it be? The answer is that God loves us. He did not create us as He created the inanimate objects of the universe. He formed us as objects of His love, with whom He could have fellowship. God said, "Let Us make man in Our image" (Gen. 1:26). God deeply desires that we have fellowship with Him; He has created us so that we can. It is a real and glorious possibility.

But as we saw in the first chapter of this book, sin has invaded the human family, and we no longer have the innate ability to walk with God "in the cool of the day" (Gen. 3:8). So God has reached out in His creative grace and has provided the means by which fellowship with Him can be restored, through the life, death, and resurrection of our Lord Jesus Christ. Now God's people not only have the possibility of walking in fellowship with the creating Father God; He fully expects them to do so. How can we experience this in all its richness?

The Means of Abiding in Christ

There are two things necessary for fellowship with Christ. First we must live a life of obedience. When Jesus admonishes us to abide in Him, it means that where He sends us, we go; where He leads us, we follow; what He prohibits, we reject; and what He expects, we perform. There can be no abiding without obedience.

Second, we must live a life of faith. We know that initially we experience salvation by grace *through faith*. Good works do not suffice. Paul made this very clear, especially in the Roman and Galatian epistles. He went so far as to say that if anyone denies or perverts this truth, the *anathema* (that is, the curse of God) rests upon that person (Gal. 1:6–9). It was the rediscovery of this marvelous truth that sparked the great Protestant Reformation in the sixteenth century. We must cling to this cherished biblical principle.

But it is here that we often err. After being saved by faith in the person and work of Jesus Christ, we have a tendency to thrust ourselves back under the "law" again. Jessie Penn-Lewis discovered this error in herself. It spells defeat in the quest for the sanctified life. This is why Paul said in Galatians 3:3, "Are you so foolish? Having begun by the Spirit, are you now being perfected by the flesh?" We must recognize that abiding in Christ is a *faith walk*, not a walk striving to keep the "law" in human strength, laboring under our own power to become more holy. We are saved by faith and we are sanctified—made holy—by faith. Striving to keep the "law" in the energy of the "flesh" through human works will always end in failure.

And so, if we aspire to abide in Christ, we do so by grace through obedience and faith. Motives abound for fastening our gaze on that goal.

The Motives for Abiding in Christ

Our primary motive for abiding in Christ should be that we wish to give glory to Him. Peter said:

> Whoever speaks, let him speak, as it were, the utterances of God; whoever serves, let him do so as by the strength which God supplies; so that in all things God may be glorified through Jesus Christ, to whom belongs the glory and dominion forever and ever. Amen. (1 Peter 4:11)

Clearly, the abiding, loving Christian becomes
a glory and praise to Christ.

The Lord Jesus Himself said, "I glorified Thee on the earth, having accomplished the work which Thou hast given Me to do" (John 17:4). Clearly, the abiding, loving Christian becomes a glory and praise to Christ.

A further motivation for abiding in Christ is the comfort it can give us. Being saved means that we will spend eternity with Jesus—but we do not have to wait to walk in His blessed presence. Christ transforms our daily experience right now. In our weakness, He gives us strength; in our trials, He gives us comfort; in our uncertainty, He gives us leadership. His joy and peace become ours. The Lord said so clearly, "I came that they might have life, and might have it abundantly" (John 10:10). What would life be without these assurances?

Another reason for abiding in Christ is its importance for others. When we abide in Christ, the life of the Lord Jesus radiates from us. The story is told of an old man of God who invited one of his novices for a walk, saying, "We are going to walk down the street and preach a sermon today. If we have to, we will even use words." The message is clear: Our lives should so radiate Christ that people will sense in us something of the gospel of Jesus Christ. That can only come about by abiding in our Lord.

This world desperately needs a word of witness, a gesture of love, a touch of concern, some simple act or word that speaks of Christ's own love. It longs to see the reality of Christ manifested in the lives of His people. The criticism that the church is filled with hypocrites has a measure of truth. It may be an exaggeration, used as an excuse to avoid the demands of Christ, nevertheless, we must grant it some credence. And it does cause seeking souls to stumble. Christians should so exemplify the Lord Jesus Christ that all such criticisms evaporate in His presence. This is motivation enough for us to abide in our Lord.

Having discovered the means of abiding in Christ and the motive for doing so, we now must look at how we can abide in our Lord. This brings us to the heart of this chapter's step toward spiritual living.

How to Abide in Christ

First we must deal with our sin problem. We considered this issue briefly in the previous chapter on the fullness of the Holy Spirit. Now we need to look at it in more depth. We begin by realizing that although God's salvation frees us from the final judgment and we rest secure in Christ (Rom. 8:38–39), still we will suffer temptation. Still, we struggle against sin. When Jessie Penn-Lewis learned God's way of victory over sin, she did not suddenly live a life of sinless perfection. We all must deal with sin in God's prescribed manner. We cannot harbor it, refusing to confront it, while aspiring to abide in Christ.

The Sin Problem

There is a puzzling paradox in our contemporary, permissive society. The "old-fashioned" ideas of sin, guilt, and remorse have been dismissed as a hangover from the "outdated" Puritan era. Yet, psychiatrists' consulting rooms are jammed with people plagued with guilt. Of course, we can paste new labels on the problem, but renaming it does not solve it. There remains that mountain of shame lurking in the background. It casts a shadow over all of life. If only we could be brave and honest enough to face the reality. And if we desire to abide in Christ we must.

Being honest with ourselves is never easy, even for Christians. In David's case, it took a fiery prophet accusing him to his face and thundering out, "You are the man" (2 Sam. 12:7). Nothing short of that sort of trauma could bring the king to himself. Yet the Bible presented David as a man after God's own heart. Believers do sin. The most difficult words we ever frame are those of the prodigal son, "I have sinned" (Luke 15:21). But frame them we must, for, "If we say that we have not sinned, we make Him [God] a liar" (1 John 1:10). We surely do not want to do that!

> *In David's case, it took a fiery prophet accusing him to his*
> *face and thundering out, "You are the man" (2 Sam. 12:7).*
> *Nothing short of that sort of trauma could bring the king*
> *to himself. Yet the Bible presented David as a man*
> *after God's own heart. Believers do sin.*

Now, how does all of this fit into the pattern of an abiding life and being in fellowship with God? A brief study of the first chapter of 1 John will perhaps clarify things and provide some answers.

John's Admonition

In John's excellent exposition on fellowship in chapter 1 of his first epistle, he describes the spiritual experience of Jesus Christ. In verse 7 he writes: "If we walk in the light, as He Himself is in the light, we have fellowship with one another." This fellowship "in the light" is key. As one Bible scholar has expressed it:

> To gaze upon the heavenly Christ in the Father's presence, to whom all things are subject, will transform us into heavenly Christians, dwelling all the day in God's presence, and overcoming every enemy.

The idea that we might have fellowship with our God is a marvel, considering that, "God is light, and in Him is no darkness at all" (1 John 1:5). The metaphor of light, often used in the Scriptures, depicts the essence of God's character, and refers primarily to His absolute and consuming holiness. We can see this attribute of God most graphically in Exodus 33–34, where Moses meets with God on the holy mountain. The picture we get of Moses is compelling. For years he had endured the criticism and constant complaints of the Israelites as they wandered through the wilderness of the Sinai Desert. They had broken God's covenant, and Moses badly needed a fresh touch from God. He prayed, "Oh God, I need You. Don't send us onward unless I can see Your goodness, Your glory, and know You are with us. If only I could see You."

God, always gracious to His servant's cry, answered Moses with words of comfort and encouragement. God said in essence, "Moses, I understand, and I honor your request to 'see' Me. I will renew My covenant relationship with the nation. However, no one can look fully upon the Holy Lord and live. I must always remain in some sense 'hidden.' Yet, I will meet your need. So that you will know I am with you, I will cause all of My glory and holiness to pass before you. But as I pass by, I will have to put you in the cleft of the rock and put My hand over your face lest you look upon the Lord and are consumed. Then you shall see only My back as I depart into the Shekinah cloud of My glory." We sing about that glorious experience in one of Fanny Crosby's insightful hymns:

> He hideth my soul in the cleft of the rock
> That shadows a dry, thirsty land;
> He hideth my life in the depths of his love,
> And covers me there with his hand.
>
> Fanny J. Crosby,
"He Hideth My Soul"

Moses came down from his encounter with God, and when the Israelites saw him, they shrank back, awestruck. Although Moses was unaware of it, the very skin of his face was glowing with the reflected light of his backward glimpse of God's consuming holiness. "God is light, and in Him there is no darkness at all" (1 John 1:5). And marvel of marvels, this is the God who invites us to come and live in abiding fellowship with Himself.

A Disturbing Dilemma

But there is a disturbing dilemma. God is holy light. No darkness can abide in His presence. And just as physical light and darkness cannot occupy the same space simultaneously, neither can God's holiness and human sinfulness. No one can walk in fellowship with the God of light and still cling to evil darkness.

We ignore our sin either in rebellion
or because we do not know how to deal with it.

This is the sting of the dilemma. Our Lord Jesus Christ says, in effect, "Come, abide with Me in the light. Yet you cannot do so if you refuse to deal with the darkness of sin in your daily life." Often we ignore our sin either in rebellion or because we do not know how to deal with it. We rationalize the problem and deny its very existence. But we must honestly face our sins. John forcefully reminds us, "If we say that we have no sin, we are deceiving ourselves, and the truth is not in us" (1 John 1:8). What are we to do?

The Answer to the Dilemma

How do we deal with the problem of sin in God's prescribed manner? The solution must be sought at all costs; abiding in Christ—the possibility of dynamic Christian spirituality—hangs in the balance.

All this emphasis on sin may seem negative. But John has not produced a somber picture, with his broad brush strokes of blacks and grays, just to make us depressed. He has done so, so that we might move from the despair of sin-ruptured fellowship with Christ into the joy of abiding in the light. That is positive indeed.

And John gives the answer to the dilemma: "If we walk in the light as He Himself is in the light, we have fellowship with one another, and the blood of Jesus His Son cleanses us from all sin" (1 John 1:7). This is the key: "The blood of Jesus . . . cleanses us from all sin." If we want to walk in the light of God's presence, we must be *constantly cleansed* by the power of Christ's forgiveness. This means a daily cleansing of sins by the efficacy of Christ's precious blood. And so we have the solution.

Often we restrict the death of Christ to the past, to the time when we first experienced salvation and were forgiven of sin. Of course, that experience does set us on the path of life. Through Christ's great redemption we received a wonderful *relationship* with God: that of Father to child. But once saved, we have a *fellowship* to maintain. And John makes it clear that if we Christians would walk in fellowship with our Lord, we must be constantly cleansed by the blood of Christ as well as being saved by it. That is to say, the death of Christ should not be restricted to conversion alone in our experience. God intends His Son's sacrifice to be effectual *every* day so that we may abide in Christ. That daily cleansing dispels the darkness and allows us to walk in the light.

> *Too few have grasped the biblical concept of how believers should deal with their sins in order to be continually cleansed and to abide in fellowship with God.*

Most of what has been said to this point seems reasonable. Yet nebulous thinking creeps in. We may agree that we need to be regularly cleansed. However, too few have grasped the biblical concept of *how* believers should deal with their sins in order to be continually cleansed and to abide in fellowship with God. Getting a firm, biblical grip on these practicalities helps our spirituality to grow tremendously.

Manifestations of Sin in Relationships

Sin exerts itself in relationships. It makes an impact on us in three ways. First, sin always involves our relationship with God since every sin is an affront to Him. Second, sin also affects our relationship with others, since others are inevitably affected. And third, sin involves the church. Sin is always *personal* and *specific*. Only as we view our sins individually and through these three categories, can they be dealt with forthrightly. And the biblical way of dealing with them is *confession*.

Confession of Sins

The Bible tells us we are to *confess* our sins. What does John mean when he urges us to bring our sins to God in confession?

The Greek word for "confession" is intriguing. In the language of the New Testament, it is a compound, comprising the verb *to say* and a prefix meaning *the same*. The word we translate "confess" in our English Bibles literally means "to say the same thing as" or "to assent to" or "to agree with." Confession means we "agree with" concerning our sins.

With whom, however, do we agree concerning our sins? The answer is obvious: the Holy Spirit (John 16:7–11). The Spirit of God places His convicting finger on specific, individual sins which have warped our abiding walk with Jesus Christ. For Christians, to confess sins means "to concede to" or "to agree with" the convicting Spirit of God that some *particular* act truly is a sin. It means getting out of our own self and standing by the Holy Spirit, being objective about the issue, and agreeing with Him.

Specific Confession

It requires a willingness to linger before God, permitting the Holy Spirit to search us out. David prayed, "Search me, O God, and know my heart; try me and know my anxious thoughts" (Ps. 139:23).

Confession is not a general, nonspecific admission of sins. How often we simply pray, "Lord, forgive all my sins"—and that's it! The Bible never addresses Christian confession in a general way. John states, "If we confess our sins, He is faithful and righteous to forgive us our sins and to cleanse us from all unrighteousness" (1 John 1:9). We are to confess each *sin*, specifically, not our *sins* as an entity. When we generalize our confession, no assurance of specific forgiveness can be experienced. Such an approach to confessing sins may be appropriate for a worship service or in a group, but in individual private prayer, it will never do. To confess sins, according to John, means to name them individually, agreeing with the Spirit of God that particular acts of which He convicts us have truly grieved our Lord. This demands heart-searching honesty and objectivity. It requires a willingness to linger before God, permitting the Holy Spirit to search us out. David prayed, "Search me, O God, and know my heart; try me and know my anxious thoughts" (Psalm 139:23). Above all, it requires a *broken heart*, a realization that our sins put Jesus on the cross and have disrupted our fellowship with God.

Of course, it goes without saying that when we confess our sins we must willingly forsake them in repentance. This is presupposed in the biblical concept of confession. True brokenness before our Lord will move us to expel the evil that so disappoints Him. And when we have acknowledged every individual known sin before God, we can live in the assurance that we have been thoroughly and completely cleansed by the blood of Jesus Christ (1 John 1:9).

A Sin Account

A deeply spiritual missionary lady of our acquaintance confesses by means of a "sin account." She numbers the lines of a page sequentially. Then in the quiet of a secret place before God, she prays that the Holy Spirit will reveal every act displeasing to Him, everything she has done that has marred her relationship with Jesus Christ. She writes down these individual sins. Finally she brings the promise of 1 John 1:9 to bear on each one. Through this exercise she experiences a sense of real forgiveness, allowing her a deeper abiding fellowship with Jesus. Then the "sin account" can be simply be destroyed. We should make something like that a part of our regular spiritual habit, even if we do not actually write down our sins.

Of course, we all have "unknown," or "secret" sins, those evils that lurk in the hidden recesses of our hearts which at our present stage of spiritual maturity we do not recognize. They must be confessed as well. Though we cannot "name" them specifically, we can pray as David did: "Cleanse Thou me from secret faults" (Ps. 19:12 KJV). God will hear that prayer of confession also. As we grow in Christ, the Holy Spirit will progressively point out these sins to us and allow us to deal with them specifically.

Forgiveness

The forgiveness of God is a marvelous experience indeed. "To forgive" in John's terminology means to wipe out a debt. "To be cleansed" implies the blotting out of a stain. Not only will God eradicate all debts, He will also blot out the stain of their memory so that we are not dragged down into spiritual depression. The Bible says, "I will be merciful to their iniquities, and I will remember their sins no more" (Heb. 8:12). God forgets; so can we. We are set free.

Other Implications

What if some sins involve relationships with other people as well as our relationship with God? In such cases, confessing these sins to God alone will not allow us to experience full liberty. We should confess them to God; all sin should be brought to our Lord for cleansing. But in the Sermon on the Mount Jesus urged: "If therefore you are presenting your offering at the altar, and there remember that your brother has something against you, leave your offering there before the altar, and go your way; first be reconciled to your brother, and then come and present your offering" (Matt. 5:23–24).

The simple truth expressed by our Lord Jesus Christ cannot be avoided: If we sin against another person and our fellowship with them is marred, restitution must be made to the offended person. We must acknowledge our sin and seek forgiveness from those we sin against, as much as possible and as God leads. If we fail to do so we cannot really expect a true abiding fellowship with Christ—or with one another (1 John 1:3).

Humble confession to another is difficult but necessary. If we cannot speak to the offended person face-to-face we can telephone, or write, or e-mail. It is important that we are right before God *and others*. After all, the Bible presents this as the only honest, ethical thing to do. Yet, it is hard; the Holy Spirit has to bring us to a place of brokenness before God (Ps. 51:17) before we are willing to humble ourselves to others (James 4:10). But God can mold and form the heart so that our lives exemplify Jesus Christ; He too was a man of contrite, humble spirit. Such a spirit among us all would revolutionize our homes, our churches, our nation, and our world.

A Final Step—A Difficult One

There can be times when sin manifests itself not simply against God, nor simply against another individual. It may be flagrant and open, bringing reproach to the church as well. Hopefully, this situation does not occur often, but what do we hear the Bible saying if it does? James tells us, "Therefore, confess your sins to one another, and pray for one another, so that you may be healed" (James 5:16). Does James mean that there are certain sins we should confess to a group in the church or even to the whole congregation? It seems to be his meaning. This is *really* difficult. It would be wonderful, though, if such fellowship existed among believers that we could always be open, honest, and candid about ourselves. The church should be like this, a place where love and acceptance can heal ruptured relationships. We have a need to be honest about ourselves to our brothers and sisters in Christ, without feeling threatened. If our churches could only be genuine caring communities, we could drop our masks there and be ourselves. Our reticence would vanish.

A Caution

In this area of confession, real care must be taken that openness does not degenerate into a simple airing of one's "dirty linen." This is a satanic trap, and it can be very damaging to spiritual health and fellowship. There are things in our lives that only God should know. The biblical mandate is to confess sins in the area of the offense. All sin should be confessed to God, and then confessed to those sinned against. Going beyond these scriptural guidelines can create serious problems. We must be honest; we must be open; but we must be Spirit-led. A sensitivity to the Holy Spirit, as we abide in Christ, will allow Him to direct and lead in the matter of what sins need to be confessed and to whom. Of course if the sins are so gross and open that reproach is brought upon the entire church and fellowship there is damaged, then forgiveness should be sought from the entire congregation. And occasionally congregations must exercise church discipline. This constitutes the real, scriptural meaning of a public "rededication."

The Bible declares that sin should be confessed. We need to confess to those we have sinned against—God, others, or the church. Only then can we be engaged in true spiritual fellowship.

More

*We cannot be perfect, but we can be
"overcomers." Abiding in Christ
makes us conquerors.*

Abiding in Christ is more than a continual round of temptation, sin, confession, and restitution. In itself, that would constitute a defeated lifestyle. Let it be understood and fully acknowledged: *Victory can be found in our Lord Jesus Christ.* We cannot be perfect, but we can be "overcomers." Abiding in Christ makes us conquerors. Paul said, "In all these things we overwhelmingly conquer through Him who loved us" (Rom. 8:37). That truth must be claimed along with the promise of forgiveness and cleansing. How can we get on that road to victory?

The Road to Victory in Christ

We can experience *victory* over temptation and sin because we are in Christ. This truth meant so much to Jessie Penn-Lewis, as we have seen. That key expression needs further investigation, however. Paul alone used the phrase—or its equivalent—more than 160 times in his letters. It must be very important indeed.

*Being a conqueror comes only through faith. Faith,
not human striving, is the key that unlocks all
of God's treasure-house.*

The Centrality of Faith

John formulated the foundation of spiritual victory when he wrote: "This is the victory that has overcome the world—our faith" (1 John 5:4). The way of victory is the way of faith. When we strive in our own energy to be overcomers, we inevitably end up having to say with Paul, "For the good that I wish, I do not do; but I practice the very evil that I do not wish" (Rom. 7:19). That is not victory—but defeat! Lack of faith forces us into the warfare of the "Wilderness." We are prevented from entering the "Promised Land" (Heb. 4:6). Being a conqueror comes only through faith. Faith, not human striving, is the key that unlocks all of God's treasure-house. Paul presents the same spiritual plan when he says, "Above all, taking the shield of faith, with which you will be able to quench all the fiery darts of the wicked one" (Eph. 6:16 NKJV). John Yates, the hymn writer, had it right: "Faith is the victory, we know, that overcomes the world."

The Object of Faith

Faith must have an object, however. It will not do simply to say, "Have faith!" That may sound spiritual and supportive, but it is too indefinite to possess any power. Genuine faith always has its basis in objective reality: the truth of God. The truth of God as the object or ground of faith, should be understood in two ways.

First, believers possess the truth of God in the Holy Scriptures. The Bible has a vital role to play as an object of vibrant belief. Second, Christians have the living Truth in Jesus Christ Himself. He is the goal of our faith. How, then can we experience victory through our faith in Jesus Christ? Paul writes:

> What shall we say then? Are we to continue in sin that grace might increase? May it never be! How shall we who died to sin still live in it? Or do you not know that all of us who have been baptized into Christ Jesus have been baptized into His death? Therefore we have been buried with Him through baptism into death, in order that as Christ was raised from the dead through the glory of the Father, so we too might walk in newness of life. For if we have become united with Him in the likeness of His death, certainly we shall be also in the likeness of His resurrection, knowing this, that our old self was crucified with Him, that our body of sin might be done away with, that we should no longer be slaves to sin; for he who has died is freed from sin. Now if we have died with Christ, we believe that we shall also live with Him, knowing that Christ, having been raised from the dead, is never to die again; death no longer is master over Him. For the death that He died, He died to sin, once for all; but the life that He lives, He lives to God. Even so consider yourselves to be dead to sin, but alive to God in Christ Jesus. (Rom. 6:1–11)

A most significant truth emerges out of what Paul is saying.

A Great Truth

Paul begins his dissertation by stating that when we die, sin's power and dominion over us are broken. Quite reasonable! When we die, we will be with our Heavenly Father and our days of temptation will be through. But what about our problem now, in this life? We are still very much alive—and prone to sin. Would it not be wonderful if we could be dead and still be alive at the same time? But such a thought seems ridiculous, at least from any human perspective. We would be what the horror story writers call "zombies." Impossible! But then Paul startles us with a seemingly incredible statement. He tells the Romans—and us—that because of *identification with Jesus Christ,* we believers have been made one with our Lord. We are "fused," as it were, *in union with Him,* and we have actually shared in the His death and resurrection. In Christ we have died to sin on the cross and have been resurrected to new life because we are *in Him.* We are actually "living-dead" people in Christ. Of course, being in union with Christ does not mean we lose our humanity and our distinction from the Deity as some Eastern religions teach. We are not "absorbed" into God. We are still limited, created beings. God alone is infinite and ultimate. Still, we find ourselves, by God's saving grace in Christ, so united with our Lord that we share in Him a sense of oneness. It is a mystery, but the Scriptures declare it to be true. So we rest in His Word. And it all has marvelous implications.

Our "oneness" with Christ is multifaceted. In the Ephesian epistle alone, Paul outlines seven aspects of our position "in Christ:"

- Ephesians 1:3:　We receive all blessing in Christ.
- Ephesians 1:4:　God chose us in Christ.
- Ephesians 1:6:　We praise His grace in Christ.
- Ephesians 1:7:　We have received redemption in Christ.
- Ephesians 1:9:　God displays His kind intention in Christ.
- Ephesians 1:10:　All things are summed up in Christ.
- Ephesians 1:13:　We are sealed by the Spirit in Christ.

The principle even relates to our prayer life. We pray in and through our Lord Jesus and His righteousness. We are literally in Christ. Let us now look at this incredible spiritual fact as it relates to victory over sin.

We are to understand that God's all-inclusive salvation, as well as providing forgiveness of sins, also makes us one with Christ. This means when Jesus hung on the old rugged cross, we hung there too. Our "old man" died with Him.

We Are Dead to Sin

We are to understand that God's all-inclusive salvation, as well as providing forgiveness of sins, also makes us one with Christ. This means when Jesus hung on the old rugged cross, we hung there too. Our "old man" died with Him. All this happened in a spiritual sense, but the spiritual is as real— actually more real—than the material. Yet, we ask, "How can it be? Jesus died two thousand years ago." Realize this: God transcends time and space and, in His infinity and ultimacy, actually identified us on the cross with

Jesus before the "foundation of the world" (Eph. 1:4). And make no mistake, He is well able to do so. Nothing is too hard for the Lord (Gen. 18:14)—including transcending our time frame. We are "boxed in" to our limited four-dimensional world—but God is not. Time and distance pose no problem for our transcendent Lord. Einstein has shown that time and space are relative even to us; how much more is God able to stand beyond our confining dimensions. This means that when Jesus died for sin and gained the victory by His blood shed on Calvary, we were there too and shared in that victory by death. Consequently, our old nature is dead, truly dead, crucified with Christ. We are new people. That is exactly what Paul, under the inspiration of the Holy Spirit, declared.

Granted, this truth appeals only to faith. Our limited reasoning powers fail us here. But since the Scriptures declare our oneness with Christ in death, by faith we accept it, knowing God can do what He wishes. Remember, "faith is the victory." As believers, we do not have an old and a new nature, each of equal strength, battling one another. The old self has been crucified with Christ. Believe it. Claim it. Our old self is dead. What appears old about us resides in the as yet unrenewed or carnal aspect of our mind. But more of that shortly. Let it be clear, the "old man," as the King James Version expresses it, stands crucified, dead, and buried *in Christ*.

We Are Alive to God

The headship of the first Adam, under which we were naturally born, has ended; sin and death have been defeated. We now live as a new race, under the headship of the last Adam, Jesus Christ. . . . Can sin lord it over us? Must we be destined to grovel as constant victims to temptation? No!

Furthermore, not only have we died and been crucified with Christ, we have also been spiritually resurrected in Him. He lives, and being in Him, we too have broken the bondage of death. We have emerged from the tomb. We now live the resurrected life of our Lord in the person of the Holy Spirit. We have been born again (John 3:3). The headship of the first Adam under which we were naturally born, has ended; sin and death have been defeated. We now live as a new race, under the headship of the last Adam, Jesus Christ (1 Cor. 15:45). Recall how Paul expressed it—we are raised to walk "in newness of life" (Rom. 6:4). Can sin lord it over us? Must we be destined to grovel as constant victims to temptation? No! We are dead to sin in Christ, our new Head, and we live the resurrected life of our Lord's new race. This is our birthright in Jesus Christ. As one writer expressed it, we are "born crucified" people in Christ. Thus Paul wrote: "I have been crucified with Christ; and it is no longer I who live, but Christ lives in me; and the life which I now live in the flesh I live by faith in the Son of God, who loved me, and delivered Himself up for me" (Gal. 2:20).

Not Easy to Grasp

Of course, assimilating these truths is not easy, especially when we see that at times we do fail and fall into sin. The problem is, we still have our old minds to contend with. Before coming to regeneration in Christ, our faithless minds moved us to act selfishly, not according to God's will. We thought and acted as rebels. It was a pattern. But now we are in Christ. By faith we see ourselves "crucified and raised with Christ." And since we are in Christ, the Holy Spirit can work to create a new mind in each of us, breaking the old pattern.

Two laws clamor for ascendancy in the Christian's life. Paul calls one the "law of sin and death" (Rom. 8:2). That law operates through the unrenewed mind when we do not surrender to Jesus Christ and His daily lordship in our lives, or if we fail to recognize that our "old man" stands dead in Christ. The other is the "law of the Spirit of life in Christ Jesus" (Rom. 8:2). This law works through our redeemed nature as the new mind is constantly enlarged by the Holy Spirit. In this latter law lies the victory. Paul said, "The law of the Spirit of life in Christ Jesus has set you free from the law of sin and death" (Rom. 8:2). Let us illustrate this.

An Illustration

We can liken the interaction of these two principles to ascending into the sky in a balloon. The law of sin is like the law of gravity. Its pull cannot be escaped. Regardless, the balloon rises. How? Another law counteracts the law of gravity. The gas in the balloon exerts a stronger force than the downward pull of gravity, so the balloon goes up. In like fashion, "The law of the Spirit of life in Christ Jesus" operates as a higher law and so overcomes the sinful law that works in the unrenewed mind. So we had better stay in the gondola of faith, for only then can we ascend to spiritual heights. As the new nature ascends, the Holy Spirit constantly renews our minds into Christlikeness. And the wind of the Spirit carries us along into the will of God.

The New Mind

When we surrender our all—"Present our bodies"—
that commitment gives the Spirit free reign to renew
our minds so we can know and understand
the will of God and do it.

By the grace of God and in faith, we ascend above the carnal thinking of the "old mind." We permit the Holy Spirit to transform us after the will of God. Paul said, "Present your bodies . . . acceptable to God . . . and do not be conformed to this world, but be *transformed by the renewing of your mind*, that you may prove what the will of God is, that which is good and acceptable and perfect" (Rom. 12:1–2, italics added). The goal is to become, as Paul again stated, "Renewed in the spirit of your mind, and put on the new self, which in the likeness of God has been created in righteousness and holiness of the truth" (Eph. 4:23–24). He went on to urge, "Whatever is true . . . pure . . . lovely . . . let your mind dwell on these things" (Phil. 4:8); and as the Old Testament writer put it: "As he thinks within himself, so he is" (Prov. 23:7). The mind, the core of the conscious will, must be transformed by the renewing power of the Holy Spirit. This lifelong process the Bible calls *sanctification,* and it comes essentially through trust in our Lord. Let it be stressed once more; sanctification does not come by striving, but by surrender and faith as we appropriate our position in Christ (Gal. 3:3). When we surrender our all—"Present our bodies"—that commitment gives the Spirit free reign to renew our minds so we can know and understand the will of God and do it. In our earthly life we will never reach perfection, but by faith we grow toward it. Moreover, when we do fail and surrender to sin, we have the promise of God's forgiveness (1 John 1:9). At such times we must confess our sin, get up, and go on toward the goal of the renewed mind, heart and life in Christ.

Believe the Bible

Now it is obvious that only by taking God at His word can we understand what it means to be "in Christ." But *therein lies the victory*. And therein we find liberty. As one author has pointedly expressed it:

> . . . When Christ died on the cross to sin, we were identified with Him in that death to sin. That is, we died *with* Him. By our union with Him in His death, we were freed from sin and the penalty of sin and emancipated from the power of sin. All our sanctification, therefore, must be traced to, and rest upon, the atoning sacrifice of our Lord Jesus Christ. The cross of Christ is the efficient cause of deliverance from the power of sin. Freedom from the dominion of sin is a blessing we may claim by faith, just as we accept pardon.[19]

Stephen Olford also makes this point poetically in his book *Not I, But Christ:*

I'm dead to sin through Christ my Lord,
For in His death I also died;
It's written clear in God's own Word,
And, praise His name, I'm justified!
I'm dead to sin, thus I must live,
To Christ alone who gave His all;
And for His love I can't but give
My life and gifts, both great and small.
I'm dead to sin, so I must serve
My God and King each day and hour;
What He commands I must observe,
And seek to do with heav'nly pow'r.
I'm dead to sin, O blessed thought!
I now can rest from care and strife;
My fight He has forever fought,
And now I live His risen life.
I'm dead to sin, O blessed thought!
I now can rest from care and strife;
My fight He has forever fought,
And now I live His risen life.[20]

The Bible goes so far as to say we are already "Raised . . . up with Him, and seated . . . with Him in the heavenly places, in Christ Jesus" (Eph. 2:6). In a very real sense, we are already in heaven. What a position is ours! We rest IN CHRIST. We have LIFE.

The Practicalities

*We dare not fight Satan on his own ground.
We fight the war by striving to stay on the field of
faith. . . . Then the battle is the Lord's.*

The "in Christ" principle works itself out in a very pragmatic fashion. Catch the dynamics of it! Let us say that we find ourselves confronted by one of our old weaknesses. The temptation hits us. Our unrenewed mind, accustomed to yielding to the things of the flesh, exerts itself (see Rom. 7:18). The battle has been fought and lost so often, it seems. But now we have a new truth. We recognize, as Paul wrote to the Romans, "We have been released from the law, having died to that by which we were bound, so that we serve in newness of the Spirit and not in oldness of the letter" (Rom. 7:6). Realizing our identification by faith with Christ in His death and resurrection, we confront the temptation and say, *This sin has no more power over me. I am dead to it. I am a new person. The old nature is crucified with Christ. I am alive to God, and the resurrected life of Jesus Christ is mine.* Resting on Christ's promise, we look in faith to God and *His power* for the victory.

The Battle of Faith

A battle does occur, of course. But during the warfare, we do not fight sin "directly," for that would certainly mean defeat. Sin is stronger than we are. In faith we take our stand, but never relying on our own strength and determination. How sin, Satan, and the world love to deceive us here! When we quit the refuge of faith, we are vulnerable to Satan's power. We dare not fight Satan on his own ground. We fight the war by striving to stay on *the field of faith*. The fight is not merely "the good fight" It is the good fight "*of* faith" (1 Tim. 6:12). Then the battle is the Lord's (see 2 Chron. 20:15).

> *We take our position in Christ by faith. That is the wonderful truth Jessie Penn-Lewis finally discovered. It is God's way to defeat "the wiles of the devil" (Eph. 6:11 KJV) and be victorious.*

In that "fight of faith," severe trials may befall us. During testing times, times when we desperately need God, it often seems He stands far off. The prophet Elijah felt that way, even to the point of praying the Lord would take his life (1 Kings 19:4–12 KJV). He had sunk into despair; all seemed lost. But it was right at that moment that *God came* (vv. 11–14). A blistering wind blasted out of the sky, but "God was not in the wind"; a shattering earthquake rent the ground under Elijah's feet, but "God was not in the earthquake"; a raging fire swept past, but "God was not in the fire." Where then was the mighty God who can blow all worries away, split mountains of problems, and with His burning fire consume all troubles? Why was He silent? After all the prodigious phenomena, the prophet heard "a still, small voice." God may not step into our trials in a mighty manner; He often comes softly. But be assured, *He will come in,* even if only as the "still, small voice." He knows our plight and will surely manifest Himself. He will do what is best, whether we understand His ways or not. Always take heart, let Him work as He will, and trust Him. God honors faith.

We take our position in Christ by faith. That is the wonderful truth Jessie Penn-Lewis finally discovered. It is God's way to defeat "the wiles of the devil" (Eph. 6:11 KJV) and be victorious. We do not "work" toward victory; by faith we work from it.

Thus we live and battle in a new arena, an arena of freedom through faith. There we find the power to abide in Christ. Deliverance from sin's dominance is as much a part of salvation as deliverance from its penalty. All of this becomes available to us through our Lord's death and resurrection. And it becomes ours in the wonderful conversion experience. This is true for all believers. Every born-again person is in Christ. We are accepted by God in Christ as we inherit the whole new nature of our Lord. Consequently, in absolute commitment, we permit the Holy Spirit to renew our minds constantly, and abiding sanctification follows.

An Important Caution

All this emphasis on faith by no means implies passivity—just saying "I believe" with no definite decision to surrender our will to God's will. On the contrary, after Paul exhaustively presents our position in Christ in Romans 6:1–11, he immediately goes on to stress, "Therefore do not let sin reign in your mortal body that you should obey its lusts" (Rom. 6:12). We have a God-given will to employ in all spiritual matters. God never bypasses our decision making any more than He ignores our faith and trust. Being an overcomer demands discipline. Recall that Paul said, "I buffet my body" (1 Cor. 9:27). In seeking victory in Christ, we must exercise our will, yield to God, and stand firm in our decision to do God's bidding, resisting sin as never before. As a great leader in the Salvation Army put it:

> Will you let Jesus have your all? You have been trying to fight the devil in your own strength, and you have failed. If you will now let the Holy Spirit lift up the standard of holiness in your heart, you will have victory where you have been defeated. You will be pure in an unclean age; you will pray in a prayerless age; you will have joy in a joyless age; you will have faith in a faithless age; and others will see Christ in you.[21]

To repeat: When we bend our will to God's will and purpose, and abide on the ground of faith, "This is the victory that has overcome the world" (1 John 5:4).

God Said It

Of course, our position in Christ does not lend itself to a purely rational understanding of the facts. It is paradoxical to say the very least. But after all, much in the Christian faith defies limited human reasoning. The nature of the Trinity and the incarnation of the Son of God are not rational. This does not mean God's *truth* is *irrational;* rather it is *supra-rational* because He is the supra-rational Lord God Almighty. And we praise Him because He is that kind of a transcendent God. We firmly believe all the Bible declares and focus our minds there until it becomes natural to us to take God at His word. Remember, that is what faith is all about. And recall what the writer of the book of Hebrews declared: "Without faith it is impossible to please [God]" (Heb. 11:6).

Why All These Words?

It took Jessie Penn-Lewis some time to assimilate it all, but when she did, she became a liberated woman in the Spirit. It may well take us time as well, but we press on. So we "walk by faith, not by sight" (2 Cor. 5:7).

These realities, although hard to grasp, are vital to abiding in Christ and experiencing victory through Him. It took Jessie Penn-Lewis some time to assimilate it all, but when she did, she became a liberated woman in the Spirit. It may well take us time as well, but we press on. So we "walk by faith, not by sight" (2 Cor. 5:7).

And there are other disciplines such as Bible study, prayer, witnessing, taking on the "whole armor of God" (Eph. 6:10–17) which are vital to abiding in Christ—the rest of this book will deal with these issues. But it all begins and ends in faith. The Spirit works in all believers according to their faith and will orchestrate a Christ-centered fellowship. Such abiding faith in Him spells victory and a deep, rich, ever-maturing Christian experience. Andrew Murray expressed it well when he said:

> When first they (Christians) found peace they learnt that they were saved by faith. They understood that pardon and acceptance and peace and life all come by faith alone . . . we must always walk by faith; that ever and increasingly we must live by faith; and that every day and every hour nothing can help us but a clear, definite, habitual faith in God's power and working, as the only possibility of growth and progress.[22]

Conclusion

We can abide in Christ and become spiritual, victorious, maturing believers in our wonderful Lord.

Prayer

Oh, Lord, You have done so much for us all in Christ. You make victory and blessings possible through our union with Him. Help me grasp all these wonderful truths, exercise faith, and become a conquering Christian. In Jesus' name and for His glory I pray. Amen.

10 Questions for Study and Discussion

1. Jessie Penn-Lewis struggled with health problems all her life. Did that help or hinder her spiritual development?
2. What were the "steps" to spiritual formation Jessie came to understand—and take? What do they mean to us?
3. What is the *glory* and *goal* of "abiding in Christ"?
4. Where does "abiding in Christ" all begin?
5. How are we to deal with the sin problem?
6. What are the results of refusing to deal with our sins?
7. Is victory over sin possible? If "yes," does that mean we can be perfect?
8. What does it mean to be "in Christ"?
9. What is the relationship between being "in Christ" and Christian victory? What does it mean to "abide"?
10. Why is the "walk of faith" the heart of it all?

The Spiritual Woman Exemplifies God

MEET MARTHA FRANKS
A WOMAN WHO EXEMPLIFIED GOD

*I gave an example that you also
should do as I did to you.
(John 13:15)*

*T*hat dear woman exemplifies God more than anyone I have ever met." Such statements surround the Christlike life and dedicated ministry of Martha Franks. Missionary, seminary professor, institution builder, and humble servant of Jesus Christ, Martha Franks exemplified the love of God in a life of service. She truly personified a spiritual woman. Her life reads like a litany to God's glory.

A Vivacious Little Girl

Such had not always been the case with Martha, especially as a young child. Friends saw her as a vivacious, lovable little girl, but she did nurse a strong personality. She was self-willed and firm-minded. Martha was born to John and Sallie Franks in the small community of Laurens, South Carolina, the youngest of six children. Her parents were devout, churchgoing folks who saw to it that Martha would never be found at home playing when the local Baptist church conducted services. And, though self-willed, she never rebelled at going to worship. Nonetheless, she had her own way of evaluating her church. The institution did not quite measure up to her ideal. Because she was an assertive, inquisitive, determined little girl she caused her parents a certain amount of consternation. Few would say she was the easiest child to raise. But she was loved, and home was always a happy and secure place for her.

The Parents

John Franks grew up with the legacy of the post-Civil War South. His father had been killed in the Civil War when John was but two years of age. Consequently, his mother had to bring him up during the Reconstruction era. Families in the Deep South—especially if there were no father in the home—had a difficult time. But John emerged from those troubled times an upstanding young man. In the early years of the twentieth century he went into what people then called the seed and feed business. He ran a general store. On his letterhead, he advertised not only seed and feed, but groceries, plantation supplies, wagons and harnesses—a typical "jot-'em-down" store.

Martha's mother, Sallie, had a more normal background than John. Her secure home life had given her a pleasant and contented disposition. She knew how to handle little Martha, and she had a deep faith in the Lord Jesus Christ. When she had finished her work for the day, she would walk on the long wraparound porch of their home singing, "I Will Guide Thee with Mine Eye." Little Martha would trot along behind her, wondering what in the world the words meant. One day she would find out for herself.

Martha—a Delight

The Franks were well respected in the small town. Martha, with her little self-willed antics, became the delight of the community. She had a keen interest in everything and could always be counted on for any new adventure. The other children in the family delighted in Martha's inquisitiveness. When the family was able to afford their first car, ten-year-old Martha begged to be allowed to drive it. Her older brothers, of course, refused to let her get behind the wheel. But she attentively watched every move they made while driving until she felt absolutely certain she could handle it as well as they. She even got the operator's handbook and thoroughly digested every word. One day all of her older brothers were away, and Martha's mother had gone to a church circle meeting. Martha saw her big opportunity. She had been ordered to run a message for her mother in the horse and buggy. However, Martha pulled up in the car! She had never driven before, but she knew how to drive nonetheless—and she did it well. Driver's licenses were not required in those days, and since John Franks never learned to drive, he made Martha his unofficial chauffeur. From then on she drove him wherever he wished. That spoke of the adventurous spirit of little Martha.

School Days

School days were a joyous time and an exciting adventure for our future servant of Christ. On the way home from school Martha would often swing onto the back of a wagon or carriage, ride for two or three blocks, and then hop down and continue walking with her friends. She was an athlete and something of a tomboy. She also was a good swimmer. This held her in good stead on more than one occasion when she and her friends went swimming. If one of the other children got into trouble, she would go to their rescue. She made an excellent lifeguard and, on occasion, actually saved lives.

Martha heard the message of Jesus Christ and of the need to send missionaries around the world. To her the most fascinating mission work took place in China. She sat enraptured as she listened to the story of Lottie Moon, who had given her life to the needy Chinese.

Much of Martha's family life revolved around the First Baptist Church of Laurens. It was here that Martha heard the message of Jesus Christ and of the need to send missionaries around the world. To her the most fascinating mission work took place in China. She sat enraptured as she listened to the story of Lottie Moon, who had given her life to the needy Chinese. During one of the great famines of China, Lottie Moon had continually shared her own meager bowls of rice. Weakened from malnutrition, she died on Christmas

Eve of 1912 as she was returning by ship to America. Such stories deeply touched many of the children, but they touched Martha especially. Seeds were being sown that would lead young Martha to dream of going to China as a missionary herself.

As she grew a little older her childish romanticism faded away. She began asking herself what kind of a person she wanted to be. She did determine one thing: She would never be one of those "religious" persons, as she put it. At least *she* understood what "religion" was! Yet she remained very involved in the life of the little Baptist church—never completely giving up the thought of mission work.

No "Religion" for Her

Martha's revulsion to being "religious" was probably caused by something that occurred far too often in the old Bible Belt. When children reached what people commonly called the "age of accountability," they were expected to make a "public profession of faith" in order to become members of the church. This could easily be perfunctory, and in too many cases, there was no true spiritual substance. Some even thought this so-called age of accountability had to be age twelve, because Jesus was twelve when he debated in the temple with the Jewish leaders. No one could really explain how the custom had started. In any case, Martha determined that she would not be that sort of "religious" person.

In the end she was the only one in her Sunday school class who would not make her "profession of faith." She had reached the age when the church folk said she should "join the church," but she felt no inclination at all to do so.

Conversion Comes

One day, however, during her church's annual evangelistic services, John Franks took his little daughter into the dining room of their home, sat her down, and asked her, "Do you know that you are a sinner?" That really put Martha off. She replied, "Certainly not!" She thought she knew what her father meant by being a "sinner." An itinerant beggar had come through the community sometime before, robbed the bank, and in the end was killed by a policeman. To Martha that beggar was what a sinner was. She felt hurt that her father would ask such a question. She knew she had never sinned like that in her life. Thus she sensed no need of a Savior.

But conviction did subtly settle on Martha. She began to see something of her own sin—even if she had never robbed a bank. Eventually she did walk down to the front of the church at the conclusion of a service to make her "profession of faith." As she did so the pastor asked her, "Do you love Jesus?" Martha said that of course she loved the Lord. She had no sooner spoken than someone urged the congregation to baptize her as well. A rather superficial decision to be sure! The church, or at least the pastor, should have taken a much more gradual and spiritual approach. Martha missed a true salvation experience. But perhaps a step toward Christ had been taken.

As she matured, Martha's need for a personal relationship with God deepened. When she turned fourteen years of age, she began to realize through the work of the Holy Spirit—that the Lord Jesus Christ stood ready to forgive her sins and save her. That summer, Mrs. Fuller, a close relative, invited several girls to her home in the country. The Baptist church in Mrs. Fuller's community was holding a summer revival meeting, and Martha attended the services. There she heard the gospel clearly proclaimed. Christ spoke to her heart distinctly—and in an unusual way. As her biographer expressed it:

> Martha had been gifted with a musical ear, and while never having the discipline to study the piano, she played, as she liked to say, "for her own amazement." One day as she sat playing, she looked at a candlestick which seemed almost to speak to her. It was in the shape of a cross and there was the Christ on it looking at her. As she played and sang and looked at the image of Jesus on that candlestick cross, she realized for the first time that it was for her, for Martha Franks, that Jesus had died. That day, as they worshiped, she felt it again and heard the Lord speak to her. She received His love and salvation on that very day, and felt Him bind her to Himself "with cords of love."[1]

New life flooded Martha's entire being. She now belonged to Jesus.

Martha went on to finish high school as a maturing, spiritual young Christian lady. Although her newfound faith in Christ had transformed her life, she never conceived that her childish dream to become a missionary to China would come true. Little did she know what God had in store for her.

During Martha's final year of high school, the state of South Carolina added an optional year of study. She really did not care to attend another year, but her father insisted. She went for a short time and, in the end, poured out her heart to her mother. "I can't stand school," she said, "All my friends are gone. I don't ever want to go back again." Her mother asked what she would like to do instead, and Martha quickly replied that she wanted to go to college. "Then go talk to your father," was her mother's answer. Her father's only question was "Where would you like to go?" Martha, without hesitancy, blurted out, "Coker!" That settled it; Martha was college bound. She had always seen Coker as the ideal choice; and the school granted her admittance. Unfortunately, when her brother Clyde heard of her plans, he had objections. He said his sister had no business going to Coker and that she should go to Winthrop College, where a friend of his had gone. So Father John called a family meeting to decide which college Martha should attend. The vote came down: Winthrop won. So Martha packed her bags and, against her will and much to her disappointment, made her way to Winthrop College in Rockhill, South Carolina. The family had decided, and that settled the issue.

Off to College

Martha did not fit in very well at Winthrop during her early weeks. She would call home regularly to tell her parents how unhappy she was. Her mother finally tired of hearing her complaints and said to Martha, "Young lady, your father and I are making a sacrifice for you to be in school. You are not coming home. Now, you dry up and get to work!"[2]

Before long, Martha met another young Winthrop student by the name of Olive Lawton. Olive had been born on the mission field in China. Martha never dreamed then how their paths, by the providence of God, would cross in the future. Martha and Olive studied and worked together and soon became fast friends. The die was cast for this strong-willed young lady. Coincidentally, Martha and Olive had been born on the same date, February 15, 1901. Martha felt so happy with her new friendship that she said, "Oh! I always wanted a twin, and now I've got one."

The Call

During her time at Winthrop Martha involved herself in the local Baptist church. Here she heard an urgent plea. At that time her denomination had launched the "Seventy-Five Million Campaign." That program's goal was to raise seventy-five million dollars to support various world missions. During the appeal Martha heard the words, "God has a plan for each of your lives." She could not escape the challenge. What would God have her to do? Could the Lord Jesus actually be calling her to His full-time service? It seemed a giant leap to take at that time. How could she ever do it? But then the light dawned, and she asked herself, "Why not let God do it for me?" Another step forward was taken.

*Martha heard the words, "God has a plan for each
of your lives." She could not escape the challenge.
What would God have her to do? Could the Lord Jesus
actually be calling her to His full-time service?
It seemed a giant leap to take at that time.
How could she ever do it? But then the light dawned
and she asked herself, "Why not let God do it for me?"*

As Martha continued to spend time with Olive Lawton, she kept wondering whether God was actually calling her to become a missionary. Olive herself had determined to return to the mission fields of China; there was no doubt about God's purpose there. But had Martha received a like call? She struggled on. As God continued to speak to her Martha continued to pray, and she finally came to the undeniable conclusion that God wanted her—as well as Olive—to be a missionary to China. As her biographer writes, "God was speaking; Martha was listening."[3] The decision was made. And she did find that "God would do it for her"; He would give her His strength to yield to His leadership. Peace at last—almost; what about her parents?

The Family Reacts

Martha felt some apprehension about telling her parents of her commitment to go to China. Her fears were well founded. Even though the Franks were a regular churchgoing family they reacted to her news with shock and dismay. Yet, they did not attempt to stand in her way. They had always known Martha's firm determination to live her life as she thought best; and now God's will was paramount to her. She would live her life His way. Martha's decision did not grow out of her strong will. The call was genuine and her determined spirit responded in true surrender to Christ. Martha set her face like a flint toward China.

But God works in the lives of all His children. He worked in Martha's family, too. Her parents and siblings came to realize that it was God's call to their Martha that mattered most. In time, they became very proud of her as her missionary service unfolded.

When Martha graduated from Winthrop College, eight women in the class of 1922 left to serve as foreign missionaries. Five went to China, including Martha and Olive.

Seminary Days

After Winthrop, Martha served as a teacher for a short time in Schoolfield, Virginia, a suburb of Danville. This gave her an opportunity to gain experience which would prove useful in China. Two years later she enrolled at the Women's Missionary Training School, attached to the Southern Baptist Theological Seminary in Louisville, Kentucky. There she finished her theological training, sitting at the feet of outstanding professors like A. T. Robertson, one of the greatest New Testament scholars of the twentieth century. Finally, in 1925, God opened the door for Martha to go to China. The Mission Board of her denomination had not been able to fund her work. Not only that, the First Baptist Church of Laurens, her home church, also found itself financially strapped—they had no help to offer. But a group of women in Richmond, Virginia, had raised enough funds to send one missionary abroad. They contacted the Baptist International Mission Board and Martha was chosen. She was on her way. God had provided to see His purpose accomplished.

> *Martha had truly learned to trust God and love Him*
> *with all of her heart, soul, strength, and mind.*
> *She had yielded to His purpose and was bearing*
> *the beautiful spiritual fruit of love.*

Martha had truly learned to trust God and love Him with all of her heart, soul, strength, and mind. She had yielded to His purpose and was bearing the beautiful spiritual fruit of love. Soon she would learn to love her neighbor —the Chinese people—as herself. Like the first rays of sun on the eastern horizon, the dawn began to rise on a ministry that would impact people for countless years to come.

China on the Horizon

As Martha made her way to the West Coast of America to sail for China, she experienced the pain of parting with her parents. But as she prepared for the long ride, she was met by Miss Bertha Smith, a native South Carolinian. Bertha had served as a missionary in China for some years and was returning to the field after a furlough back home. Like Martha she was a graduate of Winthrop College, and she also worked under the same mission board. And so they traveled together to California, and God bonded them in Christ's love. This meant much to Martha as it alleviated some of the wrench of leaving family and friends.

Martha and Bertha sailed together on the *USS President Madison*. They had a great time witnessing and sharing the message of Christ with fellow passengers and crew. As the ship slipped silently into the Shanghai harbor, a whole new world lay before Martha—a challenging world, the variety of which she had never imagined. But her love for Christ would surely see her through.

The mission leaders stationed Martha in Hwang Hsien. There she met Olive Lawton's parents, and they filled a spot in her life. Martha enthusiastically engaged in language study and found herself quite adept at Mandarin. Bertha Smith reported that "She could speak the language like a native. If you hadn't seen her as she spoke, you'd never know she was an American." Martha only laughed at those words, saying modestly, "It's hard, but fun."

She found the Chinese to be a fascinating people. As her biographer said, "She was glad to be in China and determined to learn to tell of God's love which receives the souls of those who accept His love with no strings attached."[4] After Martha finished her language studies, she gave herself unreservedly to the work of evangelism and ministry.

Revival Looms

Turmoil and unrest, especially in Shantung Province where Martha worked, were a constant source of confusion. The Chinese Communist party had been organized in 1921. National China, under Chiang Kai-shek, opposed them at every turn. This precipitated a rebellion early in Martha's ministry, and all missionaries were forced to leave their Shantung stations. Until the turmoil settled, they were quartered in the seaport city of Chefoo. The work had been progressing reasonably well, but now it seemed things were to be disrupted.

Just before Martha moved to Chefoo in April of 1927, she encountered a fellow missionary, Jane Lide, who had recently returned from furlough in the United States. While at home, Jane had begun to move into a new level of consecration to Christ. She called it "being filled with the Holy Spirit." Fellow missionaries said Jane left for furlough reading philosophy, but returned passing out gospel tracts and attempting to win people to Christ. As Jane shared what God had done, the Holy Spirit pierced Martha's heart. He touched Martha in a new way, and she too became a Spirit-filled Christian. Alice Huey, a missionary friend, described Martha's growth:

> She [Martha] was heart hungry. She wanted a closer, deeper touch with the Lord. I don't recall much that Jane said that night. We went to a nearby home [and] slept in the home of a friend who was away. As we lay there in the dark, Martha's hand in mine, I began to pray. I asked God to reveal Himself to Martha in a way she had not realized before—to satisfy her longings, etc. I hadn't prayed long till she squeezed my hand hard. No word was ever passed, but she was different. She walked like one in a dream for days and days. Fundamentally, she was the same girl, yet different. She saw the Lord high and lifted up (Isa. 6:1).

Martha knew that she had met Christ at a depth not experienced before. She realized the Holy Spirit was powerfully at work in her life. She had always thought of the Holy Spirit as One who would come by her side to help. Now, by faith, she allowed the Spirit of the Lord Jesus Christ to permeate every aspect of her life, letting Him control her, plan her every day, and live the life of Christ through her. God had begun leading her into a new, growing sphere of exemplifying her Savior. It was the beginning of a revival for her.

The Chefoo Revival—Shantung Is Next

In the setting of Chefoo, God began to pour out His spirit on all of Martha's fellow missionaries. Through the messages of a Norwegian Lutheran missionary, Miss Marie Monsen, God did a rich work, moving significantly and deeply among the "interned" servants of Christ. What later became known as "The Shantung Revival" began there in Chefoo in the spring and summer of 1927. Martha wrote home about how the Spirit wonderfully blessed the churches and Chinese believers as the missionaries returned to their fields. In a letter she related:

> Such prayer meetings! Such love for the unsaved! Such love in the Lord! . . . I believe with all my heart that the highway to victory is prayer—Oh will you not pray with us that we may reap an abundant harvest of the precious souls on this . . . field? Our heart's desire for people is that they may be saved. Hold on in prayer with us to that end. . . . May the God of peace fill you with His blessed Spirit and use you abundantly in the homeland.[5]

The power of God fell mightily upon them.
As they met for worship and praise a stillness
permeated the entire church.

The Chefoo meetings proved tremendous indeed. After the missionaries had returned to their service in Shantung Province, Marie Monsen came to Martha's station. She ministered there for several days, and the power of God fell mightily upon them. As they met for worship and praise a stillness permeated the entire church. Everyone sensed the awesome presence of the Holy Spirit.

Marie Monsen spoke very quietly and simply. Martha herself confessed that Marie did not say a word that she herself could not have said. Yet, Marie was so filled with the Spirit that her words were overwhelming. Her first desire was for the salvation of the Chinese. She constantly spoke about "new birth" and many found Christ as Savior. It was a glorious time indeed.

A New Ministry

During the Shantung Awakening, Martha and a co-worker undertook the care of three newborn babies. Even as a little girl, Martha had often prayed that the day would come when some unwanted child would be left at her door. One morning, in the midst of the revival, God answered her prayers. Martha opened her door to discover a little girl lying outside the gate. The child had a cleft palate and as a result had been abandoned by her family. Martha and another missionary lady took her in and named her Mong En (Received Grace). They soon learned of another unwanted child and took her in too. And then another! That became the beginning of a wonderful ministry to three precious little girls. Martha was learning more and more about what it meant to love others as oneself.

As the revival expanded, Martha's own spiritual experience grew apace. A common theme was the necessity of making restitution for sin. The Spirit of God probed so deeply that some might have thought it was pushed to extremes. But Martha was fully open and receptive, and she gladly responded to His convicting hand. Her biographer writes of a telling incident:

> Martha's own experience was similar to that of many of the others. Upon her graduation from Winthrop College, she took with her one of the college hymnals. She reasoned that she needed it for the Lord's work in China far worse than the college would ever miss it. She remembered Satan saying to her, "You deserve it." During that time of revival, years later, she too was reminded of her sin. She sat down one night, packed the hymnal for mailing, and included a letter of confession and apology. Upon her arrival in South Carolina on her next furlough, there to greet her was a letter from Winthrop. Martha was afraid to open the letter for fear they were recalling her degree and stripping her of her rank. Instead, it was an invitation to the college for graduation where she received the Mary Mildred Sullivan Award for her service. It is Winthrop's highest honor; they gave it to Martha.[6]

All the missionaries and many of the Chinese believers shared such experiences. In the grace of Christ's forgiveness, a fresh freedom and joy burst into their hearts. Personal relationships that had been broken were restored. Many scaled new spiritual heights. The fruit of the revival can only be described as tremendous. Before the Shantung Revival, the Baptist Seminary had a half-dozen students. After it, the seminary filled up with 150 Chinese men and women who wanted to give themselves to God's ministry.

As Martha continued her work, her devotion and love for Christ and others became so obvious that she was considered one of the most effective missionaries on the field. Bertha Smith said that no one had come to China more spiritually unprepared than Martha Franks, but she quickly became a radiant, spiritual woman of God, exemplifying her Savior. Word of Martha's powerful testimony reached one of the leading Chinese ministers of the gospel, Pastor Li. God had used him to bring more than ten thousand Chinese people to faith in Christ. He wrote a letter to Martha saying, "I want to work in the country with you." What a delight this proved to be for her.

Another "Spirit"

Not too many years after the great revival broke out, another "spirit" swept the land. The Japanese invaded northeast China, and Shantung province soon found itself under the grip of the invading armies. Martha's area of work lay right in the invaders' path, and in an incredibly short time Japanese soldiers overran the entire mission field. Martha and her missionary companions were confined to their small compound.

Many of them were crammed into one or two rooms in the upstairs of her home while a number of soldiers occupied the entire floor downstairs. The Japanese soldiers were not noted for their morality. Pillage, rape, and violence were everywhere. Of course, Martha, being a very beautiful young woman, stayed in constant prayer that God would protect her. Would she be safe? Her biographer tells the story:

> They did not have long to wait. One of the soldiers came to the foot of the stairs and called in Chinese, "Send the young woman down!" Martha was the only young one among them. What should they do? What could they do? There was no recourse but to do as they had been ordered and pray God's protection for her as she went. As the other missionaries knelt to pray for her safety, Martha started down the stairs. She felt as if God were walking beside her. Hadn't He promised to be with His own each step of the way? Martha knew that someone must be in charge. Silently, Martha prayed to God, "Lord, someone has to be in charge; let it be me. Show me what I should do."
>
> With a firm grip on herself, Martha opened the door, stepping into the dining room filled with Japanese soldiers. She smiled broadly and bowed as politely as she had ever done in her life. At once she looked at the piano and, without having planned it, walked over, sat down and began to play. She played every kindergarten march, chorus, and tune she could recall. Having exhausted her repertoire of children's music, she played "Silent Night." As the strains of that beautiful carol of our Saviour's birth filled the room, some of the soldiers hummed the tune with her. When she had finished playing "Silent Night," Martha got up from the piano, bowed very low to the soldiers, all of whom stood bowing to her in return. Without a word, she turned and left the room and walked back up the stairs. The others surrounded her, thanking the Lord for His love and mercy.[7]

God cares for and protects His own.

The internment went on for some time until a miracle changed everything. Word came that the American missionaries could be repatriated if they wished. Surprisingly, that door of opportunity was opened directly after Pearl Harbor. The interned Americans had thought when the Japanese attacked Hawaii that their lot had become serious indeed. But in the grace and providence of God, the Japanese officials decided to send the missionaries back to America. One can imagine the elation and the gratitude they expressed to God as they boarded the *USS Gripsholm* and sailed for home.

Back Home and Then to Taiwan

Back in the States during the war years (1942–1945) Martha traveled to many cities, sharing the gospel and challenging God's people. She stressed the need for missions around the world. When the war ended, she was one of the first to return to China. She could not go back to north China to work since it had fallen under control of the Communists led by Mao Tse-tung. Instead, in 1947 Martha began teaching in the old Chinese seminary in Shanghai. No one really knew what would the future hold as the Communist forces spread.

As China slipped more deeply into chaos it became clear that the days of service on the mainland were coming to an end. Chiang Kai-shek was driven to Formosa, later called Taiwan, bringing many Chinese refugees in his wake. God led Martha Franks to them, and a ministry on the "beautiful island" (the meaning of "Formosa") began to take shape. Bertha, Martha's close missionary friend, was already in Taiwan so together she and Martha joined hands as the work progressed.

While on furlough in America Martha had attended a Spiritual Life conference at Ben Lippen in North Carolina. She had been so inspired by the experience that she began to look for a suitable place in Taiwan to build a center. After much prayer and searching she found a lovely site for a minimal amount of money, and the work was undertaken. Martha called the center "Little Ridgecrest," after a Baptist retreat center near Asheville, North Carolina. Under Martha and Bertha's care it became a blessing to all who attended its many conferences. Martha and Bertha also taught at the new Taiwan Baptist seminary, founded to train Chinese men and women for Christ's ministry. Today, the seminary has become a large complex with many beautiful buildings, and the property on which Little Ridgecrest sits is worth millions of dollars.

And again Martha threw herself into helping needy children. She started a program for deaf children and learned sign language to better help them. The number soon reached 150 boys and girls—with a few blind little tots as well. It proved to be a wonderful work. Martha's love for the needy deepened more and more. Her biographer tells the following story:

One Sunday afternoon a tiny six-year-old boy groped his way in with the other children and straight into Martha's heart. It was his first year in school. Life was most difficult because he had no one to help him bathe and wash his clothes. Accompanying the smaller boy was another of about the same age whose eyes were terribly red and in constant pain. Martha engaged an elderly woman living near the school to go each Saturday to bathe the boys. She purchased two changes of clothes for each boy, and the old woman took one change home each Saturday where she washed and pressed the pieces before returning them to the boys on the following Saturday. Each little boy had two cotton underpants and shirts, two outer shirts, and two pairs of pants, which were the sum total of their possessions.[8]

That exemplified the love and the heart of Martha Franks.

Above all, Martha wanted the boys and girls to whom she ministered to come to a vibrant saving faith in the Lord Jesus Christ. In a letter home, she wrote:

My greatest thrill came the last night of the conference for young people when thirty or more of our "silent" young people made professions of faith in the Lord Jesus as their Savior. Three made dedication for life service, and already one of them is "preaching" every Sunday night in our church to the deaf.[9]

She was a dignified, cultured Southern belle,
but her love for the Lord would lead her to lay aside
American conventionalities and do anything
she could to win Chinese people for Christ.
She sought out any avenue to help others.

Martha spent fifteen years serving the Taiwanese people. She would go out into the streets of the towns and villages, playing her accordion and sharing the old gospel story to any who would stop and listen. She was a dignified, cultured Southern belle, but her love for the Lord would lead her to lay aside American conventionalities and do anything she could to win Chinese people for Christ. She sought out any avenue to help others. The people so appreciated Martha that she received an invitation to give English lessons on the largest radio station in Taiwan. The government actually granted her permission to preach the gospel if she would only teach the people to speak English. Martha seized that opportunity.

Retirement

But retirement time had to come. The policy of her sponsoring mission board was that, at the age of seventy, missionaries had to return home. This was hard for Martha. She had seen this age limitation end the career of her dear friend Bertha Smith a short time earlier. It was difficult for aging missionaries to give up their labors. Thankfully in Martha's case the work did not end, but simply changed addresses. She came home to immerse herself into Christ's ministry in America.

Home Again—Blessings Abound

Martha moved back to her hometown, and her brother Clyde built her a house on the old family property. Martha's retirement was anything but retirement. In one year alone, she spoke in forty churches, took part in six conferences, ten prayer retreats, two crusades, and one hundred fifty week-day meetings. She was a persistent servant and truly exemplified the Lord she loved.

*One cannot help but ask, "What was behind Martha's
tremendously effective ministry? How did she become
such an example of the Christ-centered life?"
The answer is simple: She had learned to give her all
to Christ, to love God with all of her heart,
soul, strength, and mind, and her neighbor as herself.*

During those busy days the Director of the South Carolina Baptist Homes for the Aging helped Martha fulfill what had been a dream of hers for years: to establish a home for the aging. In 1979, architects were hired to begin the work. Before long a fully equipped long-term nursing facility was completed. On February 4, 1985, Martha, her sister Rosalee, her friend Olive Lawton, and many others moved into the new complex. There Martha lived well into her nineties, a rich blessing and source of inspiration to all!

One cannot help but ask, "What was behind Martha's tremendously effective ministry? How did she become such an example of the Christ-centered life?" The answer is simple: she had learned to give her all to Christ, to love God with all of her heart, soul, strength, and mind, and her neighbor as herself. She radiated the presence and example of the Lord Jesus. One would never have thought that the self-willed, playful, raucous little girl from Laurens, South Carolina, could ever become this spiritually-minded woman, so filled with the Spirit that she was able to exemplify the image of Christ. But God can do anything in those who set their mind to live in the Spirit and bear His fruit.

Lessons in Godliness

*The object for which Christ became the Leader of our
salvation, the great work He has to do for us, the bond
of union between the Son and the sons of God,
the proof of their bearing His image and likeness,
and the mark of their real oneness, is Holiness."*

Godliness is never superficial. Just going to church, doing a few kind things, and being a nice person is a far cry from exemplifying God. There is a vast difference between being a "good person" and a godly person. The godly Christian permits Christ to permeate *every aspect of life*. As Andrew Murray writes, "The object for which Christ became the Leader of our salvation, the great work He has to do for us, the bond of union between the Son and the sons of God, the proof of their bearing His image and likeness, and the mark of their real oneness, is *Holiness*."[10] That *holiness* must be generated in us by the Holy Spirit Himself. It manifests itself in six ways.

Control

First, the Spirit of God desires to control our daily actions. Our Lord created us as people with will, with decision-making capabilities. That will must be committed to Him in every action in every moment of life—no exceptions. This is the foundation of godliness.

Our Words

In the second place, if we are truly yielded to the Spirit our words should exemplify the Lord Jesus Christ. The prayer of every godly Christian should be, "Lord, bind my tongue. Let my speech always be with grace, seasoned with salt" (Col. 4:6). Jesus said, "By your words you shall be justified, and by your words you shall be condemned" (Matt. 12:37). How unruly our mouths can be! How much heartache and how many ruptured relationships occur because of a loose tongue! James tells us, "If anyone thinks himself to be religious, and yet does not bridle his tongue but deceives his own heart, this man's religion is worthless." James goes on:

> The tongue is a small part of the body, and yet it boasts of great things. Behold, how great a forest is set aflame by such a small fire! And the tongue is a fire, the very world of iniquity; the tongue is set among our members as that which defiles the entire body, and sets on fire the course of our life, and is set on fire by hell. For every species of beasts and birds, of reptiles and creatures of the sea, is tamed, and has been

tamed by the human race. But no one can tame the tongue; it is a restless evil and full of deadly poison. (James 3:5–8)

That is a stern indictment from the Word of God. We must permit the Holy Spirit to control our tongues, our words, and our attitudes, so that they minister grace and not heartache.

Our Thoughts

Third, the Holy Spirit desires to bring our minds under control. We learned this in the previous step. In Paul's second letter to the Corinthians we read, "We are destroying speculations and every lofty thing raised up against the knowledge of God, and we are taking every thought captive to the obedience of Christ" (2 Cor. 10:5). Our thoughts grow out of our attitude, and it is these thoughts that determine what our life really is. As we read in Proverbs, "For as he thinketh in his heart, so is he" (Prov. 23:7 KJV). It is vital, therefore, that the Holy Spirit control that part of us if we would exemplify Jesus, as Martha did. But how do we control our mind? We do so by prayer, by Bible study, by seeking God's will, and by placing priority in spiritual things. Nothing is more important. As Paul put it, "Have this attitude [mind] in yourselves which was also in Christ Jesus" (Phil. 2:5).

Motivation

We must constantly seek the Holy Spirit's power to keep our motives pure and Christ-honoring. When we keep our motives right, our thoughts, words, and actions fall in line.

Fourth, our motivation must be pure. This seems so difficult. We easily slip into spiritual selfishness and self-seeking. Often we find we have mixed motives. We know we should seek "first the kingdom of God and His righteousness" (Matt. 6:33 KJV) but fail to do so. Thank God for the blood of the Lord Jesus Christ which cleanses us, and for the power of the Holy Spirit which delivers us from this dilemma. Remember, in Christ we are dead to sin and alive to God by faith. We must constantly seek the Holy Spirit's power to keep our motives pure and Christ-honoring. When we keep our motives right, our thoughts, words, and actions fall in line.

Relationships

Fifth, we must seek purity in our interpersonal relationships. Fellowship is central to holiness. For true fellowship there must be a spirit of understanding, acceptance, forgiveness, and submission (Eph. 5:21). An arrogant, unforgiving spirit will inevitably hurt others and disrupt relationships, especially in the home. People matter to God; godliness demands that they matter to us as well.

Fullness

The sixth manifestation of godliness is the *fullness* of the Holy Spirit in heart, mind, body, and life. God is love; that is the spiritual fruit we must bear. To be spiritual means to love. We risk all God would work in us if we fail to remember Paul's words, "But now abide faith, hope, love, these three; but the greatest of these is love" (1 Cor. 13:13).

Spirituality Means Love

Love is an intriguing word. It conjures up dreams, creates fantasies, and brings all sorts of emotions to the surface. This is not only true on a human plane; it is also true on a spiritual level. John tells us that God is love (1 John 4:8), and the Bible verifies and emphasizes that reality over and over again.

In the original Greek of the New Testament there are three words for love: *agape, philia*, and *eros*. In English we translate all three words by our word *love*, but there are vast differences in their meanings. Only two of the words are actually used in the New Testament; *eros* does not appear. It is from that term that we get the English word *erotic*, and God is certainly not *eros* love. The philosopher Plato saw *eros* as essentially egocentric. It does not necessarily manifest itself on an erotic level, but it revolves around a self-centered quest for happiness and satisfaction. And it seems to drive countless lives. Even believers ask such selfish questions as "What can Jesus do for me?" or "How can the Lord help me here?" or "How can I find satisfaction in my religion?" Christ does meet such needs. But the Christian life goal must remain: Love God and love one another. *Eros* is far from where God would have us be in our spirituality.

A Higher Love

The second Greek word for love is *philia*. This form of love accepts another in relationship, and is on a higher level than *eros*. It describes a natural attraction to those who belong to our own "group" and it means "brotherly affection." As a matter of fact, the name of the American city of Philadelphia has this word as its root. Literally *Philadelphia* means "the city of brotherly love." We also get our word "philanthropy" from it. A Christian can exemplify *philia*. To be benevolent, to be gracious, to be kind—these are all important for a stable society—as well as for a healthy church and true Christian fellowship.

God's Kind of Love

Agape is the highest love; it is our final goal. Agape is God's kind of love—His only kind. Our Lord wants us to live in that level of love.

But when we come to *agape* love, we get to the real heart of the love issue, even though *philia* love is incumbent upon us as believers. *Agape* is the highest love; it is our final goal. *Agape* is *God's* kind of love—His only kind. Our Lord wants us to live in that level of love.

The essence of *agape* is found in 1 Corinthians 13, the so-called love chapter. A marvelous little devotional booklet on this chapter was written by Henry Drummond, a deeply devout Scottish scientist. It is entitled *The Greatest Thing in the World,* and it has become a classic, with more than ten million copies sold. In it the author presents the essence of the "love chapter" and the core meaning of *agape* love.

Henry Drummond calls God's *agape* love the *summum bonum* of life. Of what does it consist? First Corinthians 13 makes that clear; *agape* love reflects nine graces:

- Patience—"Love is patient."
- Kindness—"Love is kind."
- Generosity—"And is not jealous."
- Humility—"Love does not brag and is not arrogant."
- Courtesy—"Does not act unbecomingly."
- Unselfishness—"Does not seek its own."
- Good Temper—"Is not provoked."
- Guilelessness—"Does not take into account a wrong suffered."
- Sincerity—"Does not rejoice in unrighteousness, but rejoices with the truth."

These are all godly attributes. Jesus personified each one, for *agape* is of God. This love God has for us is demonstrated in the ways He reaches out to us, not by our efforts to reach up to Him. Through *agape* we have been given Christ's glorious salvation. As has been said by R. C. L. Lenski:

> Jesus makes all things new. The newness Jesus has in mind is not strange and startling to the disciples, it has a familiar and a pleasant mien. Jesus has brought a new love into the world, a love that is not only faultless and perfect as love but one that is intelligently bent on salvation for the one loved. Only the disciples know from Jesus what this love is, only

they have enjoyed the experience of his love; hence this precept is for them alone—it would be useless to give it to the
world. So also this love is to be for "each other" in the circle
of his disciples. It cannot be otherwise, because the tie that
binds the disciples of Jesus is a thing apart and cannot include others. Just as Jesus loves his "little children," and there
is an intimate exchange of love between him and them, so it
is with regard to the exchange of love between these "little
children" themselves.[11]

And the beauty of the *agape* love life is that God gives it to us by His
Holy Spirit. Think of it. God enables us to have His love life poured into our
lives. Glorious indeed!

The Essence of Spirituality

Because of this we are thrust back to this chapter's step to spirituality.
When we love on the *agape* plane, we exemplify our God who is Spirit
(John 4:24)—and that is beautiful. Little wonder, as Lenski expressed it,

We have therefore every right to say that *agape* is the centre
of Christianity, the Christian fundamental motif *par excellence,*
the answer to both the religious and the ethical question.
Agape comes to us as a quite new creation of Christianity.
It sets the mark on everything in Christianity. Without it
nothing that is Christian would be Christian. *Agape* is
Christianity's own original basic conception.[12]

The Practicalities of Agape

*Agape love accepts people as they are and ministers
to them in their need. We do not seek out people just
because we like them. In love we seek them out to help
them whether they are "likable" or not. Jesus Himself
consorted with "publicans and sinners."*

This *agape* love life is practical. For example, Jesus said, "He who has My
commandments and keeps them, he it is who loves Me" (John 14:21). There
are ethical and moral implications to *agape;* we must keep Christ's commandments. We must move from an egocentric existence into a Christ-centered
life of submission to His will, because we love Him. Further, love on the
agape plane must be spontaneous, with no hidden motives. We love and obey
simply because the Lord Jesus Christ loved like that, even to death on the

cross (Phil. 2:8). *Agape* love accepts people as they are and ministers to them in their need. We do not seek out people just because we like them. In love we seek them out to help them whether they are "likable" or not. Jesus Himself consorted with "publicans and sinners." We reach out because Christ reaches out to us and through us. Not only that, but *agape* is indifferent to human status. It is not for us to judge who stands righteous before God and who does not. After all, as Paul said, "There is none righteous, no not one." How could we have a right to pass judgment on others? This does not mean we should close our eyes to violations of Scripture—but we leave the judging to God.

Agape love is creative. We encounter God in love, and God is the Creator of everything good and meaningful. Thus the loving Christian seeks creative ways to manifest love to God and others.

Finally, *agape* is the foundation of our fellowship with God and one another. If we walk "in the light," we walk in God's love, giving of ourselves, seeking the good of others, and glorifying the Lord Jesus Christ in all things. In this way we can exemplify our Lord, as Martha discovered.

Now if *agape* love is God's quality of love, and God alone possesses this beautiful attribute, how in the world can we love like that as He demands? How can we exemplify our Holy God?

Fruit-Bearing

The Bible shows us how to exemplify God through living the *agape* love life. The principle? *We bear the "fruit of the Spirit"* (Gal. 5:22) through the inner work of the Holy Spirit.

> *The spiritual principle so central to this theme can be found in Romans 5:5: "The love* [agape] *of God has been poured out within our hearts through the Holy Spirit who was given to us." Because "God is love" (1 John 4:8), by the Holy Spirit He pours His* agape *love in our hearts. In that way alone we can love God with all our heart, and our neighbor as ourselves.*

We have seen in a previous step the importance of walking in the fullness of the Spirit. The Spirit leads us, directs us, and gives us power for ministry. He also creates love within us. The spiritual principle so central to this theme can be found in Romans 5:5: "The love [*agape*] of God has been poured out within our hearts through the Holy Spirit who was given to us." Because "God is love" (1 John 4:8), by the Holy Spirit He pours His *agape* love in our hearts. In that way alone can we can love God with all our heart, and our neighbor as ourselves. Apart from that work of the Holy Spirit, we can never fulfill the "Great Commandment." By our feeble human efforts we simply cannot love on the *agape* level. It is "Mission Impossible." We should stop trying and start trusting the Holy Spirit to create *agape* within us. Paul said in Galatians 5:22–25:

> The fruit of the Spirit is *love*, joy, peace, patience, kindness, goodness, faithfulness, gentleness, self-control; against such things there is no law. Now those who belong to Christ Jesus have crucified the flesh with its passions and desires. If we live by the Spirit, let us also walk by the Spirit. (emphasis added)

Implications

There are important implications in this passage. The disciple of the Lord Jesus, abiding in Him as a grafted branch, daily draws spiritual, life-giving sustenance from the Vine, the Lord Jesus Christ Himself. When we abide in Him, the Holy Spirit fills us and we begin to bear the marvelous "fruit of the Spirit." Significantly, in the Galatian passage Paul uses the term *fruit* in the singular. There is only one essential fruit of the Spirit—love. Out of love flows all of the other wonderful graces, not only those in the Galatian passage but also in the love chapter of 1 Corinthians 13. The parallel between these two passages is striking.

1 Corinthians 13—Love	Galatians 5:22–23—Fruit
Patient	Patient
Kind	Kind
Not jealous	Joyful
Not arrogant	Gentle
Not counting evil	Self-controlled
Not provoked	At peace
Holy	Good
Selfless	
Enduring	Faithful
Humble	

Because of this parallelism a Bible scholar has pointed out that Paul's passage in Galatians 5:22–23 should have a colon following the word "love" and not a comma as most translations have it. Thus it would read, "The fruit of the Spirit is love: joy, peace . . ." not "The fruit of the Spirit is love, joy, peace. . . ." There is one fruit of the Spirit out of which flow different aspects of it. This would make 1 Corinthians 13 and Galatians 5:22–23 virtually synonymous.

The conclusion to all this rests in our loving on the *agape* level, for that is the word the apostle uses throughout both passages. The Holy Spirit enables the flow of *agape* into us as we abide in the Vine, and thus bear His fruit.

But now we will look more closely at the various aspects of love, as seen in Galatians 5, to determine how we can exemplify our Lord Jesus Christ and His love.

The Fruit of Love

Joy

Joy is a beautiful blossom that sends forth its fragrance to all parts of the Christian experience. The prophet Nehemiah said, "The joy of the Lord is your strength" (Neh. 8:10). Nothing appears quite so contagious or winsomely attractive as Christian joy. But notice, the prophet calls it "the *joy of the Lord.*" Peter expresses it as "joy inexpressible and full of glory" (1 Peter 1:8). This joy is not an earthly, temporary happiness. Christians do not experience joy simply because circumstances are pleasant or because they know how to think positively. Christian joy is a deep satisfaction that wells up because of the Holy Spirit and His work in the heart—regardless of life's circumstances. That joy is *His* joy, and hence is "full of glory." True joy comes from the knowledge that no matter what life hurls our way, God stands with us and in us. (Rom. 8:28). When trials come, as Andrew Murray has said:

> The salvation God has provided for us, the blessed life in the new and living way into the Holiest, through Jesus Christ, has such power that it can enable us amid every trial to be more than conqueror through Him that loves us. Give up yourself absolutely and entirely to God in Christ Jesus, as into the hands of infinite love; firmly believing this great and infallible truth, that God has no will towards you, but that of infinite love, and infinite desire to make you partaker of His divine nature; and that is as absolutely impossible for the Father of our Lord Jesus Christ to refuse all that is good, and life, and salvation which you want as it is for you to take it by your own power.[13]

When we live in that arena of faith the fruit of joy—even in sorrow—springs forth in our lives. We can rejoice in the knowledge and assurance of God's love. And that leads to peace.

Peace

Walking in obedience to the Spirit and drawing on His love will produce fruit the Bible calls "peace." Paul described it as "the peace of God, which surpasses all comprehension" (Phil. 4:7). Notice once again, the peace is *God's peace*. Our bookstores are filled with volumes on how to obtain inner peace. Everyone wants to know how to find that mysterious something called "peace of mind." As F. B. Meyer said, "Our natures sigh for rest, as an ocean shell, when placed to the ear, seems to cry for the untroubled depths of its native home."[14] People turn everywhere except to the *one and only* source where such peace can be found: our Lord Jesus Christ. His promise remains true: "Peace I leave with you; My peace I give to you; not as the world gives, do I give to you. Let not your heart be troubled, nor let it be fearful" (John 14:27). We do not have to strive for His peace. Hard work will not produce it. Peace is Christ's gift to those who faithfully abide in Him.

Now make no mistake here. Life is still difficult. Fruit-bearing believers do not deny that. But they can have victory even in the midst of trouble. This is why Christians can weep and have peace at the same moment.

Patience

Patience can be defined as "the strength to defer anger, and the contentedness to bear injuries." It depicts a quality primarily concerned with *people*. Chrysostom, the great preacher of Constantinople, said that patience is the quality of grace God gives to the Christian who could in justice seek revenge but refuses to do so. The gospel writers show the Lord Jesus Christ displaying this attitude toward the people He encountered. If we bear the kind of fruit that flows from Christ, patience should characterize all our relationships in all the various and trying circumstances of life.

Kindness

Kindness is another beautiful love-fruit that Christian branches bear. *Kindness* is sometimes defined as "goodness" or "Christlikeness." Another definition is "a sweetness of temper that moves us to be gracious, courteous, and easy to be reconciled when we have been wronged." Only the fruit-bearing, loving Christian can display this quality in real depth. Kindness challenges the world.

Goodness

Goodness, as a fruit, takes its rightful place on the believer's branch as an expression of *agape* love. An incident during our Lord's earthly ministry illustrates its meaning. A man came to Him on one occasion and asked, "Teacher, what good thing shall I do that I may obtain eternal life?" Jesus retorted, "Why are you asking Me about what is good? There is only One who is good" (Matt. 19:16–17). The man had asked a common question. The anomaly of our nature seems to be that even though we are sinful we appear concerned about doing and being good. Jesus put the record straight. Only God is good. He alone forms the basis of all true goodness. Therefore, doing good and being good display God's nature.

This grace of goodness does not mean being a "do-gooder." It denotes a "strong goodness," the kind God inspires. It signifies, as one commentator expressed it, "Living virtuously and equipped at every point." A genuine godly attempt to be helpful to others in every phase of life is at the core of goodness. Paul said, "So then, while we have opportunity, let us do good to all men, and especially to those who are of the household of the faith" (Gal. 6:10).

Faithfulness

Faithfulness is another beautiful fruit of the Spirit and is a manifestation of God's love. *Faithfulness* means "trustworthiness." It denotes a person who is totally reliable, like God. Honesty, fidelity, and integrity are at the heart of it. Faithfulness grows out of love and vibrant faith in Christ.

Gentleness

The next fruit of the Spirit is what the Bible calls "gentleness." It displays the glory of the Vine, Jesus Christ, for He was such a man. Jesus said, "I am gentle and humble in heart" (Matt. 11:29). He also said, "Blessed are the gentle, for they shall inherit the earth" (Matt. 5:5). This grace expresses itself in three ways. A gentle Christian submits to the will of God (Matt. 11:29). A gentle Christian is teachable and is never too proud to learn (James 1:21). Finally, a gentle Christian is considerate in spirit and attitude (1 Cor. 4:21). The companion to gentleness is humility. The adjectival form of the word refers to an animal that has been trained and brought under control. Gentleness must not be confused with weakness. Jesus was anything but a weak man, but He called Himself meek and gentle (Matt. 11:29). Gentleness actually means great strength.

Self-Control

The Greek philosophers used the word *self-control* to convey self-mastery. It applied to the person who had mastered his desires and love of pleasure. Paul employed the term in relation to an athlete's discipline of his body (1 Cor. 9:25) and to the Christian's mastery of sexual desire (1 Cor. 7:9). Strength of character lies at the heart of the idea. Christians can by faith so master themselves that they are able to be self-giving servants to others, displaying God and His love.

Now what is the summation of it all for God's redeemed people? Loving service to others. As Murray said:

All the redeemed form one body. Each one is dependent on the other, each one is for the welfare of the other. Let us beware of the self-deception that thinks it possible to enter the Holiest, into the nearest intercourse with God, in the spirit of selfishness. It cannot be. The new and living way Jesus opened up is the way of self-sacrificing love. The entrance into the Holiest is given to us as priests, there to be filled with the Spirit and the love of Christ, and to go out and bring God's blessing to others.[15]

All of these spiritual graces must continually grow and mature. Our Lord made this clear in John 15. Jesus put fruit-bearing in the progression of "fruit," "more fruit" (v. 2), and "much fruit" (v. 5). That is the upward path we should take. Notice, there will be pruning (v. 2), but only in order to produce "much fruit." To grow in fruit-bearing means growing in grace. May we ever continue to grow in Christ.

A Big Order

*Is it really attainable? Yes! As we have seen, it comes
by abiding in Christ, walking by faith in the fullness
of the Holy Spirit, and living the Christ-centered life.*

All this constitutes what it means to be a fruit-bearing branch. A beautiful life to be sure—love in the highest sense of the word and making its contribution to the world! But it seems an almost unbelievable order. Is it really attainable? Yes! As we have seen, it comes by abiding in Christ, walking by faith in the fullness of the Holy Spirit, and living the Christ-centered life. Then "the love of God . . . (is) poured out within our hearts through the Holy Spirit who was given to us" (Rom. 5:5). In that way, and in that way alone, do we exemplify God. As Miles Stanford expressed it,

> Christian living is not our living with Christ's help, it is Christ living His life in us. Therefore, that portion of our lives that is not His living is not Christian living, and that portion of our service that is not His doing is not Christian service; for all such life and service have but a human and natural source, and Christian life and service have a supernatural and spiritual source.[16]

And Paul said, "For me to live is Christ" (Phil. 1:21).

Conclusion

So we conclude that to be spiritually alive means to demonstrate Christ's love in all its aspects. When we love as the Spirit empowers us to do, it brings glory to Him, and it can even brings the world to embrace Him for "Love never fails" (1 Cor. 13:8). Living a loving life, as Martha Franks discovered, exemplifies the Savior, for "God is love" (1 John 4:8).

Prayer

Dear God, our Father, thank You for Your great love. I long to be like Jesus and love as He loved. Grant Your grace to enable me to live a Spirit-filled, fruitful life of love as I simply abide in our precious Savior, the Lord Jesus Christ; in whose name I pray. Amen.

10 Questions for Study and Discussion

1. Did Martha Franks' young personality help her in the service of Christ? What did God need to tame in her life? Why?
2. Martha Franks was "called"; how does God's "call" come to us? Are all Christians "called"?
3. What is the meaning of real revival like the Shantung Awakening? Do we need it today? How will it come about?
4. What areas of our lives does the Holy Spirit strive to control? Why? What are the results?
5. What are the three kinds of love and how do they relate to a Christian exemplifying God?
6. What roles do fullness, abiding, and discipline play in attaining love?
7. How can we love on the *agape* level?
8. How do love and the "fruit of the Spirit" relate to each other?
9. Why do so few seem to love on God's level?
10. What are the simple principles and daily disciplines to exemplify God—*and are we going to do them?*

The Spiritual Woman Grows in God

MEET KAY ARTHUR
A WOMAN WHO GROWS IN GOD

---

*Like newborn babes, long for the pure
milk of the word, that by it you may grow
in respect to salvation.*
(1 Peter 2:2)

$\mathcal{T}$he Bible declares that spiritual growth stagnates unless we saturate ourselves in the Scriptures. The Word of God is the light of our life. As the psalmist said, "Thy word is a lamp to my feet, and a light to my path." (Ps. 119:105). Spirituality is rooted and grounded in the Scriptures. The quest for it takes off on the wings of the Word.

It is here that Kay Arthur has made her magnificent contribution. She is an avid and perceptive Bible scholar and, in her work to encourage spiritual growth through the study of Holy Scriptures, she herself epitomizes what it means to grow in the grace of God through the Word.

A New Life Arrives

Kay was born on the eleventh day of the eleventh month of 1933 in lovely Jackson, Mississippi. She had the wonderful privilege of being raised in a loving home by parents who were all mature parenthood ought to be. Kay has the happy testimony that she never saw her mother and father quarrel. She always expresses gratitude for the love and security her parents provided for her sister, her brother, and for her. It is easy to see why Kay was a well-adjusted girl.

Kay's family moved quite often because of her father's career. In all, Kay attended twelve elementary schools and four high schools in the course of her early education. At the time it seemed a chore for her to have to uproot so often; little did she realize God was teaching her how to be open to new people, how to reach out to them. He was preparing her to travel, even to the ends of the earth.

Nursing

After Kay finished her high school days in Jackson, she enrolled in St. Luke's School of Nursing and became a registered nurse. She loved her job, and the work she did in restoring people to physical health was a symbol for what, one day, she would be doing—restoring ailing Christians to spiritual vitality. Kay also attended the Case Western Reserve University in Cleveland, Ohio, and later Tennessee Temple University in Chattanooga, Tennessee. Temple University had been founded by the well-known minister of the gospel, Lee Robinson. This fine institution instilled in Kay a deep love, appreciation, and knowledge of the Scriptures. A foundation was clearly being laid for her future ministry.

A New Home

While studying to become a nurse, Kay met her future husband. She had always dreamed of loving a man for the rest of her life, of raising a happy family, of being the perfect wife and mother. She wanted her home to have all the qualities of the one she grew up in. When she met Frank Thomas Goeth, Jr., everything seemed to come together. "Tom" was a handsome man from a prominent family in the community. Moreover, he was a fine sportsman. He had been offered contracts to pitch for the Yankees, the Phillies, the Indians, and the Pirates. Kay could hardly believe that a man like that had fallen in love with her. They soon married, and it seemed as though a great future lay ahead of them. But cracks in the foundation of their union began to appear very early. Tom sat Kay down one day and said, "Kay, now you are Mrs. Frank Thomas Goeth, Jr., and there are things that I don't like about you. I want them changed." Kay was horrified. Tom's arrogant, negative attitude toward her shot through her heart. She could only think this must be some kind of a nightmare, that she would wake the next day to find Tom lovingly standing by her side. But it was no dream. Tom had fallen into a serious depression, and it seemed as though all happiness disappeared.

Shattered Hopes

Kay's hopes had been shattered. Through six years and the birth of two sons she valiantly tried to keep their lives on an even keel. But it was impossible. One night Tom was so upset by some angry words Kay had let slip that he actually backhanded her. Kay admits that her husband was a gentleman and that she had pushed him to the brink, but she felt so miserable, she really did not care. She had all the things that made for happiness. As she expressed it, she had "money, milk, modeling," but for all that, she found her marriage in pieces. It was inexplicable, a mystery that only eternity would be able to unravel. At the age of twenty-seven, her dream for a happy home was dashed. Tom divorced Kay and left her with their two small sons. She had hoped to rear her boys in an environment of joy and security much like the one she had experienced. Instead she had come to a dead end.

Going Astray

In the wake of this tragedy Kay turned from her Christian upbringing. All she wanted was to find, as she expresses it, "someone to love me whether I was having a good day or a bad day." Kay went astray. Life went from bad to worse. She frankly admits that she became a slave to sin. She would make resolution after resolution, but she could not to break the bondage. Then, right at that terrible point in her life, the grace and goodness of God dramatically intervened and stopped her. At a party one evening, someone turned to her and said, "Kay, why don't you stop telling God what you want and tell Him that Jesus Christ is all you need." This remark infuriated Kay. She shot back, "Jesus Christ is not all that I need. I need a husband, my boys need a father. I need . . ." and she stomped off and went home. The next day Kay felt sick at heart. She tried to rationalize the situation, telling herself her problems were caused by something deep inside her that simply could not be treated or healed.

Conversion Comes

She cried out, "God, I don't care what You do to me.
I don't care what You do to my sons. I don't care if I never see
another man . . . if You will just give me peace."
And then a miracle. God's wonderful grace, forgiveness,
and peace flooded her heart.

Kay's boys were to go to summer camp, and Kay found herself preparing for the trip in a turmoil of conflicting thoughts and emotions. A day or so before they were to leave, she went into the kitchen to bake a cake. Her younger son, Mark, was clinging to her apron. Suddenly Kay had to get away. She knelt down to the boy, embraced him, and said, "Mark honey, Mommy has to be alone for a moment." He turned her loose, and Kay bolted up the stairs to her bedroom. There she collapsed on her knees, and from the depths of her heart, under conviction and in confusion, she cried out, "God, I don't care what You do to me. I don't care what You do to my sons. I don't care if I never see another man . . . if You will just give me peace." And then a miracle. God's wonderful grace, forgiveness, and peace flooded her heart. Jesus really was the Prince of Peace for her at that moment—all she needed. Kay did not even know what had happened. She did not have the religious terms to express it. But she had truly opened her heart to Jesus Christ and had been born again. She did know that everything would be all right.

In the Word

After Kay's rich experience of salvation in Christ, she immersed herself in the Word of God. No longer was Kay all alone; now she had God. In the days following her conversion she thought hard about her life and all that had happened. She told the Lord that she would be willing to remarry Tom if God could just reach him as He had her. Then came the horrifying news; Tom had committed suicide. Kay was stunned. She was so deeply upset that she could hardly process what had happened. The man with whom she had hoped to spend all of her days, the father of her two precious sons, had hung himself and was gone.

In desperation she ran to the telephone and called her pastor. As she later said, "I felt numb—I needed understanding." He was not at home. Later she was able thank God for that. Her unheeded call forced her to turn to the Lord, and through the Scriptures she found the comfort she so badly needed. Kay had only been a Christian a very short time but she had been, as she put it, "saturating myself in the Word and getting to know my God." It was this that answered her anguish. In her great moment of need, God used the Word she had "hidden in her heart" to give her understanding and solace. As Kay cried out in pain, God spoke to her. She relates,

> Oh, I did not hear an audible voice, but I did hear that still small voice in the chambers of my heart that I have now come to recognize quickly over the years. He said three things to me and they were all from the Word I was hiding in my heart. Yet I don't even think that I even realized that at the time. He said, "Kay, in every thing give thanks for this is the will of God in Christ Jesus concerning you. All things work together for good to those who are called according to His purpose. I will not give you anything you cannot bear." In one of my moments of darkest need as a baby Christian, I saw the way God used His Word to lead, to direct, to comfort, to speak, to give understanding about what to do in the moment. As the years have passed, I have continued to saturate myself in it. It is in His Word that I find all I need for life and godliness, and it is in His Word that I continue to discover my God—who He is, how He acts and reacts, what He is like, what He desires of me, for me. It is in my time alone in the Word that I have developed an intimate, personal, vital relationship with the living God of the Universe. I am absolutely, totally irrevocably convinced beyond a shadow of any doubt that the most valuable pursuit man can embark upon is that of knowing God. I know that knowing the Word of God and the God of the Word has radically changed me—from the inside out—and has established my life on an immovable and sure foundation.

Peace was hers. The lesson was learned.

Trials Come—and a Prophecy

Kay faced many difficulties and challenges in her early Christian life. Once she tried to share her faith with a family member, and she was utterly rejected for her efforts. Again Kay found herself crying out to the Lord for His comfort and strength. But she was learning.

During those days, the Lord seemed to reveal to Kay that one day she would marry a wonderful man by the name of Jack Arthur. All Kay knew about Jack was what she had learned from a prayer request card she had picked up. He was serving as a missionary in South America and had been there for some time. He had even suffered persecution for his faith. At one point he had been stoned for preaching the gospel. As Kay faithfully prayed for Jack she wondered what he looked like. So she picked up a prayer card that had his picture on it. He was a nice-looking man.

God gave her the promises of His Word. She knew she should be thankful for all things—even a lost job.

Then, in June of 1965, Kay was told the eleven-bed diagnostic hospital where she was working would be closed. And there she was, without a job and with two young children to take care of. But again, God gave her the promises of His Word. She knew she should be thankful for all things—even a lost job. In simple childlike faith, Kay lifted up her heart to her Lord, "Father, I don't know why, but thanks anyway." That very night, Kay took her boys to a concert. Little did she know that Jack, who happened to be a graduate of the same school she was attending at the time, had come to town for one night—that night! When the concert concluded, Kay and the children made their way to an ice cream store on the campus. While they sat eating ice cream, Kay heard Mark say, "Mr. Arthur, would you sign my Bible?" At that very moment Kay understood God's providence—in the closing of the hospital, in everything that had happened. Kay and Jack talked briefly. Jack mentioned that he would be returning to the mission field in a few months. And Kay thought in her heart, "Well, you don't know it, but I am going with you."

A New Home

Jack returned to the mission field without Kay, but only briefly. Within three months he was back on the campus as a missionary speaker. The rest is history. In December of 1965, to make a wonderful courtship story short, Kay and Jack were married, and together they were off to Mexico—as missionaries. God had at last fulfilled Kay's deep desire. He had given her a godly husband and the opportunity to serve Him. Life began taking on a whole new aura.

By this time the children were teenagers. The educational situation in Mexico left much to be desired, so Kay taught her children herself. This was God's way of showing Kay that she had the spiritual gift of teaching.

While in Mexico, the Lord blessed Kay and Jack with their first son, and Kay's third. They named him David, after the great Israelite king. Three years later, Kay became seriously ill with a heart infection. The doctors insisted the Arthurs return home. While it was true that Kay was physically sick of heart, she became spiritually sick of heart at the thought of abandoning their ministry in Mexico. Little did she realize their missionary outreach would one day span the globe.

Expanding Ministry

Back in America, the Arthurs settled down in Chattanooga, Tennessee. The Lord led them into a wonderful ministry with teenagers. The young people would gather in their home, and Kay and Jack would teach them the Bible. By the hand of God, this teaching ministry was multiplied many times over. Women began to come to Kay, asking her to share the Word of God with them. In a very short time the living room of their home proved too small. The Lord opened up an opportunity for Kay and Jack to acquire a thirty-two-acre farm near Chattanooga for their teaching ministry. At the time of the purchase, four buildings dotted the property: a farm house, a large barn, a chicken house, and a gatehouse located at the top of the drive-way. Kay, Jack, and the three boys moved into their new home and, the very next Tuesday morning, Bible studies began in the old chicken house. For the first few weeks the numbers were slim. There were so few people that each one present could share their name and prayer requests. But the numbers soon grew, so much so that before long Kay and Jack had to clean out the barn, put in a new floor and loft, and move the Tuesday morning Bible study in there! In this way and in that setting, Precept Ministries, as the Bible study program is now known, was born. By 1970 it was fully incorporated. And still it grew.

An Unfolding Ministry

In the end the chicken house and the barn together could not hold the numbers who came to study God's Word. Kay and Jack set to constructing an administration building, then an auditorium, a production building, and finally the great Grace Kinser Memorial Training Center. (In 1971 Grace Kinser had invited Kay to come to Atlanta, Georgia, to teach the Bible in her home, and that experience became a significant landmark in the ministry.) As the work continued to grow, office buildings were built, along with two dorms to house those who attended conferences. In 1989 the old barn and chicken house were torn down to create parking space.

*The Lord began to impress a world vision
on Kay and Jack.*

The Lord began to impress a world vision on Kay and Jack. Every week Kay would travel to Atlanta to teach. Her ministry grew until thousands were attending her Bible sessions. Kay became burdened for a way to teach people to study God's Word more effectively. Many attended the conferences, but what of all those who could not travel to her, who desperately wanted to learn how to study the Scriptures? Growing out of her burden were the principles for the inductive study technique she came to call

"Precept upon Precept." In 1976 this new phase of ministry began. Kay Arthur became one of the leading Bible-teaching women of the late twentieth century.

A Personal Testimony

God has spoken to many lives through Kay's ministry. The authors have had personal experience of this. Our sister-in-law attended one of Kay Arthur's Bible study conferences. Although she had been a professing Christian for many years, she had seemingly never come to know Christ. While hearing the Word of God there, she was so moved by the Holy Spirit that she sank to her knees and gave her heart completely to Jesus Christ. Her life was transformed. Thousands have been so touched. The ministry now supports a staff of more than 120, with offices in several foreign countries. At this time Bible study courses are conducted in every state in the United States and in more than seventy other countries as well. Each course is accompanied by a companion set of audio and video teaching tapes. Studies can be acquired in Spanish, Korean, Romanian, Chinese, Japanese, Portuguese, Russian, Czech, and German.

Into the Media World

The Bible study ministry has expanded into broadcasting. Kay has hosted a fifteen-minute daily radio program, "How Can I Then Live," answering questions on "How to Live in the Fullness." She also has anchored an hour-long television program that was syndicated to hundreds of television stations. Kay has written at least fifteen books, including one award-winning volume, *Lord, I Need Grace to Make It*. Although Kay's ministry at the beginning was primarily directed toward women, men have begun taking the study courses as well. Her leadership seminars help other Bible teachers prepare effective study programs.

Kay and Jack together continue to do all the administrative work of Precept Ministries. They travel continually and have seen ministries develop in Israel, India, Romania, Japan, Korea, and parts of Europe. The constant moving Kay did as a little schoolgirl has paid off. More than twenty books besides Kay's own works have come out of the ministry, and the list continues to grow. Kay has also written for *Decision, Moody,* and *Virtue* magazines. She serves on thirteen ministry boards, either as adviser or in some other capacity. She works with the National Day of Prayer, the Institute of Evangelism, the Congress on Biblical Exposition, Christian Women United, and on and on. National radio and television programs repeatedly have invited her to be a guest. Her Bible teaching is in constant demand.

The Heart of It All

What constitutes the heart, the mission of Precept Ministries as Kay and Jack envision it? Their mission statement is simple:

> The mission of Precept Ministries is to establish God's people at home and abroad and God's word as that which produces reverence for Him. This mission is being accomplished by teaching the word of God through various means such as inductive Bible study courses, devotional studies, training programs, conferences, radio, and television. These are designed to motivate, communicate, cultivate, instruct, and train in such a way that people will become Christlike and equipped to fulfill the Lord Jesus Christ's mission for them.

A Tribute to Grace

Kay Arthur came to know Christ through her trials, heartaches, and tragedies. She knows what is means to grow in grace through the Word of God. Many have come to a deeper, richer understanding of the Scriptures through her life of service.

As with Kay, our spiritual life and development really depend on our ability to grasp and assimilate the Bible. One poet wrote of searching the world over for truth, culling it from all the greatest writings, and from the wisest men and women. Then he returned weary from his quest only to find that "all the sages said is in the book God's faithful ones read." This simple poetic testimony to the Word of God is right and true. It has been affirmed by millions of believers through the ages.

Testimonies to the Scriptures

William E. Gladstone, the "Grand Old Man" of the British Parliament, said:

> I have known ninety-five great men of the world in my time, and of these eighty-seven were all followers of the Bible.
>
> Talk about questions of the day, there is but one question and that is the gospel. It can and will correct anything that needs correction. My only hope for the world is in bringing the human mind into contact with Divine Revelation.
>
> Though assailed by camp, by battery, and by mine, the Holy Scriptures are nevertheless a house built upon a rock, and that rock impregnable.[1]

*Helen Keller . . . said, "The Bible seems to me like a river
of light flowing through my darkness and it has kept
my hope of accomplishments bright when things
seemed too difficult to overcome."*

The French thinker Jean-Jacques Rousseau hated Christianity, but he said, "I must confess to you that the majesty of the Scriptures astonishes me. . . . If it had been the invention of men, the inventor would be greater than the greatest heroes."[2] Helen Keller, the blind and deaf Alabama woman who so touched the world, said, "The Bible seems to me like a river of light flowing through my darkness and it has kept my hope of accomplishments bright when things seemed too difficult to overcome."[3] And the English author John Ruskin urged, "Read your Bible—make it your daily business to obey in it all you understand. To my early knowledge of the Bible I owe the best part of my taste in literature."[4] The list of the "greats" who eulogize the Scriptures seems endless, not to mention the multitudes of ordinary people who have found God's Word to be "a lamp to my feet, and a light to my path" (Ps. 119:105). The woman who seeks true spirituality must imbibe the precious elixir of the Word of God, for

> These have God married
> And no man shall part,
> Dust on the Bible
> And drought in the heart.

Through the Holy Scriptures we draw closer to God and He to us. Let us look at the nature of this Book in this our sixth step towards spirituality.

What the Bible Is

*Behind and beneath the Bible, above and beyond
the Bible, is the God of the Bible. The Bible is God's
written revelation of His will to men.
Its central theme is salvation through Jesus Christ."*

So much has been said, so many books have been written, and so many sermons preached on the Bible that it hardly seems necessary to say anything more. Nevertheless, as Simon Peter said, "stirring up your sincere mind by way of reminder" (2 Peter 3:1), we will look into what it is we are actually holding when we pick up the Bible to read.

Henrietta Mears said, "Behind and beneath the Bible, above and beyond the Bible, is the God of the Bible. The Bible is God's written revelation of His will to men. Its central theme is salvation through Jesus Christ."[5] The Bible, being God's own Word, leads us to the living Word: Jesus Christ. To further our spiritual development we are now going to delve into the nature of the Scriptures, their purpose, and their interpretation. We promise not to be technical or pedantic, because after all, the Bible is alive (Heb. 4:12) and imparts a living truth to us.

Divine Inspiration

The Bible is inspired by God's Holy Spirit. Scripture itself attests to this fact in passages such as Psalm 19, Psalm 119, Luke 24:25–27, John 10:34–35, Hebrews 1:1–3, 2 Peter 3:16, and so on. The most quoted witness of the Bible to its own inspiration is found in 2 Timothy 3:16–17 which says, "All Scripture is inspired by God and profitable for teaching, for reproof, for correction, for training in righteousness; that the man of God may be adequate, equipped for every good work." The secular use of the word *inspiration* usually implies human genius. The Bible presents an entirely different understanding of the term. The word Paul used for inspiration, *theopneustos*, literally translates "God-breathed." The New Testament stresses the fact that God breathed into the sacred writers so that what we have in the Bible is the very Word of God. The astute theologian Carl F. H. Henry said, "In short, the Bible's life-breath as a literary deposit is Divine." Although God clearly allowed the human factor in the production of the Scriptures, an issue we shall address in a moment, the Bible came from the inspiration, motivation, and work of the Holy Spirit. How did God actually inspire the authors of the Bible? We simply do not know what took place in the psyches of those writers when they penned their works. We can understand in most instances *why* they wrote, but just how God inspired them is beyond our grasp.

Methods

Several "theories of inspiration" have been proposed down through the years. A brief look at a few of them will help us arrive at a solid view of inspiration that will, in turn, enhance our appreciation of the divine nature of the Bible. One such theory is called "inspiration by intuition." It says that the biblical writers were merely people of religious genius who had profound spiritual insight. Of course, this idea of inspiration could apply to any talented person, from a gifted writer like Shakespeare to a great scientist like Steven Hawking. Surely the Bible is more than a work of mere human ingenuity, however brilliant the authors were. This is not a very satisfactory theory.

Another popular view can be described as "inspiration by illumination." It declares that each biblical author had a deep experience of God and was inspired to record it. Such an approach does not eliminate the work of the Holy Spirit, but it implies God's contribution is no more than an intensification of the illumination all believers share. This tends to oversimplify the dynamic personal work God performed when the writers penned their pages.

The third view is known as "inspiration by dictation." This particular approach is the opposite to human inspiration or illumination. Some have even called it the "mechanical view" of inspiration. It holds that the writers were no more than typewriters or word processors in the hands of God. The human factor is all but eliminated. Of course, such passages as Exodus 31:18, where the Ten Commandments were written "with the finger of God," imply this approach, but the Bible as a whole makes it obvious that the human writers were more than passive tools in God's hands. Each writer's personality, culture, background, and purpose in writing clearly played a part. At the same time, God so inspired the biblical writers that nothing they wrote was outside the control of God.

The Best View

The "plenary view" or the "dynamic view" of inspiration boasts a large following. It states that the entire Bible is inspired by God. No portion of the Scriptures arose from human generation alone, nor can any segment be seen as less inspired than any other. The entire Bible is the product of the Spirit of God using human writers. This view carefully balances the Holy Spirit's influence and the human writers' role in the production of the Word. It maintains the integrity of both. This is the position that has been held by evangelical scholars and Bible-believing Christians down through the ages.

To further understand the nature of the Scriptures it would be helpful now to have a quick look at certain key words.

Key Words About the Bible

The general consensus of theological history up until the last two or three hundred years was . . . that revelation, a Word from God, could be propositional as well as personal . . . not only could be but actually was.

The first important word is *revelation*. It has been argued that revelation only occurs when God confronts a person and reveals Himself to him or her. This has certainly occurred countless times. Look at Moses on the Holy Mount when God addressed him face-to-face and gave him the Law. Look also at the apostle Paul on the Damascus Road when he met Jesus Christ. And such experiences are not recorded in the Bible alone; down through history people have encountered God. We all meet Him personally at some time—although not always so dramatically as Moses and Paul. Some people claim, however, that such an experience is the *only* means of revelation, that there is no such thing as a written or *propositional* revelation of God. Those who hold such a position say the Bible, therefore, is not true revelation but only the *record* of revelation. The existentialist theologian Friedrich Schleiermacher (1768–1839) propounded this theory. Archbishop William Temple also expressed the same belief, saying, "There is no such thing as revealed truth. There are truths of revelation, that is to say propositions . . . which are not themselves directly revealed."[6] But for millennia God's people have contended that the Bible itself is a revelation of God. As one scholar pointed out,

> The general consensus of theological history up until the last two or three hundred years was . . . that revelation, a Word from God, could be propositional as well as personal . . . not only *could* be but actually was.[7]

Why should one sort of revelation preclude the other? There is no reason for it to be so. Actually, one complements the other. People, for example, need to learn about each other both ways. If a woman we do not know walks up to us and stands in silence, we can learn a few things—her height and the color of her clothes, for example. But that is not very much. We certainly cannot tell whether we want to get to know her better, or whether we might become friends. We get some hints by her presence, but hardly enough to establish a relationship. We have to hear her communicate; she must truthfully tell us about herself. Only then can we know her. If human encounters are like that, could it be different with God? That is why we have the Bible. Through it we get to know God.

Beyond Words

At the same time, God's revelation of Himself in the Scriptures is far more than mere theological statements. In the Bible we do learn about God, but He actually reveals Himself as well. We can encounter God *personally* through the Scriptures. It often becomes His "tool" to encounter us. We cannot divorce the personal *and* propositional aspects of full revelation in the Bible. Both are essential. We need to dynamically know God as well as know *about* Him. Charles Haddon Spurgeon stated in a sermon delivered May 17, 1887, "What God has joined together these [existential] . . . thinkers willfully put asunder, and separate the Revealer from his own revelation . . . Christ and his Word must go together." It makes no sense to cut up or divide revelation into Word and encounter. J. I. Packer explained: "To deny that revelation is propositional in order to emphasize its personal character is like trying to safeguard the truth that cricket is played with a bat by denying that it is played with a ball. The denial undercuts the assertion."[8]

Or to put it another way: it is nice to have one's spouse stand before us and smile; it is also nice to hear the words, "I love you." Both kinds of encounter deepen the relationship. So it is with God.

Testimonies to Revelation

How grateful we should be that God has given us a clear revelation of Himself in the Holy Bible. We should treasure it. To delve into its pages regularly, open-heartedly seeking God's message for our lives is a discipline we dare not neglect.

The church has historically held the view that the Bible is God's Word and revelation to us. For example, the *Thirty-Nine Articles* of the Church of England states the Holy Scriptures are "God's Word written" (Article XX). The famous Westminster Confession of 1647 declares the Bible is "to be received, because it is the Word of God." The Baptist London Confession of 1644 stated: "In this written Word God hath plainly revealed whatsoever he hath thought needful for us to know."[9] Go back as far as the early church fathers and trace the question through the ages of church history. It is answered virtually the same everywhere in all times. The objective revelation of God can be found in the Holy Scriptures. How grateful we should be that God has given us this clear revelation of Himself in the Holy Bible. We should treasure it. To delve into its pages regularly, open-heartedly seeking God's message for our lives, is a discipline we dare not neglect.

We praise God that we encounter Him personally in the Word for, as we saw in step two, the Bible states concerning itself,

> For the word of God is living and active and sharper than any two-edged sword, and piercing as far as the division of soul and spirit, of both joints and marrow, and able to judge the thoughts and intentions of the heart. And there is no creature hidden from His sight, but all things are open and laid bare to the eyes of Him with whom we have to do. (Heb. 4:12–13)

That is revelation: that is the role of the Bible. Biblical inspiration as God's revelation has been succinctly defined in a statement at the Lausanne Congress on World Evangelism:

> We affirm the divine inspiration, truthfulness and authority of both the Old and New Testament Scriptures in their entirety as the only written word of God, without error in all that it affirms, and the only infallible rule of faith and practice.

We also affirm the power of God's word to accomplish His purpose of salvation. The message of the Bible is addressed to all mankind. For God's revelation in Christ and in Scriptures is unchangeable. Through it the Holy Spirit still speaks today. He illumines the minds of God's people in every culture to perceive its truth freshly through their own eyes and thus discloses to the whole church even more of the many-colored wisdom of God (2 Tim. 3:16; 2 Peter 1:21; John 10:35; Isa. 55:11; 1 Cor. 1:21; Rom. 1:16; Matt. 5:17–18; Jude 3; Eph. 1:17–18; 3:10, 18).[10]

As long as we believe that, we will not go astray. It is awesome to think that when we pick up the Bible with an open heart and mind, we may well meet God. This leads to the next term, *authority*.

A Word of Authority

The authority of God's Word means we should hold the Bible in grateful reverence and let it speak for itself.

Since the Bible is the inspired, truthful Word of God, it has absolute *authority*, and that means we must *obey* it. Many creedal statements talk about the Bible as being the "authoritative rule" for faith and practice. This authoritative rule applies to the church, regardless of time or denomination. It also relates to the individual believer. As Dr. Dewey Beegle put it, "Scripture becomes the basis of appeal in all matters pertaining to the content of faith and the practice of Christian living."[11]

The authority of God's Word means we should hold the Bible in grateful reverence and let it speak for itself. To force the Holy Scriptures into some preconceived mold often does violence to its authority. For example, so-called "liberation" or "process" views, as well as "feminist" and "masculine" views have all, at different times, been superimposed on the Bible simply to justify an agenda. This cannot be warranted. God gave us His Word for all people and to meet every need. We must let it say what it says. Billy Graham was right when he wrote, "Millions of people today are searching for a reliable voice of authority. The Word of God is the only real authority we have. His Word sheds light on human nature, world problems, and human suffering. But beyond that, it clearly reveals the way to God."[12]

The Bible Harmonizes

Another important term concerning the Scriptures is *harmonization*. This simply means the Bible does not contradict itself. Granted, the fact that our human understanding is limited may occasionally make it difficult to reconcile certain verses. Nevertheless, the Bible does ultimately harmonize. It was written over a period of one thousand years by writers from diverse backgrounds yet its message remains essentially the same throughout. This is nothing less than miraculous. We can only conclude that Scripture was inspired by the Holy Spirit. As David Dockery wrote, "The theological, ethical, and historical message of the Scripture is known to be true because of the general, overall consistency of the biblical writings, even though this consistency is expressed in great variety."[13]

All of this is to say that we can rely on the Scriptures. It stands on its own as fully true, authoritative, and effectively functional in our spiritual life. Thank God for His providential hand in giving the Bible to us.

The Human Element

This human factor becomes important if for no other reason than it can save us from "bibliolatry," that is, worshiping the Bible. The Scriptures are God's Word, but not God Himself.

But what about the fact that the Holy Spirit used human authors in the production of the Bible? What does that mean? This human factor becomes important if for no other reason than it can save us from "bibliolatry," that is, worshiping the Bible. The Scriptures are God's Word, but *not* God Himself. We must never make the Bible into an idol; the Word of God informs and leads us to God.

This marvelous book can produce grace and growth in our lives through the Holy Spirit. It is an instrument

- of conviction (Heb. 4:12)
- of regeneration (1 Peter 1:23)
- of sanctification (John 17:17)
- of Christian growth (1 Peter 2:2)
- of God's leadership (Ps. 119:105)
- to increase faith (Rom. 10:17)
- of defense against temptation (Matt. 4:1–11)
- of effective Christian service (Eph. 6:17)

Each one deserves a brief word of comment.

The Bible Is the Instrument of Conviction

The most difficult admission for us to make is that we sin. We excuse ourselves, rationalize, blame others, and do almost anything but admit we have failed God. But before we can ever find genuine peace, we must acknowledge our evil transgressions. If we listen, the Holy Spirit will convict us, especially as we search God's Word. Remember our oft-quoted verse from Hebrews: "For the word of God is living and active and sharper than any two-edged sword" (4:12).

The Bible Is the Instrument of Regeneration

The Holy Spirit becomes the agent in regeneration. And again, His instrument in this mighty act is the Bible. First Peter 1:23 reads: "Being born again, not of corruptible seed, but of incorruptible, by the word of God, which liveth and abideth forever" (KJV). The Scriptures can transform a sinful person into a saint.

The Bible Is the Instrument of Sanctification

Sanctification, an often-used biblical word, simply means "set apart." The word "holy" has the same root. This being "set apart" works two ways. The Holy Spirit sets us apart *from* sin. As we read God's Word the Spirit convicts us, helps us to yield to His promptings, and eradicates sin from our lives. The Holy Spirit also set us apart *for* God. Sanctification is a daily dynamic process whereby increasingly we live solely for God; to worship, to serve, to obey, and to magnify Him through a holy life. How does it come about? Jesus prayed, "Sanctify them in the truth; Thy word is truth" (John 17:17). In the same spirit David said, "How can a young man keep his way pure? By keeping it according to Thy word" (Ps. 119:9). Sanctification is accomplished through dedication to the Word of God.

The Bible Is the Instrument of Christian Growth

Peter, as we have seen, admonished all Christians to "Grow in the grace and knowledge of our Lord and Savior Jesus Christ" (2 Peter 3:18). We have emphasized again and again that such growth is vital to our spiritual well-being. And recall again, in Peter's word, "Like newborn babes, long for the pure milk of the word, that by it you may grow in respect to salvation" (1 Peter 2:2). The Bible, as our spiritual nourishment, enables us to grow in grace and faith.

The Bible Is the Instrument of God's Leadership

God has said, "For all who are being led by the Spirit of God, these are sons of God" (Rom. 8:14). That is a wonderful promise, but the question is often asked, "Although I know I'm a child of God, how can I be led into the full will and purpose of God?" David found the answer: "Open my eyes, that I may behold wonderful things from Thy law" (Ps. 119:18). The Bible, God's law, holds the solution. When we study God's Word daily and consistently we come to an ever-increasing knowledge of the will of God. We need to "search the Scriptures" (John 5:39).

The Bible Is the Instrument to Increase Faith

Jesus said if we had faith we could remove mountains (Matt. 17:20). Through faith many miracles take place and many needs are met. We all should cry out for more faith. D. L. Moody, the great evangelist of the last half of the nineteenth century, shared how he longed for more faith. He said he prayed and prayed, asking for his faith to increase, seemingly to no avail. Then God brought to his mind Romans 10:17: "Faith cometh by hearing, and hearing by the word of God" (KJV). When he saw that verse, the light dawned. Faith grows by Bible study. Do you want a deeper and richer faith? Then you must study God's Word regularly.

The Bible Is the Instrument of Defense Against Temptation

Christ gained His victory over the Devil by His use of Scripture. The Bible serves as a mighty weapon of defense. It can give us victory over sin and Satan in spiritual warfare. Jesus set the pattern.

Throughout His time of temptation (Matt. 4:1–11) Christ consistently resisted Satan with the words, "It is written." He gained His victory over the Devil by His use of Scripture. The Bible serves as a mighty weapon of defense. It can give us victory over sin and Satan in spiritual warfare. Jesus set the pattern. Little wonder then the Bible itself admonished all Christians to "Study to show thyself approved unto God, a workman that needeth not to be ashamed, rightly dividing the word of truth" (2 Tim. 2:15 KJV).

The Bible Is the Instrument of Effective Service

A grand and joyous old hymn of the faith states:

The service of Jesus, true pleasure affords;
In Him there is joy, without an alloy;
'Tis heaven to trust Him and rest on His words;
It pays to serve Jesus each day.

Serving in Jesus' name is one of the great pleasures of the Christian life. The Bible is not only a defensive weapon in the battle against Satan, it is also becomes an effective offensive weapon in Christ's service. Paul tells us in Ephesians 6:17 to take "the sword of the Spirit, which is the word of God." With God's Word in hand, we can do great things for our Lord.

How precious Scripture becomes for the spiritually-minded, growing believer. But we must learn to use it wisely. This leads to a major issue: How do we interpret the Bible? If it is to point us to Christ and develop our spiritual life, how can we be sure we are getting out of it what God wants us to? What principles do we follow?

A Big Word

The study of how to interpret the Bible properly is called *hermeneutics*. It is possible to extract and develop quite bizarre views of the Christian faith from the Bible while still believing it is the inspired, inerrant Word of God. How can people with different beliefs support their various positions from the same Bible? Dewey M. Beegle explains: "The problem eventually comes down to the quality of the interpretation. . . . The basic criterion for determining God's truth is the proper use of reason working with all the available data. Without this approach there is no way to break into the vicious circle of theological deductions."[14]

Good Principles of Interpretation

In order to understand what the Bible really says, it is not enough to believe it is fully inspired and authoritative. We must interpret it properly. That involves what is called biblical criticism. The word "criticism" does not mean being negative about the Scriptures or questioning their truthfulness. Rather it means discovering the proper hermeneutics. Let us now look at some principles of interpretation.

Purpose and Style

Biblical criticism must take into consideration the writer's purpose and style. Each biblical writer had a definite message in mind and constructed a style that would best express it. For example, the gospel of Matthew was written primarily to convince Jewish people that Jesus was their Messiah. On the other hand, John's gospel was written to appeal to the Gentile reader. John, therefore, refers to Jesus more often as the Son of God than as the Messiah since this designation would be better understood by the Roman world. There is no conflict between the gospel of Matthew and the gospel of John to be sure, but there is a difference.

We can see the principle again in the writings of Paul. When he wrote his letter to the Galatians he had a particular problem in mind. The churches there were slipping back into the belief that they could be saved by the works of the law rather than by God's grace alone through faith. That was a serious issue, and to them Paul wrote his "strongest" letter. On the other hand the author of the book of Hebrews wrote to warn his readers not to slip back into their old ways, since Christ had inaugurated a superior convenant with them.

Right behavior was important. The emphasis and style of these two epistles are different because their purpose was different. They were addressing two contrasting problems. When we read God's Word, keeping an eye out for these kinds of things is important for proper interpretation. Consulting good commentaries becomes a wise procedure.

All Kinds of Literature

Furthermore, there are many types of *literary* genres in the Bible. Taking this into account in the interpretation of the Scriptures has sometimes been called "literary criticism." What types of literature do we discover in the Bible? Here are a few:

- Poetry (virtually all of the Psalms)
- History (Joshua, Judges, and so on)
- Law (Leviticus, Deuteronomy, and so on)
- Biography (the four Gospels)
- Ethics and Morals (the Sermon on the Mount)
- Narrative (Jonah)

And the list goes on. The Bible abounds in literary forms.

We should be aware of what kind of literature we are dealing with. Reading a poem is different from reading history—and certainly different from reading today's newspaper. There are those who would tell us not to accept the Bible as literally true. But we say the Bible *is* literally true. It does not contain one word that is not literally true. However, the Scriptures do encompass different kinds of literature. Just because the Word of God has poetry does not mean that part of the Bible is not true—it is truth expressed poetically. Nor does Bible history contain errors. It is true history of the distant past, expressed as old historians would express it. The Bible was produced in the language and cultural setting of the time. Moreover, it speaks phenomenologically, that is, it does not pretend to be a precise dissertation on current science. The writers expressed ideas and truths in the context of their everyday experience. Had they not done so, no one would have understood them. These human factors are to be kept in mind as we seek a proper interpretation of a book or passage in Scripture. Realizing the literary genre we are dealing with really helps in our interpretation and understand of God's Word.

A Conflict? Not Really!

The Bible does not contradict itself, nor does it contradict genuine truth in any area. At the same time we must realize that, though the Bible does not conflict with true science, it is not a scientific textbook. It tells us God created the universe, but it does not give us the details of how He did it. The Scriptures were never intended to give us detailed answers in any area of contemporary technical research; they were written to point us to God and "explain Him." Of course, some biblical critics would tell us a conflict exists between science, history, and biblical truth. But they miss the point; truth is truth, be it scientific or spiritual—and all truth ultimately comes from God. Therefore real science and proper biblical understanding never conflict. Sir Winston Churchill, concerning the Bible and the imagined conflict of science and the Scriptures said,

> When professors with high sounding titles attempt to palm off their pernicious denials of the Holy Scriptures by labelling them: "The Findings of Science" or "The Consensus of Scholarship," some folks take them seriously and are ready to throw away their Bibles. . . . We may be sure that all these things (what the Bible says) happened just as they are set out according to Holy Writ. We may believe that they happened to people not so very different from ourselves, and that the impressions those people received were faithfully recorded and have been transmitted across the centuries with far more accuracy than many of the telegraphed accounts we read of goings on of today. In the words of a forgotten work of Mr. Gladstone, we rest with assurance upon "THE IMPREGNABLE ROCK OF HOLY SCRIPTURE."
> Let the men of science and learning expand their knowledge and probe with their researches every detail of the records which have been preserved to us from these dim ages. All they will do is to fortify the grand simplicity and essential accuracy of the recorded truths which have lighted so far the pilgrimage of man."—*Now*[15]

It is not incidental that modern research in cosmology and quantum mechanics is beginning to demonstrate a striking affinity between the Scriptures and science. For this we should be thankful.

In other words, the Bible does not deal with the question of whether or not the big bang theory of Creation is correct. The Scriptures do not give us Newton's three laws of motion nor Einstein's concept of relativity. Paul did not have a word processor when he wrote Romans. We must see the Bible for what it is, a book about God, and not try to read into the it things that cannot be found there. Nor should the scientific mind-set make the same error and propose conflict. Again let it be said, no disagreement arises between *true* science and *correct* Bible interpretation. Actually, they imply one another; after all truth *is* truth. Truth prevails wherever we may find it, in the laboratory or on our knees before an open Bible. And we simply thank God that we have in the Scriptures a revelation of God. Our minds as well as our hearts need to be *humble* and submit to Him. This will do much to eliminate problems and so-called contradictions in the Bible. It is not incidental that modern research in cosmology and quantum mechanics is beginning to demonstrate a striking affinity between the Scriptures and science. For this we should be thankful.

Preservation

The Holy Spirit has providentially and wonderfully preserved the purity of the biblical text and has protected the quality of manuscripts down through the years. The Dead Sea Scrolls are an example. We have such incredibly accurate early copies that we certainly should again thank God. What we have comes so close to the originals that we can say with confidence that this Bible of ours is verily the Word of God.

Gratitude for Thinkers

Furthermore, how grateful we should be for Bible scholars and archeologists who help us in so many ways to understand God's Word. Some say, "Who needs the scholars?" We do; we need them desperately, and God has raised up men and women of high caliber, using them to hand on the Scriptures to us.

We also thank God for the biblical linguists who, through the years, have given us excellent Bible translations. There have been a number of authoritative translations in the English language down through the ages. A sample list of them follows:

- The Septuagint Version—285 B.C.
- The Vulgate Version—A.D. 400
- The Wycliffe Version—A.D. 1380
- The Tyndale Version—A.D. 1525
- The King James Version—A.D. 1611
- The American Standard Version—A.D. 1900–1901
- The Revised Standard Version—A.D. 1946–1952

Today we have many new English translations and paraphrases, among them:

- The Phillips Version
- The Williams Version

- The New American Standard Version
- The New International Version

May we not fail to use the research the scholarly world has given us. It can help us tremendously in our interpretation of the Word.

Exegesis

Exegesis is another principle of biblical interpretation. Exegesis means the careful and extensive study of what the writer actually said and what he meant to communicate. This demands contextualization. Six steps become helpful here:

1. Grasp the surface, simple message.
2. Get at the deeper, structural principles.
3. Understand the historical-cultural situation addressed.
4. Ask: How would the first hearers understand the passage?
5. Ask: Is the passage relevant today? What does it mean to me today?
6. Ask: What is the general and specific application?

All this means we take language seriously, treating history as history, poetry as poetry, and figurative language as just that. Again, good commentaries and writings prove most helpful here.

The Context

Understanding the *context* of a passage within the Bible itself greatly aids correct interpretation. It is important to place a passage in the coherent whole of the entire Bible. Scholars call this the "analogy of faith" principle. Scripture is compared with Scripture, always recognizing the coherent, noncontradictory nature of the entire Bible. Passages are seen in the light of the central theme of the Scriptures as well as in their contemporary situations. Relevancy must be sought.

The "Center"

> *The Christ-centeredness of all Scripture must be constantly kept in the foreground. Jesus said of the Scriptures, "It is these that bear witness of Me" (John 5:39). Christ is the final Word, the final authority. "I am . . . the truth," Jesus said (John 14:6).*

For correct interpretation the *Christ-centeredness* of all Scripture must be constantly kept in the foreground. Jesus said of the Scriptures, "It is these that bear witness of Me" (John 5:39). Christ is the final Word, the final authority. "I am . . . the truth," Jesus declared (John 14:6). The Bible points essentially and centrally to Jesus Christ.

Application

Finally, *application* becomes vital. God intends us to discover how the truth works out in our own daily life. The Bible gives us something to *do*. We read and study it to discern God's will, purpose, and direction. And what God says in the Scriptures to do, as obedient children we do. May we ever remember, as James tells us, to "Prove yourselves doers of the word, and not merely hearers who delude themselves" (James 1:22). All the other important principles of interpretation fall to the ground if we do not approach the Word of God with an attitude of obedience to what He reveals to us.

These basic hermeneutical approaches should help us better to understand God's Word so that we can continue to grow spiritually and fashion our lives on a divine basis.

God Said It

So there it is: In the Holy Scriptures God has delivered an authoritative, trustworthy, true propositional revelation of Himself that will endure all the tests of the critics and provide for believers "food for the soul." As J. I. Packer has correctly told us:

> The mental discipline of systematically submitting our thoughts, views, and purposes to the judgment of Scripture as it interprets itself to us in regard to our relationship with God, is more than one Christian tradition among many; it is a discipline intrinsic to Christianity itself.[16]

Perhaps the simple cliché is not quite as simplistic as may at first be thought:

> God said it,
> I believe it, and
> That settles it.

Now a great deal of what has been said on the Bible up to this point may seem rather theological and on the intellectual side. The Bible does contain real food for thought, of course, but the basic point is that we must understand and assimilate the spiritual aspects of Bible study if we would grow in Christ. To that important point we finally address ourselves.

Assimilating God's Truth

In order to grow through Scripture study we should realize two things. First, the Holy Spirit inspired the Bible. As we meditate on the it it the Holy Spirit also becomes the interpreter. As one faithful Bible reader put it,

> It is only the heart that yields to be led by the Holy Spirit that can expect to profit by the teaching of the word, and truly to know Christ in His divine saving power. The truths of Christ's sonship and divinity and priesthood and redemption *were given in charge to the Holy Spirit;* He revealed them from time to time; *He alone can reveal them to us.*[17]

Before we begin reading the Bible we should come to our Lord in *earnest prayer*. We should thank God for the Scriptures that He has so graciously given us, then sincerely ask the Heavenly Father to guide us, open our minds, give us a receptive heart, and grant us a revelation of Himself by the power of the Holy Spirit. That is why Paul said to the Corinthians,

> As it is written, "Things which eye has not seen and ear has not heard, and which have not entered the heart of man, all that God has prepared for those who love Him." For to us God revealed them through the Spirit; for the Spirit searches all things, even the depths of God.... Now we have received, not the spirit of the world, but the Spirit who is from God, that we might know the things freely given to us by God. (1 Cor. 2:9–12)

We are utterly dependent on the Spirit of God to teach us from the pages of our Bible. Because of this we yield humbly in heart and mind to His speaking.

Second, we must attempt to read the Bible with a desire to grow. We need not elaborate on this point since this is what this entire step sixth is all about. But now we must look at a few, final, practical suggestions to get the most out of our Bibles.

Some Practical Ideas

There are a few practical things we can do to make our Bible study time all that God would have it be. We should work toward having a regular study time using a definite program of study. Regularity and planning have psychological value, if nothing else. A haphazard reading of a portion here and a portion there will never suffice. We eat regular, balanced meals for bodily health. Why not have a regular plan for feasting on the Holy Scriptures? This should not be seen in a legalistic sense; at times circumstances may prevent us from keeping our commitment. We should not carry a burden of guilt if we cannot keep our study schedule for a real reason. The Bible liberates us, not enslaves us. But we do need to spend an adequate amount of time in the Word of God on a regular, planned basis. The Holy Spirit will lead us, and we are wise when we give ourselves to this discipline.

Further, let us make use of all the help available. Different translations can often produce a clearer insight into the truth of God. Bible study guides, helpful books, and above all, good commentaries are invaluable. God's great truths can often be made more clear by diligent scholars who know the scriptural languages and the significant ideas they convey. From time to time it is good to read a commentary straight through to get the feel of an entire book of the Bible. Another great resource is the Internet. There are more helps for the Christian life and Bible study on that medium than could ever be imagined. God has not only given us the Scriptures, He has given us excellent helps as well. We would do well to take advantage of them.

And finally, we need to keep in mind the major themes of the Bible. We do not need to get hung up on "secondary" issues. This does not mean that secondary doctrines are not important, but we should never let the real purpose of the Bible fade into the background.

A Basic Fact

If we neglect the Bible, we do so at the peril
of our spiritual development.
The Bible does truly change lives.

The Word of God is paramount in the Christian's life. If we neglect the Bible, we do so at the peril of our spiritual development. The Bible does truly change lives. To make this point, the story is told of a converted cannibal who one day was sitting reading his Bible as a trader passed by. The trader asked him what he was doing. "Reading the Bible," he replied. "That book is out of date in my country," said the trader. "If it had been out of date here," said the cannibal, "you would have been eaten long ago."

Andrew Murray reminds us that a wise Christian will be "full of the conviction that Scripture is indeed God's Word; that God Himself, through His Spirit, spoke in the prophets, and that it has the power of God dwelling in it."[18] The first-century Christians were called those who "have upset the world" (Acts 17:6). They upset it by sharing the Word of God. And the Word of God can transform our world today; it can turn it upside down, or more correctly, right side up. That is the Bible's power, as Kay Arthur learned. May we learn it too.

Conclusion

We should now better appreciate the Bible God has so graciously given to us. We should also be more committed to learning about it and studying it, allowing it to become in our lives all that the Lord would wish. The spiritual woman digs deep in the Word and through it, grows in grace, daily becoming more like Christ.

Prayer

I thank You for Your wonderful Word. Grant me the ability to love it, be found in it, understand it, and live it out in my daily life. May I come to the place where I can say with David, "Thy Word I have treasured in my heart, that I may not sin against Thee" (Ps. 119:11). Through the Living Word, our Lord Jesus Christ, I pray. Amen.

10 Questions for Study and Discussion

1. Do you think Kay Arthur's divorce had anything to do with her conversion? Why and how?
2. How do circumstances force us into God's Word? How does it affect us?
3. Why is it so important that we "grow in grace"?
4. What role does the Bible play in our Christian maturity?
5. What is the basic nature of the Scriptures, and what does that mean to our study of it?
6. What "helps" do we have in Bible study today, and how can we evaluate and use them?
7. Do the principles of interpretation have an important place in Bible study? Why? What are they?
8. How do we handle problems in the Bible, such as "conflicts"?
9. What are the rules of discipline to follow to profit most from Bible study?
10. What can the Bible mean to me and why am I not getting the most out of the Scriptures as I read?

The Spiritual Woman Talks with God

MEET EVELYN CHRISTENSON
A WOMAN WHO TALKS WITH GOD

Pray without ceasing.
(1 Thessalonians 5:17)

$\mathcal{T}$he day: January 31, 1922; the place: Muskegon, Michigan. On that date and in that picturesque place, Edna and Edward Luhman celebrated the birth of their beautiful daughter Evelyn. And it was a fine home and family little Evelyn entered.

The Family

Edward Luhman owned a greenhouse and worked as a florist at the time. He enjoyed this work, although later in life he changed careers to become a state highway contractor. Everyone knew his wife, Edna, as a faithful, godly homemaker, a deeply spiritual woman who always prayed diligently for her family's salvation. God heard her pleas and one bright day Evelyn's older sister accepted Jesus as her personal Savior. Then the mother and her oldest daughter claimed Evelyn for Christ. Again, God answered and Evelyn believed.

Conversion

The story of Evelyn's conversion as a child unwinds as a thrilling story. When Evelyn reached nine years of age, an evangelist named Harry McCormick Lentz came to Lakeside Baptist Church in Muskegon. Under his preaching, Evelyn fell under strong conviction of sin during a Sunday morning worship service. She cried all afternoon over her "nine-year-old sins," as she put it. She could not wait to get back to church. That night, when the evangelist invited forward those who wished to make a public commitment to Christ, Evelyn responded with her whole heart. She shot down the aisle and knelt at the altar. The Sunday school superintendent of her church knelt beside her and led her to Jesus. What a night for the little girl! Wonderful things came out of that service.

The Family's Spiritual Journeys

Evelyn had a bright brother, affectionately known as "Bud," who had received Jesus as a little boy. Tragically, he turned his back on God for thirty years, saying he no longer believed in Him. During this time he traveled with Evelyn's father as a contractor and lived a very rough life. The family earnestly prayed for him over the years until Evelyn's mother finally just surrendered her wayward son to God, asking Him to do anything needed to bring him to Christ. Not long after, Bud suffered a serious automobile accident in Detroit. The whole family flew across Michigan to be with him. They wanted to talk with him in the hospital, but his condition was so serious the doctors would not allow it. It was not thought possible that he would ever regain consciousness again. He was kept alive only by machines and tubes.

The family earnestly prayed for God to grant mercy and the opportunity to speak to Bud. He needed Christ so urgently. The next morning, the doctors allowed Evelyn and her mother ten minutes alone with him. Evelyn leaned over to her brother and said, "Bud, God loves you." Suddenly, he stirred. She leaned over a second time and said, "Bud, can you trust Jesus today?" Her brother came out of the coma, and through all the tubes going down his throat, he said, "Uh-huh!" He went on to recover from the accident and was able to live a life dedicated to Christ for two more years, before cancer took him. Still, his return to God had been the answer to prayer. Prayer was a vital part of Evelyn's life.

Sadness, Yet Joy

Evelyn's father also died at a relatively young age, but not before he found Christ. For twenty-five years Evelyn had prayed for his conversion, joined in heart and hand by her mother and her older sister. Edward had lived a loose life on the road with Bud. One day he became ill, so ill he suspected that he was going to die. The doctor was summoned but he only confirmed Edward's suspicions. Deeply disturbed, Edward sent for the minister who had not seen him since he was baptized as a baby. The pastor administered last rites and left. Edward looked over at his wife and a flood of memories swept over him. Down through the years she had lived a holy life before her husband. On one occasion Edward remembered coming home from a trip to find his wife reading the Bible. He told her he felt sure he had seen angels around her. Now as he lay on his sickbed, he looked up at her and said, "There's more to it than what the minister did, isn't there?" She said, "Do you think so?" He replied, "Yes. Call for your pastor." Edna's pastor, an evangelical minister, came and led Edward to Christ. Joy filled every heart; the "prodigal" had come home. Evelyn's father lived as an invalid for two more years. Day after day, he sat with his Bible open on his lap and his oxygen mask strapped on. There were tears of sadness when he died, but there were also tears of joy that Evelyn's father had found eternal life through Jesus Christ.

Evelyn inherited a great, praying family
—a marvelous heritage indeed!

By this time Evelyn had begun to see a life of service and ministry for Christ before her. Edna married Raleigh Moss, a devout Baptist minister. The couple became prayer warriors, spending two hours every day praying for Evelyn's developing ministry. After some years Raleigh died, but Evelyn's mother continued praying for her daughter at least two hours a day throughout the rest of her life. Evelyn described her mother as "an absolutely holy woman, an awesome example," and though they never lived geographically close to each other after Evelyn grew up, they shared a precious prayer relationship. Evelyn's sister, Maxine, is still living and, as Evelyn says, is "her greatest prayer support." Evelyn inherited a great, praying family—a marvelous heritage indeed!

Evelyn's School Days

Now that we have been introduced to the family and their spiritual journeys we can turn the calendar back and look at Evelyn's childhood and how it led her to a marvelous ministry of prayer. Her earlier years were difficult. The Depression of the 1930s had the entire country in its grasp. Though the family had few resources, they had each other. Evelyn always knew where to find her mother when she needed her. She would be in their greenhouse, deep in prayer among the calla lilies. Edna said she could almost feel the beautiful three-feet tall white flowers "breathing up to God." Having a mother who knew God—and how to pray to Him—made up for their stringent circumstances.

During her schooling Evelyn was always a competitor. She would challenge two or three friends in her classes to see who would come out on top after a test. She also assumed the role of protector and took it upon herself to safeguard other little girls who were afraid of the boys. She would walk her friends home, watching over them carefully, and then walk home by herself. No one wanted to take on Evelyn!

Evelyn gave herself to the church as a growing child. She began her actual Christian service at age fourteen by playing the organ and teaching in the beginner's department of Sunday school. She involved herself in youth groups, usually as a leader—that was her gift.

Meeting "Chris"

At age fourteen Evelyn met Harold Christenson, the man who would one day become her husband. They played football together, roller-skated "in a gang" down the middle of the street, and went tobogganing on the high snowy hills outside their town. After finishing high school, Evelyn felt led to further her education. "Chris," as everyone called Harold, was the only boy she had ever dated, and together in January of 1941, Evelyn and Chris enrolled in the Moody Bible Institute at Chicago. Just after midnight, as they were riding the train from Muskegon to Chicago, Chris slipped an engagement ring on her finger. A new day—and a new life—began to unfold. Their romance had a few restrictions. In 1941 Moody did not allow students to date during the first semester, even if they were engaged. But their love deepened as God prepared them for a great future together in His service.

The War

That fall semester, on December 7—"a day that shall live in infamy"—the startling announcement came that Pearl Harbor in Hawaii had been attacked. Chris immediately quit school and enlisted in the Air Force air cadet program. Evelyn finished out the semester at Moody, then returned home. On February 14, 1942, Valentine's Day, Evelyn and Chris were married, just before Chris was to begin pilot training. Once his training was completed Chris remained in the States until his squadron received its orders. Finally, in February of 1943, he left for Europe to serve as a B-17 bomber pilot.

Evelyn soon learned she was expecting their first child. The child was stillborn, and Evelyn herself almost died. This heartbreaking time was made even more difficult by the lack of good medical care. Evelyn's convalescence was excruciating.

On one of Chris's bombing missions, his B-17 was hit and caught fire over Berlin. Chris promised God that if he made it back to neutral territory he would serve Him for the rest of His life. It proved to be no "foxhole" commitment. God saw the crew back to base, and when Chris came home from the war, he and Evelyn immediately enrolled in Bethel College, preparing to serve Christ faithfully. Chris went on to Bethel Seminary. While they were there, Evelyn lost another child.

The Pastorates

In 1952, after seminary, Chris and Evelyn moved to Stansfield, Minnesota, where they took up their first pastorate. In Stansfield, Jan was born—a healthy little girl. A short time later, the couple had another child, Judy, who was born with spina bifida. During the three and a half years the Christensons spent in their first pastorate, Evelyn needed to spend a great deal of time nursing and caring for little Judy. The family then left Minnesota and took up a new pastorate in Rockford, Illinois. By this time, Jan was two years old. Evelyn and Chris eventually had another daughter, Nancy, and a son, Kurt. And today they enjoy eight grandchildren!

*God honored and blessed the Christensons—
the church membership doubled during the first four
years of their ministry there.*

In Rockford, the Christensons gave themselves to the building up of the Temple Baptist Church, which later became known as the "What Happens When Women Pray" Church. In Rockford, Evelyn taught a large adult Sunday school class that included many lawyers and teachers. She wrote all of her own material and carefully prepared for the class, using her husband's library. She taught for over fourteen years and averaged at least twenty-five hours per week in preparation and study. The class covered all the major Christian doctrines, many books of the Bible, the life of Christ, and other important topics. Through this intensive study and research Evelyn gained an excellent knowledge of the Christian experience. God honored and blessed the Christensons—church membership doubled during the first four years of their ministry there.

The Prayer Ministry Begins

In November 1967, some leaders of the "Crusade of the Americas" evangelistic campaign asked Evelyn to conduct a prayer experiment. The challenge was to find exactly what happened when women prayed. She confesses she really had no idea how to go about the task. The crusade did not want more "theories" on prayer; they wanted results—they wanted to understand how God worked when earnest, sustained prayer was made by faithful women. The first thing Evelyn did was ask God how to begin—*if* indeed such a thing was in His will. Could God really want this? Evelyn had to have an answer. One morning, while studying the Bible, she read: "Behold, I have put before you an open door" (Rev. 3:8). The verse resonated deeply in her heart. Evelyn had her answer; she told God she would participate in the experiment, trusting His leadership and wisdom. She involved the women of her church in the experiment for six months. By the time it was completed a tremendous spirit of prayer had developed in the congregation. The amazing results are documented in *What Happens When Women Pray.*

Off to Seminary

At this crucial time, Chris received a call to become a seminary professor at Bethel College and Seminary in St. Paul, Minnesota. Evelyn was devastated. Everything seemed to be going so well at the church. Chris was an effective pastor; and prayer permeated the atmosphere. The wonderful spirit of prayer in Rockford was not the only thing Evelyn had seen develop. She had started an evangelistic neighborhood Bible study. A good number of people participated in the study, and only two of that entire number failed to accept Christ. Could God really be directing them to move?

The president of the seminary had been a good friend for several years. When Chris and Evelyn had their interview with him he asked, "Evie, how do you feel about moving up here?" Evelyn looked at him and said, "Chris is being called *to* something, I am being called *from* something." It was difficult to be suddenly torn away from these rewarding ministries. Nonetheless, it was clear that God was leading them to move, so off to Bethel the Christensons went. Before long God opened new doors for service. Evelyn began conducting "prayer seminars" and then went on to start a tape ministry. The world was going to hear of this woman of prayer whether she lived in Illinois or Minnesota.

God's Providential Leading

Evelyn was asked, "What produces a million-copy book?" Her most appropriate reply was, "Prayer!"

The story of how Evelyn actually wrote her first book *What Happens When Women Pray* is a lesson in God's providential leading. While visiting with the Christensons Jim Lemmon of Victor Books, an old college friend, had asked Evelyn about her ministry. She told him about the prayer seminars they had developed. He asked if she had any of them on tape. Slightly embarrassed, Evelyn told him she had a suitcase full of them. Jim took a set of the tapes to Victor Books. Evelyn soon received a call from the company telling her they wanted to publish her work. She admits she had never dreamed of writing a book, even though people had often suggested it. As friends pressed her to write, Evelyn urged them to talk to God about it, because He had not told her to do so. Finally when Victor Books forced the issue, she went to work. When she finished the manuscript and put it in the mail, she had serious second thoughts. She flew to the phone, dialed the editor, and said, "Do not print that thing! The manuscript contains nothing that every Christian does not already know." He just laughed. When *What Happens When Women Pray* hit the bookstores it became an immediate success, selling more than two million copies in the United States alone. It has been translated into many foreign languages and is now read all over the world. Evelyn testifies that God truly had His hand in the writing. She never would have had the confidence to produce such a work on her own.

Victor Books asked Evelyn to come for a celebration after the first million copies had been sold. At the festivities, Evelyn was asked, "What produces a million-copy book?" Her reply was, "Prayer!" Evelyn had a prayer-support team who prayed with her often and prayed for her continually. In itself this clearly demonstrated what can happen "when women pray." And these faithful women still pray for Evelyn and her ministry. Once a week the prayer team leader calls Evelyn to hear her requests, needs, and joys. Then the entire group meets once a month for prayer. They also gather in an annual retreat to seek God and learn how He will lead Evelyn the next year. Evelyn's entire ministry is permeated with prayer. She constantly claims Jeremiah 33:3: "Call to Me, and I will answer you, and I will tell you great and mighty things, which you do not know." She desires most deeply that God receive glory through what her ministry accomplishes. That kind of attitude can only be achieved through victorious praying. Evelyn has said, "God can get a lot done if we don't care who gets the credit." Evelyn knows that our Lord must be in control, for, as she says, she is not "an administrator, an advertising agent, or any of those things." The Holy Spirit does the work.

Seeking Direction

Evelyn constantly seeks God's direction in the challenges she faces. From the day she read Revelation 3:8 and was led to write her first book, she has clung to it as God's commission and used it as her guiding principle through the years.

The Practical Ministry

In 1980, Evelyn felt God calling her to take her ministry overseas. She believes that when God asks her to do something, she must do it.

Because of increasing travel responsibilities, Evelyn found herself unable to conduct week-long studies on prayer as she had in earlier years. As a result she developed a one-day, intensive prayer seminar. This approach has been a significant help for busy women who desire a vibrant prayer life. Invitations to conduct such seminars flood in. In 1980, Evelyn felt God calling her to take her ministry overseas. She believes that when God asks her to do something, she must do it. She has said that even if she were sick, or if circumstances seemed to be working against her, she would still do whatever the Lord asked. And He has always been faithful, giving her strength, and clearing the way for her to accomplish each task. With God's help, not only has she taught in every state in America but she has taught in every continent on the globe!

A Door Closes—Or So It Seems

In their early days Evelyn and Chris had dearly wanted to become missionaries, and they had actually received an appointment to India. Then the doctors discovered that Chris had a bleeding ulcer. The only treatment at the time for this problem was to give the patient cream and milk; but in India, cows are sacred and milk is hard to come by. The missionary doctor refused to let the Christensons go. Evelyn mourned this disappointment for years. She even found it difficult to attend a missionary commissioning service without tears, so certain had she been that God's call would send her to India. Thirty years later God began to fulfill her dream. Evelyn was invited to India to teach on prayer. She packed bags and bags of tapes and materials, and set out. Juliet Thomas, the International Prayer Director for the Lausanne Committee sponsored by the Billy Graham Association, was also the director of Operation Mobilization in India. It was she who helped Evelyn with all the arrangements for her ministry there. Over time the work has grown and spread.

Through Trans-World Radio, Evelyn has developed an India prayer ministry. She broadcasts to that vast nation every week, even up in Nagaland. With Juliet's help Evelyn communicates to both Hindi and English listeners. The ministry uses an old Communist transmitter from just outside of Moscow, of all places. And so as it turns out, Evelyn did become a "missionary" to that huge nation after all. God is good.

New Writings

Evelyn has written several more books. Translated into at least forty languages, *A Study Guide for Evangelism Praying* has become part of the curriculum of the women's track of A.D. 2000 International, a movement to share Christ with the whole world by the dawn of the new millennium. Evelyn serves as co-chair of the movement. This book has also become the basis for the broadcast on Trans-World Radio. It has been written in such a way that it can be accessed by ordinary people of any culture who want to learn more about Christ.

Evelyn's works include *What Happens When Women Pray; Lord, Change Me; Gaining Through Losing; What Happens When God Answers; Battling the Prince of Darkness; What Happens When We Pray for Our Families; A Study Guide for Evangelism Praying;* and its companion, *A Time to Pray God's Way.* Chariot Victor Books has developed a whole new line of books for Evelyn's ministry, including two children's books: *What Happens When Children Pray,* which includes actual prayers of each of Evelyn's grandchildren, and *My First Prayer Journal.* She has also produced another prayer journal, *Prayers and Answers.* Writing has become a mission field in itself for Evelyn.

In May 1992, a group of sixty-five Christian women leaders met, bringing together charismatics, evangelicals, Pentecostals, mainline denominations, and many different ethnic groups. In the context of the A.D. 2000 movement, the group used *A Study Guide for Evangelism Praying.* Kay Arthur wrote *God, Are You There?* on the gospel of John, which served as follow-up material. The group decided to open its 1995 meeting at Wheaton College to the public. By 1997 there were four regional meetings, taking place in Miami, Florida; Portland, Oregon; Grand Rapids, Michigan; and Bakersfield, California. Evelyn feels convinced that a great moving of God comes about at these meetings because of the prayer that goes into their preparations.

The Impact of Evelyn's Work and Book on Evangelism

*In every evangelistic meeting where Evelyn has
spoken, an average of 25 percent of those attending
have made a profession of faith to receive Christ. That is
phenomenal. Behind it is fervent prayer.*

In 1980, Evelyn felt a distinct call from the Holy Spirit to do evangelistic work coupled with her prayer ministry. Since that time, in every evangelistic meeting where Evelyn has spoken, an average of 25 percent of those attending have made a profession of faith to receive Christ. That is phenomenal. Behind it is fervent prayer. Evelyn's book on evangelism "covers the waterfront" on the vital ministry of prayer for effective witnessing. The first chapter in *A Study Guide for Evangelism Praying* is "Why Evangelize?" It explains God's provision for us in His Son, Jesus Christ. Other chapters include "The Cleansed Life," "Don't Go Without Power," "Intercessory Praying," and "Praying for Each Other." The last chapter explains the methods of evangelistic prayer. Evelyn explains the concept of "triplet praying," conceived by Brian Mills of England. Three people meet once a week, praying in concert for three non-Christians and seeking ways to reach out to them. Evelyn encountered this concept in England when involved in "Mission England 1984," a Billy Graham-sponsored project. There she met Brian Mills, the director of the Triplet Program, who told her that ninety thousand people prayed with the program all over England. Billy Graham later said he considered this the greatest thing he had ever seen in a concerted prayer effort. Evelyn encourages her readers to participate in the ministry.

The Foundation

Evelyn has always felt called to the hidden mission field in the local congregation. The church, God's people, should be led and instructed in prayer and evangelism. In Evelyn's view, if the entire church were aroused to their task, the whole world could be reached with the gospel, and the Great Commission would be fulfilled. Evelyn feels that America's future rests in experiencing such a great revival. And prayer, along with the declaration of the gospel, becomes the key to true spiritual awakening.

The prayer theme of Evelyn's entire ministry is found in 1 Timothy 2:1–4:

> First of all, then, I urge that entreaties and prayer, petitions and thanksgivings, be made on behalf of all men, for kings and all who are in authority, in order that we may lead a tranquil and quiet life in all godliness and dignity. This is good and acceptable in the sight of God our Savior, who desires all men to be saved and to come to the knowledge of the truth.

All God's children, no matter what their background, must adopt a praying lifestyle. And Evelyn speaks from experience. She is a woman of prayer herself. She exemplifies what Spurgeon, the great London preacher, said concerning prayer: "If the anointing which we bear come not from the Lord of hosts, we are deceivers, since only in prayer can we obtain it. Let us continue instant, constant, fervent in supplication. Let your fleece lie on the thrashing floor of supplication till it is wet with the dew of heaven."

Prayer is absolutely essential to the development of godliness. We surely know that no prayer means no power; no groaning before God spells no growth in God. This teacher for prayer has learned it all and had become a servant teacher to show what happens when women—and men—pray.

The Wonder of Prayer

We cannot but be struck by the wonder of actually talking with God. As Evelyn wrote in her classic book *What Happens When Women Pray*:

> I also learned the simple process of envisioning my God when approaching Him in prayer. The joy that floods my whole being as I find myself visualizing all God is—all His love, all His power, all His concern for me—defies description. What greater privilege could there be for a human being than to actually draw nigh to the omnipotent, omniscient God, high and lifted up on His throne in glory? This to me is the most precious part of my prayer time.[1]

The Bible invites us over and over to present our requests to our Lord and promises that the great God of the universe will answer our cry. He is our omnipotent Lord. There is nothing He cannot do. What He wills, He accomplishes. And God possesses all wisdom and knowledge. "Indeed, the very hairs of your head are all numbered" (Luke 12:7). Having all wisdom, He knows what is best for His creation.

And wonderful thought! God the omnipresent One comes to stand with us, right beside us, to help in all aspects of our lives. Just as the psalmist said:

> Where can I go from Thy Spirit? Or where can I flee from Thy presence? If I ascend to heaven, Thou art there; if I make my bed in Sheol, behold, Thou art there. If I take the wings of the dawn, if I dwell in the remotest part of the sea, even there Thy hand will lead me, and Thy right hand will lay hold of me. If I say, "Surely the darkness will overwhelm me, and the light around me will be night," even the darkness is not dark to Thee, and the night is as bright as the day. Darkness and light are alike to Thee. (Ps. 139:7–12)

He is there—always.

*Through the life, death, and resurrection of
our Lord Jesus Christ, His presence has become a
"throne of grace." God has promised that we can,
in Christ, come to Him with confidence.*

We can actually converse with the Lord of the universe. But we also must see prayer in the light of who we are. Paul told us clearly when he put together pieces of Psalms 14 and 53 with Ecclesiastes 7:20, that, "There is none righteous, not even one; there is none who understands, there is none who seeks for God; all have turned aside, together they have become useless; there is none who does good, there is not even one" (Rom. 3:9–12).

This does not paint a very pretty picture of how the Lord evaluates us. How could a God like the our Holy Lord ever consent to hear us, considering who and what we are? Yet, through redemption in Jesus Christ we can come to God in prayer, for He now sees us as *in Christ*. Our sins have been forgiven. Through the life, death, and resurrection of our Lord Jesus Christ, His presence has become a "throne of grace." God has promised that we can, in Christ, come to Him with confidence: "Let us therefore draw near with confidence to the throne of grace, that we may receive mercy and may find grace to help in time of need" (Heb. 4:16). This verse needs to be repeated continually because of the wonderful grace of God it manifests. Holy God accepts sinful people like us in Christ—*and answers our prayers*. You see, He loves us—truly loves us.

Why and How?

How can all this be? In a previous step, we saw the "in Christ" motif of the New Testament. In Him we stand before God, righteous, just, holy, sanctified, and acceptable in His gracious sight. We can draw on the bank of glory in the name of Christ and receive answers to our prayers. It is incredible indeed that we pray so little in light of our position before God. Hopefully, what we learn in this step will challenge us to greater prayer.

It goes without saying that our lack of meaningful prayer makes us culpable before God. A great praying believer, Andrew Murray, wrote, "There is probably no single sin which each one of us ought to acknowledge with deeper shame—'Guilty, verily guilty'—than the sin of prayerlessness."[2] The most glorious and Holy God invites us to come into His presence and converse with Him; to spurn such an invitation is a reproach to God. Furthermore, a weak prayer life means a deficient spiritual life as well. Murray says prayer becomes the very "pulse of life." Not only that, the church as a whole suffers when God's people do not pray. And note: It is impossible to share Christ effectively unless we undergird our witness with earnest prayer. Evelyn has shown us that.

Why the Prayerlessness?

Why do we not pray more? There is an old saying: "Satan trembles when he sees the weakest saints upon their knees." Satan and the demons attack our prayer life more than any other ministry in which we engage. If we set our hand to the plowshare of prayer, we must be ready to do battle with the Devil. But we know we can have victory through our Lord Jesus Christ.

Not only does Satan oppose a consistent, effective prayer life, the "flesh" rebels against praying as well. There are many reasons for this. We may see ourselves as self-sufficient, or perhaps we may not really believe that God answers prayer. We may simply lack discipline. One thing is certain. The "law of sin and death" operating in our old mind of the "flesh" will battle us at every turn of the prayer path. As Paul said, "The mind set on the flesh is hostile toward God; for it does not subject itself to the law of God, for it is not even able to do so" (Rom. 8:7). Only as the "law of the Spirit of life in Christ Jesus" assumes ascendancy in us will we be able to pray as God wants us to. We must fight if we would win—but remember we battle on the ground of faith, not by our own striving. And what a blessed experience it is when we engage in fervent prayer. The ways God works through prayer are limitless. These blessed workings, though well known, need to be remembered as an encouragement.

Six Blessed Workings of Prayer

Strength

First, prayer brings strength. We often think that we can succeed in life by our own power, ability, or gifts. True, God gives us a mind with which to think, a body with which to move, and a will with which to make decisions. But our natural abilities have been so warped and twisted by our fallen nature that we have become very weak creatures indeed. We do not live in Eden anymore. We desperately need the strength of God if we want to find life fulfilling. And that strength comes largely through prayer. Mary Slesser, a missionary from Scotland, lived out her life in Africa sharing the gospel. People were amazed that she, a quite average woman, could move so many in that very different culture to the will of God. Everyone who knew her asked how she acquired such power over people. One African chief whose life was dramatically changed through Mary Slesser's ministry said, "You have evidently forgotten to take into account the woman's God." God works in answer to prayer. Many have hung on their wall the little plaque that reads, "Prayer changes things." Very wise—it does!

Comfort

Secondly, prayer is a source of great comfort. The poet expressed it this way:

> Just a whispered prayer,
> And the load of care
> From the burdened heart is lifted;
> And a gleam of light,
> Makes the pathway bright,
> For the heavy clouds are rifted.
> Do not travel on in darkness,
> When you may walk in sunshine fair.
> You can find the light,
> And the pathway bright,
> By the aid of whispered prayer.[3]

Take a moment and reflect on the times when through prayer the comfort of Christ has, like a gentle rain, cooled and refreshed your disturbed, heated heart.

Power

Prayer was central, for example, to the Day of Pentecost. Acts 1:14 reads, "These all with one mind were continually devoting themselves to prayer."

In the third place, prayer brings great spiritual power into our service to Christ. Prayer was central, for example, to the Day of Pentecost. Acts 1:14 reads, "These all with one mind were continually devoting themselves to prayer." For ten days the infant church prayed; suddenly Pentecost burst upon them as the sound of a "violent, rushing wind," and "tongues as of fire distributing themselves . . . rested on each one of them, and they were all filled with the Holy Spirit" (Acts 2:2–4). Then Peter, though he had been a weak, vacillating follower of Jesus, proclaimed the gospel in power. The result? Three thousand were converted in a day (Acts 2:41). The price of prayer had been paid. What if those early disciples had not prayed? Suppose they had prayed no more than most of God's people do today? But they did pray! And God fulfilled His promise. Bertha Smith, whom we have previously met, told the story of what prayer meant in the ministry of missionaries to China. She wrote:

When the Chinese observed the week of prayer for foreign mission work, the congregations would meet for prayer an hour or two each day. On Friday, when they prayed for the whole world, they met all day. A globe was put up and places pointed out as the group prayed. They went home thrilled, saying, "We have prayed around the world today!"[4]

And the blessings fell.

Witnessing

We become more effective in our personal witness for Christ through prayer. How can we possibly witness with any effect for Christ if our prayer life waxes weak? The story of one great Christian witness, called Brother O'Neal, reads like a leaf from the book of Acts. Brother O'Neal was a simple man with only a fifth-grade education though he was a successful businessman. He loved his church and, though he never held any position of leadership, he led scores of people to Christ with his simple sharing of the gospel. He would constantly seek out people. Often he would call on a family, and the entire family would accept Christ. He would share with people in their businesses, and he would invariably witness to waitresses in restaurants. When he lovingly shared the truths of Jesus Christ with people, they would all but melt under the conviction of the Holy Spirit. One day Brother O'Neal became seriously ill. Surgery was mandatory, and when the nurse came in to prepare him for the operating room, he did his best to win that nurse to Christ. Though he lived for a short time afterward, he never regained his strength. And although he was able to speak a few words to his family, his last full conversation on earth had been that effort to win another soul for Jesus. What undergirded his life? He was a man who knew how to get hold of God, ask for blessing, and see God do great things. Prayer is effective in the ministry of Christ's witnesses.

Leadership

Prayer brings the leadership of God to life. So often we do not know what we should do, where we should go, or to what we should give our time and energy. But prayer opens the door to God's leadership. We have the Bible to guide us, to be sure. Yet we face a multitude of decisions each day, and earnest prayer is always answered with guidance.

Maturity

Finally, prayer helps us to develop genuine spirituality. Through it we become more mature by the work of the Holy Spirit. Prayer can even awaken the entire world. It lays the foundation for both personal and worldwide renewal. Let us spend one more moment on that theme.

Prayer for Personal and World Revival

The "divine mix" for revival is a willing God and dedicated prayer warriors.

The world waits to be moved to God—to be revived—and that blessing comes through unusual and sacrificial prayer. The "divine mix" for revival is a willing God and dedicated prayer warriors. Together they can stir spiritual awakenings.

In John Wesley's London home there is a tiny room with a single kneeling bench where he spent the early hours of every day interceding for an English awakening. From these prayers came one of the most profound, godly movements in church history. What will it take for it to happen in our time? Samuel Chadwick expressed it correctly:

> There is no power like that of prevailing prayer—of Abraham pleading over Sodom, Jacob wrestling in the stillness of the night, Moses standing in the breach, Hannah intoxicated with sorrow, David brokenhearted with remorse and grief, Jesus in a sweat of blood. Add to this list from the records of the church your personal observation and experience, and always there will be the cost of passion unto blood. Such prayer prevails. It turns ordinary mortals into people of power. It brings power. It brings fire. It brings rain. It brings life. It brings God.[5]

Matthew Henry said, "When God is ready to pour out unusual mercies, He first sets His people a-praying." The psalmist cried out, "Wilt Thou not Thyself revive us again, that Thy people may rejoice in Thee? Show us Thy lovingkindness, O Lord, and grant us Thy salvation" (Ps. 85:6–7). So we too ought to pray.

How can we engage in the kind and quality of prayer that will change us—and the world? What does the Holy Spirit teach us about correct, prevailing, personal prayer?

Praying Correctly

We do well to hear from Andrew Murray:

> "Lord, teach us to pray." Yes, to *pray*. This is what we need to be taught. Though in its beginnings prayer is so simple that a feeble child can pray, yet it is at the same time the highest and holiest work to which man can rise. It is fellowship with the Unseen and Most Holy One. The powers of the eternal

world have been placed at its disposal. It is the very essence of true religion, the channel of all blessings, the secret and power of life. Not only for ourselves, but for others, for the Church, for the world, it is to prayer that God has given us the right to take hold of Him and His strength. It is on prayer that the promises wait for their fulfillment, the kingdom for its coming, the glory of God for its full revelation. And for this blessed work, how slothful and unfit we are. It is only the Spirit of God that can enable us to do it right. . . . Jesus has opened a school, in which He trains His redeemed ones, who especially desire it, to have power in prayer. Shall we not enter it with the petition, Lord! It is just this we need to be taught! O teach us to *pray*.[6]

If prayer can do all that, we surely need to learn the "rules" or principles of prayer. The Bible tells us what these "rules" are. And the Holy Spirit is ready to guide us, to be our "Teacher" in the "school of prayer."

If there be any experience in the Christian life
where real liberty can be found, prayer is it.
In the final analysis, prayer is simply inviting
Jesus into our lives to meet needs.

When we speak about "rules" of prayer, it by no means implies that prayer is an inflexible, legalistic spiritual exercise. If there is any experience in the Christian life where real liberty can be found, prayer is it. In the final analysis, prayer is simply inviting Jesus into our lives to meet needs. When we liken the Holy Spirit to a teacher in the art of prayer we do not picture Him as a stern school principal, ready to suspend privileges if we do not pray exactly according to plan. Remember, "Where the Spirit of the Lord is, there is liberty" (2 Cor. 3:17). The Father is amazingly understanding, and when He finds sincerity and genuine longing, He is well pleased. We must never get so preoccupied with the form, pattern, or routine of prayer that a simple look to a loving Father or a pouring out of the deepest desires of the heart somehow get missed. There is a very simple outline that can guide us and get us started in our prayer experience. Think of JOY:

Jesus: Thank Him for His many blessings.
Others: Intercede for friends, family, and various needs.
Yourself: Pray for your own specific needs.

An approach as elementary as that will bring JOY into prayer. And, of course, the so-called "Lord's Prayer" is a basic, biblical model and guide (Matt. 6:9–13). It contains all the vital elements of effective praying, not surprisingly since it was Jesus who taught it to us. But the important thing is *to pray*.

There are several biblical principles that can lead us into a more meaningful and purposeful prayer life.

Praying Without Ceasing

Paul urged believers: "Pray without ceasing" (1 Thess. 5:17). Let's imagine a dialogue with Paul. We ask, "What do you mean by this challenge, Paul?" He answers, "First of all, God expects us to have a consistent, disciplined prayer life. Daily needs always arise. A definite prayer time should become a daily spiritual habit, as God wills and permits." "But, Paul, will we run out of things to pray for?" Paul would probably answer, "It can be helpful to make a regular prayer list or calendar. For example, on Monday pray for the family—by name; on Tuesday intercede for friends; on Wednesday pray for regular specific needs; and so on through the week. Such a discipline can help keep you on the right track. You can even write down the daily list. Establishing a regular time and place—as much as possible—can be a real aid to prayer." Paul, of course, would further want us to know that the specific time of day is not important nor is any particular posture of the body. We can pray at any hour and in any physical position. Seeking God's presence in all sincerity and humility is the essential thing.

Some time ago we visited in the home of some Christian friends. Over the kitchen sink a motto hung: "Divine services are conducted here daily." That demonstrates an important aspect of praying "without ceasing." We should pray in our daily pursuits. Whether we are washing the dishes, working on the job, or merely walking down the street, the Spirit challenges us constantly to pray. The Lord Jesus Christ is always open to our cries. We do not need to go through some series of religious exercises to bring our needs and desires before God. We can call on our gracious heavenly Father at any moment and be assured He will hear.

Praying Specifically

It is possible to pray in such nebulous terms that we really are saying nothing. Asking God to meet needs or to bless in a general way is not specific enough. We must guard against using "meaningless repetition," as Jesus warned (Matt. 6:7). The Bible urges us to get to *real issues*. If you need wisdom to make a decision, ask God for that specifically. If you need power to witness to a friend, ask for it. If a family member does not know Christ, pray specifically for their conversion. Physical needs should not be excluded either. If you need a new coat, ask for a new coat. Christians who pray in this manner find that in seeking definite things, they receive far more answers to their prayer. And, of course, this principle applies to praise. We should praise, bless, and thank the Lord for all His goodnesses—and name them one by one.

Praying in God's Will

As Jesus agonized in the Garden of Gethsemane, He ended His earnest petition with the phrase, "Yet not as I will, but as Thou wilt" (Matt. 26:39). We too must ask for things only as they are in keeping with the will of God. John tells us, "This is the confidence which we have before Him, that, if we ask anything according to His will, He hears us" (1 John 5:14). Prayer becomes effective only when offered according to God's purpose.

The question is: How can we know the will of God in prayer? First, as we have already seen, reading the Bible is essential. When we pray in keeping with the Scriptures, we know the petition accords with God's will. Moreover, Paul has told us:

> In the same way the Spirit also helps our weakness; for we do not know how to pray as we should, but the Spirit Himself intercedes for us with groanings too deep for words; and He who searches the hearts knows what the mind of the Spirit is, because He intercedes for the saints according to the will of God. (Rom. 8:26–27)

Prayer should never be seen as a mere monologue. On the contrary, praying is a dialogue between God and ourselves.

As we quiet ourselves before God, the Holy Spirit will speak and show us what to pray for. Remember, He is the Teacher in the school of prayer. Prayer should never be seen as a mere monologue. On the contrary, praying is a dialogue between God and ourselves. The Holy Spirit abides within, and reveals to us the mind of our heavenly Father on every particular aspect of our daily lives. We should use all means to seek God's will, and if any question still arises, conclude our prayer by *sincerely* saying, "Yet not My will, but Thine be done" (Luke 22:42).

Praying in Faith

A word of caution: Ending our prayer with the phrase "not my will, but Thine be done" must never be used as an excuse for failing to pray what the Bible calls *"the prayer of faith."* The Epistle of James states:

> Ask of God, who gives to all men generously and without
> reproach, and it will be given to him. But let him ask in faith
> without any doubting, for the one who doubts is like the surf
> of the sea driven and tossed by the wind. For let not that
> man expect that he will receive anything from the Lord.
> (James 1:5–7)

God places a premium on faith in prayer—as in all of life. Our Lord went so far as to say, "If you have faith as a mustard seed, you shall say to this mountain, 'Move from here to there,' and it shall move" (Matt. 17:20). Mountains of problems and difficulties can be removed by prayer, but it must be the prayer of faith. Clearly, such faith does not come easily. How do we achieve it? The Bible promises: "So faith comes from hearing, and hearing by the word of Christ" (Rom. 10:17). Faith comes through meditating on the character and word of Christ, reading the scriptural promises that relate to prayer, and knowing that the things we ask for are in keeping with God's will. Moreover, as the Holy Spirit guides us in prayer, He will generate in us, by grace, the gift of faith. We do not just "psyche ourselves up"; faith is God's gift (Rom. 12:3).

One more brief caution: We must be careful not to put faith in prayer itself. Our heavenly Father is the object of our faith. No power resides in prayer as such. "Power belongs to God" (Ps. 62:11). Yet even in this, we can rely on the Holy Spirit to help us. He will keep pointing us to the Father and ensure that we pray properly in faith. For our part, we must ask for His help, guidance, and faith that our prayers may be pleasing to our Lord.

Praying in Jesus' Name

The Savior said, "Truly, truly, I say to you, if you shall ask the Father for anything, He will give it to you in My name. Until now you have asked for nothing in My name; ask, and you will receive, that your joy may be made full" (John 16:23–24). These verses, along with several others, emphasize the centrality of praying in Jesus' name. People usually end their prayers with that phrase or something like it. There is far more to our Lord's request, however, than just pinning a pious platitude on the end of our prayers out of mere habit or custom. What does it mean to pray *in Jesus' name?*

No one can come before God and be acceptable in His sight except through the righteousness of Jesus Christ. Human righteousness never prevails. But Jesus Christ, we have learned, has made access to God possible by His life, death, and resurrection. Through Him believers are declared righteous before God and are welcomed into His Holy presence. That is why we can actually address Holy God in prayer as *Abba* ("Daddy") Father (Rom. 8:15). What a privilege; what an invitation!

Our prayers, as well as everything else, become
acceptable before the Father only in and through Jesus. . . .
Realizing this truth and being conscious of it is
the essence of confident prayer (Heb. 4:16).

Therefore, when we pray we must come before God humbly, not because of our own righteousness, but in the name of our Lord and Savior Jesus Christ. Our prayers, as well as everything else, become acceptable before the Father only in and through Jesus. Fervor, zeal, or even sincerity do not make our prayers acceptable before a righteous God, even though they have their place in prayer. Rather, praying in *Jesus' name*—in all He is and has done and does—permits the loving Father to hear and answer. Realizing this truth and being conscious of it is the essence of confident prayer (Heb. 4:16).

Praying from a Pure Heart

The psalmist tells us, "If I regard wickedness in my heart, the Lord will not hear" (Ps. 66:18). Perhaps the greatest hindrance to prayer is unconfessed, unforsaken sin. Consciously harboring any sin at all destroys our fellowship with God. Because of this we should begin our prayers by coming before the Father, listening to the voice of the Spirit as He points out some particular sin, and then honestly acknowledging that sin and confessing it. In the Lord's Prayer, which is ever our model, Jesus told us to ask: "Forgive us our debts, as we also forgive our debtors" (Matt. 6:12). Failure to confess transgressions—as well as failing to forgive anyone who may have sinned against us—sets a roadblock on the path to effective prayer. But when we do "come clean" before God and others, the channel of communication opens between ourselves and God once again, and assurance comes that He hears and answers.

Praying Sacrificially

The Holy Spirit gives us another condition of prevailing prayer—*praying sacrificially*. We must learn what the Bible means by "striving in prayer." The apostle Paul put it this way: "Now I urge you, brethren, by our Lord Jesus Christ and by the love of the Spirit, to strive together with me in your prayers to God for me, that I may be delivered from those who are disobedient in Judea, and that my service for Jerusalem may prove acceptable to the saints" (Rom. 15:30–31). If we do not recognize that we are in spiritual warfare we will not learn to strive and wrestle through to an effective prayer life. Hallesby, the Norwegian professor and prayer warrior, said:

> When those hours of the day come in which we should be having our prayer-sessions with God, it often appears as though everything has entered into a conspiracy to prevent

it, human beings, animals and, above all, the telephone. It is not difficult to see that there is a veiled hand in the complot.

Woe to the Christian who is unacquainted with these foes!

The first and the decisive battle in connection with prayer is the conflict which arises when we are to make arrangements to be alone with God every day. If the battle is lost for any length of time at this point, the enemy has already won the first skirmish.[7]

How true. We must sacrifice other things if we want to experience a victorious prayer life.

> *Fasting has its place. . . . Fasting does not only mean abstinence from food. It may mean abstinence from any number of things that would divert us from prayer.*

In this struggle of sacrificial prayer, it may be necessary at times to fast as well as pray. Fasting has its place. Jesus said, "They will fast in those days" (Luke 5:35). Fasting does not only mean abstinence from food. It may mean abstinence from any number of things that would divert us from prayer. With rugged determination we must focus, fight and struggle. Though prayer is not always easy, pray we must.

Praying in the Spirit

All that has been said concerning the various elements of prayer can perhaps be best summed up in the phrase "praying in the Spirit." Paul states that Christians should "pray at all times in the Spirit" (Eph. 6:18). We must never forget, as Paul wrote, "The Spirit Himself intercedes for us with groaning too deep for words" (Rom. 8:26). The Holy Spirit, as the Teacher in the school of prayer, instructs us both in the rudiments and in the sophistications of prayer. He inspires our faith, convicts us of sin, empowers us, and prays through us. He lifts our very souls into the presence of the Savior. Andrew Murray put it this way:

> Blessed Savior! with my whole heart I do bless Thee for the appointment of the inner chamber, as the school where Thou meetest each of Thy pupils alone, and revealest to him the Father. O my Lord! strengthen my faith so in the Father's tender love and kindness, that as often as I feel sinful or troubled, the first instinctive thought may be to go where I know the Father waits for me, and where prayer can never go unblessed. Let the thought that He knows my need before I

ask, bring me, in great restfulness of faith, to trust that He will give what His child requires. O let the place of secret prayer become to me the most beloved spot on earth.[8]

This is "praying in the Spirit." All dynamic prayer arises through the activity of the blessed Spirit of God. Dr. O. Hallesby expressed the great power in Spirit-led prayer in his book entitled *Prayer*:

> The powers of heaven are at our disposal.
>
> Have we made the proper contacts with these powers? Let us pray for the Spirit of prayer. He will take us into the workshop where the power conduits lie. Above the door of this room is written: "Nothing shall be impossible unto you."
>
> The future of the Christian work which is now being carried on with such great intensity does not depend upon curtailment or re-organization.
>
> It depends upon whether the Spirit of God can persuade us to take up the work of prayer.[9]

We must hear the Spirit's voice and permit Him to encourage and speak through our heart to God. In this manner, prayer becomes actual communication with the Almighty Father in heaven.

Conclusion

Thus we conclude that the spiritual woman—and church—must nurture, mature, and develop a true life of prayer. It is no exaggeration to say that our prayer life directly parallels our spiritual life. Not only does prayer move and mature us individually; the entire kingdom of God moves forward on the wings of prevailing prayer. How the weary, wayward world needs more prayer warriors such as Evelyn Christenson. An unknown poet expressed it this way:

> The day was long, the burden I had borne
> Seemed heavier than I could longer bear;
> And then it lifted—but I did not know
> Someone had knelt in prayer.
> Had taken me to God that very hour,
> And asked the easing of the load, and He
> In infinite compassion, had stooped down
> And lifted the burden from me.
> We cannot tell how often as we pray
> For some bewildered one, hurt and distressed

The answer comes, and many times these hearts
Find sudden peace and rest.
Someone had prayed, in faith, and lifted hand
Reached up to God and He reached down that day
So many, many hearts have need of prayer—
Then, let us, let us pray.

Prayer

*Dear Lord, Abba Father, my prayer is very simple, but I mean it so
deeply: Lord, teach me to pray. In Christ's name. Amen.*

10 Questions for Study and Discussion

1. How did prayer affect Evelyn Christenson's family?
2. Will it do the same for us? Always? Why?
3. What did prayer have to do with the Day of Pentecost? What does that mean to us today?
4. What makes prayer such a marvel?
5. How can we come before God in prayer in the light of who He is and what we are?
6. How do we save ourselves from "vain repetitions" in our prayer life?
7. What are the essential "rules" of prayer?
8. Why do we not pray more? What are results of prayerlessness?
9. What is a "prayer warrior"? How can we become one?
10. What could be accomplished through prayer—personal and otherwise?

The Spiritual Woman Serves God

MEET HENRIETTA MEARS
A WOMAN WHO SERVED GOD

Serve Him only.
(Matthew 4:10)

$\mathscr{M}$any consider Dr. Henrietta Mears one of the greatest Christian women of the twentieth century. Billy Graham said of her:

> Dr. Henrietta C. Mears . . . has had a remarkable influence, both directly and indirectly on my life. In fact, I doubt if any other woman outside of my wife and mother has had such a marked influence. Her gracious spirit, her devotional life, her steadfastness for the simple gospel and her knowledge of the Bible have been a continual inspiration and amazement to me. She is certainly one of the greatest Christians I have ever known![1]

Henrietta must be numbered as one of God's great servants. Her life demonstrates that the spiritual woman is people-involved, moving both church and society.

The Early Life of Henrietta

Henrietta was born in Fargo, North Dakota, on October 3, 1890, into a family with a godly heritage. Her maternal grandfather, William Wallace Everts, served as pastor of the Walnut Street Baptist Church of Louisville, Kentucky, in the middle of the nineteenth century. William made a tremendous contribution to the spiritual life of Louisville. In 1859, William and his wife, Margaret, moved to Chicago, Illinois. In August of that year, they began their ministry at the First Baptist Church of Chicago. Margaret was a marvelous woman of God and an asset to her husband. She had an evangelist's heart and would go into the neighborhoods, knocking on doors, distributing tracts, and sharing Christ.

Their daughter, also named Margaret, became the mother of Henrietta Mears. Margaret was a tiny woman who never weighed over one hundred pounds. Though small in stature, she grew into a giant of the Spirit. Margaret studied music and art in Europe. On returning to Chicago she married Elisha Ashley Mears, a Vermonter who was in Chicago to study law and who became one of the youngest practicing lawyers in Chicago. They later moved to Minneapolis, Minnesota, and there joined the First Baptist Church.

An early biographer of Henrietta Mears described the spiritual background of the family.

> One thrilling thing . . . about the life of Henrietta Mears is the great spiritual heritage she has received. The scope of her life has been tremendous; even more tremendous is the spiritual influence of her forebears, which can be traced back

through at least five generations, and the spiritual "mantle" that has been handed down on the maternal side from one generation to the next. Truly this is a witness to the scriptural promise "that it may go well with thee, and with thy children after thee."[2]

Stressful Times

Henrietta was the last of Margaret and Elisha's seven children. While God blessed her home and family in so many ways, there were also hard times. Her eldest brother died suddenly on his twentieth birthday; Will, another brother, came down with spinal meningitis and lost his hearing; sister Florence died of typhoid when she was only seven years of age. Despite its sorrows, the family found strength in the joy of the Lord.

The Mears family enjoyed wealth and luxury until 1893 when the "Great Panic" devastated the stock market. Railways collapsed, mines and farms closed, and businesses failed. Financial hardship struck the Mears family as well. Henrietta would say later, "I was born with a silver spoon in my mouth, but it was yanked out before I got the taste of it." God used what seemed a tragedy to teach this future servant that material things were only temporal but spiritual realities lasted forever.

Coming to Christ

Henrietta had keen spiritual perception for such a young child. She replied to her mother, "I realize that I am a sinner. Why, Mother, you know how sinful I am! And I know that Jesus is my Savior. You are always trying to get everyone to accept Christ as Savior, and I am ready."

Even as a young child Henrietta had a zest for learning. Not only that, she began to develop a profound interest in the things of Christ. Her mother regularly took her to church, though with a certain amount of trepidation. She feared Henrietta would think she was forcing her to accept Christian ideals and rebel. But this did not happen. Henrietta's hunger for God continued to broaden and deepen in her little heart. One Easter Sunday morning, when Henrietta was about seven years of age, she told her mother that she felt quite ready to become a Christian and join the church. Mrs. Mears responded cautiously, fearful that Henrietta would not understand what it meant to receive Christ. But Henrietta had keen spiritual perception for such a young child. She replied to her mother, "I realize that I am a sinner. Why, Mother, you know how sinful I am! And I know that Jesus is my Savior. You are always trying to get everyone to accept Christ as Savior, and I am ready. I want to join the church." That settled the issue. A few weeks later, little Henrietta, along with her cousin Marguerite, presented themselves before the First Baptist Church, responding very well to questions concerning the genuineness of their spiritual experience. Dr. Riley baptized both of the girls and the curtain lifted on a great church ministry for Henrietta Mears, spiritual woman of God.

Spiritual Growth

Henrietta possessed a scintillating mind. When her mother read the Bible and tried to explain some of the words, Henrietta would stop her. She informed her mother that she understood the words very well and her mother should read on. This spirit and the acuteness of the girl astounded the whole family.

Henrietta's mother exerted a continual influence on her young life. She disciplined the children well and made sure they came face-to-face with the realities of life—even the harsh ones. She would take them, for example, to the Florence Crittenden Home where needy people were housed. Henrietta grew up recognizing that struggles made up a real part of life. And Margaret would always keep a number of New Testaments with salvation verses clearly marked for visitors or salesmen. Henrietta's later effectiveness as a personal witness for Christ found its first nurturing through her godly mother. She never strayed from the effects of those influences.

Health Problems

Although Henrietta enjoyed good health, she developed a serious eye condition in her early years. She had hoped to attend the University of Minnesota, but her doctors advised her to give up any thought of studies beyond high school. They warned she would be blind by the age of thirty if she overtaxed her eyes. This brought Henrietta to the first of many significant decisions she would have to make throughout her life. What should she do? When her mother confronted her with the issue, she unhesitatingly replied, "If I am going to be blind by thirty, then blind I shall be! But I want something in my head to think about. I'm going to study as hard as I can as long as I can."[3] She entered the University of Minnesota and plunged into the work there. Henrietta's discipline and tenacity brought her excellent academic results. She made the highest of grades, and her parents pointed with pride to their brilliant daughter.

Early Service

Life at the university was not all study, however. In her freshman year, Henrietta also gave herself to the service of Christ. She became the superintendent of the junior Sunday school of her church, and this became a very significant part of her life. Already the foundation was being laid for the contribution she would later make in Christian education.

In Henrietta's second year of college her mother fell critically ill. Henrietta dropped out of university to care for her. Death came a few days after Christmas. William Bell Riley, theologian and pastor of the First Baptist Church of Minneapolis, put his arms around Henrietta at the funeral and said, "Henrietta, I hope the spiritual mantle of your mother will fall upon you." There can be no doubt that she took these words to heart.

A Deepening Experience

During this period in her life Henrietta found herself facing a profound challenge. Paul Rader, pastor of Moody Memorial Church in Chicago, was conducting meetings in Minneapolis. He called the people to full surrender to Christ. As she wrestled with grief over the loss of her mother, the young woman made a total commitment to Christ. One winter night, while all alone in her room, Henrietta fell before the Lord in prayer. She "saw the Lord" and surrendered herself utterly to Him. God's gracious hand of blessing so settled upon her that she found deep, profound peace.

> God met her heart-cry, and she was able to pray,
> "Thank You, Lord. I accept by faith
> the filling and the power of the Holy Spirit,
> just as I accepted Christ as my Savior."

That night during Henrietta's encounter with Christ, she earnestly asked God for spiritual power. God met her heart-cry, and she was able to pray, "Thank You, Lord. I accept by faith the filling and the power of the Holy Spirit, just as I accepted Christ as my Savior." She walked away from the experience a Spirit-filled woman, ready to serve Christ and His church. Henrietta was now utterly committed to the Lord. She expressed this experience in these words:

> I [had] felt absolutely powerless . . . and I prayed that if God had anything for me to do that He would supply the power. I read my Bible for every reference to the Holy Spirit and His power. The greatest realization came to me when I saw that there was nothing I had to do to receive His power but to submit to Christ, to allow Him to control me.
>
> I had been trying to do everything myself; now I let Christ take me completely. I said to Christ that if He wanted anything from me that He would have to do it Himself. My life was changed from that moment on.[4]

And so Henrietta threw herself into the service of Christ. Back at university, during her junior year, she started and taught a Bible class for university women. This work expanded until sixty women her own age were gathering each week to study and pray together. When Henrietta graduated from the university in 1913, she had an exemplary scholastic record. Had she not dropped out of class during her mother's final illness, she would have received a Phi Beta Kappa key, the highest academic award in American higher education. And the wonder of it was—she had also retained her eyesight.

Teaching and Serving

Henrietta began working as a public school teacher in Beardsley, Minnesota, a town of only one hundred fifty people. She taught chemistry, speech, and dramatics in the high school, and even served as its principal. The small community was tightly knit, and spiritual needs were many. Henrietta determined to be a positive influence for Christ. She did what she could to influence students and friends. In the Beardsley church, as might be expected, Henrietta taught Sunday school—her first love.

The small congregation had several fine programs. For example, they conducted a contest that always concluded on what the church called Missionary Sunday. The Sunday school classes would collect money for mission work over a period of time. On Missionary Sunday the minister would call out each class, and the children would report how much they had collected to aid the cause of Christ worldwide. Of course, each class hoped their collection would be the highest. Normally these collections would be in the region of two or three dollars. On rare occasions they went as high as fifteen. But when the pastor called out Henrietta's youth class, they leaped to their feet and shouted, "One hundred and twenty dollars!" Henrietta had led them well.

Love?

Henrietta left Beardsley to spend a school year at North Branch, Minnesota, where she served the local high school as both chemistry teacher and principal. It was here that she met a handsome young banker, a graduate of Dartmouth. Friendship developed into love, but Henrietta's friend did not share her faith. While she dated him regularly she could find no relief from the burden on her heart. In the end she knew she would have to end the relationship. Although he was an upstanding citizen and the first man she had ever really loved, Henrietta knew that marriage to him would lack one essential thing—a deep fellowship in Christ. Her inner conflict heightened until one night in her room, she cried out to God:

> Lord, You have made me the way I am. I love a home, I love serenity, I love children, and I love him. Yet I feel that marriage

under these conditions would draw me away from You. I surrender even this, Lord, and leave it in your hands. Lead me, Lord, and strengthen me. You have promised to fulfill all my needs. I trust in You alone.[5]

Henrietta terminated the relationship. The decision proved far-reaching, more than she could have recognized at the time. She never married. The Lord in His wisdom satisfied her heart in other ways—with a host of friends, and a ministry that brought many people to Christ.

In 1915, two years after graduating from the University of Minnesota, Henrietta moved back to Minneapolis to become a teacher and senior adviser in Central High School. She held that position for some thirteen years. And once again Henrietta devoted herself to Sunday school work. During that time her teaching gift grew, and her commitment to serve Christ deepened. Increasingly God blessed and used her.

The Church and Scriptures

God was preparing her for her life's work. Henrietta knew her Bible exceedingly well and believed without a doubt that it was the inspired Word of God.

In each town where Henrietta had lived she had always taught Sunday school. God was preparing her for her life's work. Henrietta knew her Bible exceedingly well and believed without a doubt that it was the inspired Word of God. She memorized long passages of Scripture. It seemed as though she had the Word of God right at her fingertips in every situation. She would advise others, "If you would be pure, saturate yourself with the Word of God."[6] Kay Arthur and Henrietta shared a kindred spirit on that issue.

A Door Begins to Open

One Sunday when Henrietta arrived at church, she discovered that Pastor Riley had gone out of town for an engagement. A Dr. Stewart P. MacLennan, pastor of the First Presbyterian Church of Hollywood, California, was to fill the pulpit. He preached on "The Love of Christ," and his sermon deeply impressed her. Henrietta was living with her sister Margaret at the time, and the two of them invited Dr. MacLennan home for dinner. As it turned out Henrietta made a deep impression on the preacher as well; he invited her to visit California. The year was 1927.

At that time Henrietta had been wrestling with her future. She was unsure just what God wanted her to do with the rest of her life. The choice, as she felt impressed by the Holy Spirit, was whether she should give herself full time to Christian education or carry on as she was, doing all she could for her church while keeping her position as a public school teacher.

In the throes of painful indecision, Henrietta took a year's sabbatical from her high school. Dr. Riley, her pastor, felt this a wise move and encouraged her to travel. "It may give you a vision of this world that will determine the direction of your life." He was right. Henrietta and her sister traveled to Europe. They also decided to spend the winter in California.

In Hollywood

During her stay Dr. MacLennan invited Henrietta to speak to the congregation of his Hollywood church. She so impressed the people that he offered her the position of director of Christian education. The time had come for Henrietta to settle the issue of her future once and for all. She to returned to Minneapolis with no peace in her heart. What did God want? Dr. MacLennan gave her no peace either—he wrote and telegraphed and telephoned. But was this truly God's choice? Henrietta's decision, of course, is now well-known. In 1928, with her sister Margaret by her side, she said good-bye to all her family and friends and moved to Hollywood. At the age of thirty-eight Henrietta had become the director of education for First Presbyterian Church of Hollywood. There she would spend the rest of her life, making a tremendous contribution both to that church and to churches around the world.

The New Work

When she took up her position at Hollywood Presbyterian Church the enrollment in the Sunday school was four hundred fifty. In just two and a half years it had grown to forty-two hundred.

Henrietta's contribution to Christian education was phenomenal. When she took up her position at Hollywood Presbyterian Church the enrollment in the Sunday school was four hundred fifty. In just two and a half years it had grown to forty-two hundred. Henrietta became convinced that if Sunday school were all that it should be, people would respond. "Dreams do come true," she said. But she was no mere dreamer. She had a solid, practical approach to teaching the Word of God that made Sunday school well worth attending.

Henrietta's Methods

Henrietta approached her work methodically. "The first thing I did in Hollywood," she said, "was to write out what I wanted for my Sunday school.

I set down my objectives for the first five years. They included improvements in organization, teaching staff, curriculums, and spirit." To reach these goals Henrietta then developed a closely graded teaching program and sought good biblical material that would present Christ and His claims in every lesson. She carefully trained her teaching staff and even saw to the building of a new educational building. She developed choirs, clubs, and a camping program and encouraged the youth of the church with missionary zeal. With her wide experience in teaching she established a fine rapport with the rest of the church staff. She so exemplified the Lord Jesus Christ in her own life that she was able to bring out latent talents in others.

Of course, Henrietta well knew that increased numbers do not necessarily mean success. She committed everything to the lifting up of God's Word. Above all, she wanted to see true spiritual growth and kingdom extension. She concentrated on what she called quality management, by which she meant that each person was expected to make his or her best effort to serve the Lord. God honored this approach and through it many people came to faith in Christ. The whole church felt the impact of her ministry.

A Philosophy of Service

Henrietta insisted that everyone should be taught in their peer group by a good teacher, from infancy through old age. Furthermore, she included a worship element in her educational programming. All this was new in the 1920s. Henrietta was years ahead of her time.

She felt a deep commitment to reaching young people for Christ. For that vision to be fulfilled, she needed all her teachers to be well-prepared.

If Henrietta had a special interest, as far as age-groups were concerned, it was young people. She felt a deep commitment to reaching young people for Christ. For that vision to be fulfilled she needed all her teachers to be well prepared. She told her teachers to ask themselves four questions:

(1) Do I study the lesson thoroughly myself so that I understand it? (2) Am I doing all I can to help my pupils understand the lesson and to retain it in their memories? (3) Do I have them try to deduce their own applications from what they have heard? (4) Does my teaching really influence their lives, or does it seem dull and removed from their immediate interests?[7]

She would often say, "The key is in one word—work. Webster's spells it 'w-o-r-k,' and it means just what he says it does. Wishful thinking will never take the place of hard work." She went on to say, "There are no ideas that work unless you do!" This was the secret of her success from a human perspective. But above all, the Spirit and power of God rested on her.

New Ventures

One day Henrietta picked up a Sunday school manual that the children's primary department was using. One lesson had the title, "Amos Denounces Self-Indulgence." *How in the world could a primary-age child grasp that?* As she thumbed through the Sunday school material, she saw its irrelevance for little children. In amazement she amassed a number of Sunday school publications and brought her Sunday school teachers together to have a look at them all. They were all the same. There were no pictures, nothing to attract the children's interest, and the lessons seemed to jump all over the Bible. Henrietta called it "the grasshopper method." She remembered a young junior boy who had told her, "I don't wanna go to Sunday school anymore. All they do is tell you the same old story over and over and over again. Only it gets dumber and dumber."[8] Worse than that, a young man had told her that though he held a Phi Beta Kappa key and had been in Sunday school all of his life, he knew he would fail an examination on the Bible if he were made to take one.

Henrietta sat down to write Sunday school lessons herself. It was a huge undertaking, but she was determined and she persisted. Page after page of Bible lessons appeared. As each level was completed she would have her manuscripts typed, mimeographed, and stapled together in books. Before very long the task became overwhelming, and Henrietta recruited help. In 1933, along with others, she launched what later became Gospel Light Publications. Under Henrietta's leadership, excellent graded and intelligible Sunday school lesson material at last became available to churches. By 1936 the demand for her lessons had so increased that the whole operation had to be moved into its own large building. By the time Henrietta had been at First Presbyterian Church for twelve short years, Gospel Light had become one of the four largest independent publishers of Christian Sunday schools material in the United States. Orders came in from every state in the country. It multiplied its early-on sales 120 times in its first year alone. Henrietta's commitment to the dissemination of the Bible was firm and strong. She said:

> We are standing on holy ground. The Lord said to Moses: "Put off thy shoes from off thy feet, for the place whereon thou standest is holy ground" (Exod. 3:5). This is the place where God meets men, and today He is looking for those who will do His will. Does not God want us to be concerned with the youth of our age? What am I to do about taking the gospel to them? I must stand at attention before the Lord of

Israel. I can hear Him speaking to me, as He did to Moses:
Go, deliver My people.[9]

This ministry touched the world. It blazed the trail for the teaching of
the Word of God in a sensible, communicative fashion for millions. And it all
grew out of Henrietta's love for her church, for people, for the Lord Jesus
Christ whom she served.

Teaching Effectiveness

*The impact he and Henrietta made among the movie
stars will probably never be known until we all stand
before Christ and receive our rewards.*

Everyone knew Henrietta as a beloved teacher in her own right. In particular she concentrated on college-age students and worked with them for
decades. As her biographer said, "Henrietta's success with college-age students bordered on the phenomenal."[10]

Hollywood Presbyterian Church, largely through Henrietta's bold direction and influence, began to impact the Hollywood entertainment scene.
A so-called Hollywood Christian Group was founded for Bible study, and
several famous film stars began to attend. Eventually J. Edwin Orr became a
regular contributor to the group. Henrietta had met him at a conference where
they had both been speaking, and she knew instantly that he would be the
perfect communicator to the Hollywood scene. Dr. Orr had a keen mind and
was a scholar. Even more than that, he had a great heart for God and a desire
to see true revival.

The impact he and Henrietta made among the movie stars will probably
never be known until we all stand before Christ and receive our rewards.

Conference Ministries

Henrietta involved herself in many spiritual-life conferences through the
years, and she developed several conferences of her own. By the summer of
1937 Henrietta felt the need for a permanent conference venue. She looked
at various spots to conduct such a ministry and finally settled on a beautiful
campsite called Forest Home. There Henrietta shared the Word of God and,
in the peaceful surroundings, many men, women, and young people were
able to move into a deep experience of Christ:

Henrietta Mears ended every conference at Forest Home with
a great bonfire in Victory Circle, the camp's outdoor amphi-
theater. Campers came forward at this closing campfire and

placed small sticks in the fire to represent Christian decisions they had made, committing themselves to the fire of the Holy Spirit. A Book of Remembrance was signed by each person after he had placed his bit of wood in the fire and publicly given his decision. As a result, thousands of campers ever after traced their spiritual histories back to the signatures they wrote in the Book of Remembrance and to the campfires preceding those signings.[11]

Henrietta administered the camping program herself for twenty-five years. Outside of Forest Home's conference center a sign was displayed: "One Mile from Heaven." Henrietta wanted God's people, and the unsaved as well, to know how close they were to facing their Lord.

The Church

The church always took center stage in Henrietta's ministry. She believed her real service to her Lord was worked out in that context.

Henrietta had a deep desire not only to see Christians deepened in the faith, but also to help unbelievers come to saving faith. God honored that commitment. An incalculable number of people received Christ through the ministry of Gospel Light, the conferences, the work in the Hollywood Presbyterian Church, and Henrietta's own personal witness. All this came about because of her commitment to Christ's service. It is important to note, however, that the church always took center stage in Henrietta's ministry. She believed her real service to her Lord was worked out in that context. Through her example we can learn that a truly spiritual woman involves herself in her local church. The church, as the body of Christ, is God's primary instrument for bringing the truth of Jesus Christ to the world. The Christian faith must always be seen as shared, shared in a glowing fellowship of believers. And this fellowship is the church.

The Work Goes On

Pastors of First Presbyterian Church came to prominence, in part because of the influence of Henrietta. Richard Halverson and Lloyd John Ogilvie both became chaplains to the United States Senate. Henrietta held high Christ's banner during many difficult times in American society. Through the great Depression of the 1930s, through World War II, and even into the prosperous 1950s and early 1960s (sometimes prosperous times seem more difficult from the spiritual perspective than do the bad times) Henrietta continually influenced, taught, and encouraged.

Paul wrote to Timothy, the young church leader, "The things which you have heard from me in the presence of many witnesses, these entrust to faithful men, who will be able to teach others also" (2 Tim. 2:2). Just as Jesus infused His life in that of the disciples, so Henrietta planted her life in the lives of others and they in turn made great contributions to the cause of Christ. In that very manner, a ministry can be multiplied many times. We serve others, beginning a chain reaction of grace, that they in turn will serve others. That is why life in a local church takes on such importance.

Another Program

In Henrietta's later years she launched one more major program. Under the organizational title of GLINT, Christian teaching material was provided to overseas missions. Paul Fretz, formerly a missionary to Brazil, served as an early executive director. Excellent materials for missionaries have been produced. This work can be added to the many significant contributions Henrietta Mears accomplished. As her biographer said, she left so "many enduring monuments."

The End Draws Near

In the early months of 1963, at a garden party sponsored by the women of Hollywood Church, Henrietta spotted an old friend, a fine musician. She asked this friend to play something on the piano. The woman apologized, saying that she was not prepared, but that she would play the next year. Henrietta seemed strangely disappointed and was overheard to say in a whisper, "I'll not be here next year."

That March Henrietta spent a day with a friend, driving past new construction sites in the San Fernando Valley and making plans. She spoke of reaching many new people with the gospel. That evening she spent a long time on the telephone, talking over ideas for the Forest Home ministry. Then she went to bed and, during the night, she simply and quietly slipped off to God. Someone remarked, "It was nothing new for her to meet her Lord alone, for she had often done so. This time she just went with Him."

A Memorial

Nearly two thousand people filled the sanctuary of First Presbyterian Church to share in the triumphant memorial service for this great woman of God. A telegram from Billy Graham was read: "I am certain that Henrietta Mears had a great reception in heaven. She made a tremendous impact upon my life and ministry." Various Christian leaders praised God for her service to Christ and His church. The service aptly concluded with a choir singing Handel's "Hallelujah Chorus."

Of all that could be said about Henrietta Mears perhaps the most important is that she lived as a servant of her Lord in and through the life of her
church. In this she is but one in a noble line of great women of God. God
needs spiritual women to serve in His church. That does not mean all service
must be channeled this way. Many ministries are worked out in society generally. Nonetheless, the local church has a *central role* in the service of the
Savior, and spiritual believers should show commitment to their church and
congregations.

Motives for Answering the Call

Henrietta was a spiritual woman who served God through the church. We,
too, must always obey God's call to serve Him. There are many reasons for this.

Our Status

We listen to God's call because of our status before Him in Christ. He is
Savior; we are the saved. He is the Sustainer, we the sustained. Because of
this He demands service. How can we do less when we know the price that
it cost the heavenly Father to redeem us. Desire to serve the body of Christ
should simply well up within. Peter reminded us of this when he said, "Knowing that you were not redeemed with perishable things like silver or gold
from your futile way of life inherited from your forefathers, but with precious blood, as of a lamb unblemished and spotless, the blood of Christ" (1
Peter 1:18–19). The cost of our salvation is so great that we will never fully
comprehend it until we see the Lord Jesus face-to-face. Meanwhile, Paul urges
us to be "steadfast, immovable, always abounding in the work of the Lord,
knowing that your toil is not in vain in the Lord" (1 Cor. 15:58). Our status of
salvation requires nothing less.

Rewards

> *We shall stand before God and receive eternal
> rewards for all that we have done in the service
> of Christ—even if it be no more than giving someone
> a drink of cold water in His name.*

Paul reminds us, in his epistle to the Corinthians, that "our toil is not in
vain in the Lord." This should be a high incentive to serve Christ: We shall
one day receive rich rewards. Never forget that Jesus said, "Whoever in the
name of a disciple gives to one of these little ones even a cup of cold water to
drink, truly I say to you he shall not lose his reward" (Matt. 10:42). What a
captivating thought: We shall stand before God and receive eternal rewards

for all that we have done in the service of Christ—even if it be no more than giving someone a drink of cold water in His name. We must be cautious here, though; Jesus warned His disciples that the Pharisees, when they served for human praise, have already received their reward (Matt. 6:2). We would be wise to store up rewards in heaven rather than here on earth. There we will be given "stars for our crown" so glorious that they will shine through the endless ages. Surely, that is a reason to serve Christ.

The Needs

As we look about us and see the incredible poverty of this world, both physical and spiritual, we realize how desperately people need the touch of the believer's hand to alleviate suffering. God can meet those needs and He does so through His people, the church. That is His plan; it always has been and it always will be. If the church of the Savior does not respond to the call for help, then people's lives and society in general will continue to disintegrate. And remember, it is we who are the church.

Love Motivates

Our love for God is the primary reason we should wish to serve Him, and our love for others is built on that foundation. Jesus said, "He who has My commandments and keeps them, he it is who loves Me; and he who loves Me shall be loved by My Father, and I will love him, and will disclose Myself to him" (John 14:21). If we love God, we keep His commandments. And God commands us to serve our Lord Jesus Christ. Love leaves no option.

The Channel of Service

*God's plan for world redemption involves the church
as the functioning body of Christ. It remains
the Holy Spirit's key instrument for kingdom extension.
Service to Christ through the church is the world's hope.*

Service for Jesus Christ should primarily be channeled through His church. Henrietta understood that clearly, and though she had a ministry that touched the world, she never left First Presbyterian Church of Hollywood. She worked essentially through that great congregation. The Bible says, "Christ . . . loved the church and gave Himself up for her" (Eph. 5:25). All of Paul's epistles were written to specific churches, as was most of the New Testament. Granted, the church has many weaknesses and foibles. It is often divided, hypocritical, and weak. Yet, it remains the body of Christ. And God's plan for world redemption involves the church as the functioning body of Christ. It remains the Holy Spirit's key instrument for kingdom extension. Service to God through the church is the world's hope.

A Brief Note

Now note, this is not to say God does not use so-called parachurch organizations to further His work. The Holy Spirit does raise up such organizations to meet needs that, at times, churches fail to address. And that is good. But even then, the closer such ministries align themselves with local congregations, the richer the blessings they bestow.

The Nature of the Church

All that has been said to this point leads us to look at the nature of the church. We need to understand more thoroughly its makeup and examine why service in that setting is so important to kingdom progress. To begin with, we must understand that the term "church" can refer to two different but related things.

First, the Bible presents the church as the universal body of believers. Everyone who has come to "repentance toward God and faith in our Lord Jesus Christ" (Acts 20:21) is a member of the church in that sense. Church here encompasses all the redeemed people of all times, races, cultures, and backgrounds. It is this glorious, victorious church the Scriptures call the "bride" of Christ (Rev. 21:9). How wonderful that through faith in our Lord Jesus we can become a part of that grand, living, eternal organism.

Second, the church manifests itself as one of many tangible, practical, visible local communities of faith. We sometimes think of the church as a building that sits on the street corner. Really, the building is no more than the place where the church meets. For that reason the building might more correctly be called the "meeting house." The church itself is the local body of believers, who gather together in the fellowship of Christ for worship, ministry, and the extension of the kingdom. They may come together in a large building, under a brush arbor, or even on the street They may have a denominational label like "Baptist," "Methodist," "Presbyterian," "Catholic," or "Independent." Whenever believers come together in an ordered fashion with some regularity and structure, in obedience to Christ and in order to worship Him, that constitutes a local church or congregation. All believers ought to affiliate themselves with a local congregation. The New Testament makes it clear that a negligent attitude toward the local church is a serious error. The book of Hebrews urges: "Not forsaking our own assembling together, as is the habit of some, but encouraging one another; and all the more, as you see the day drawing near" (Heb. 10:25). God's plan is plain, and we must be faithful to it. We pray, "Thy Kingdom come," and the local church is the channel for the "coming."

The Body of Christ

One of the significant names for the church in the New Testament, especially as it relates to service and ministry, is the term *body of Christ*. Paul told the Ephesians:

> Speaking the truth in love, we are to grow up in all aspects into Him, who is the head, even Christ, from whom the whole body, being fitted and held together by that which every joint supplies, according to the proper working of each individual part, causes the growth of the body for the building up of itself in love. (Eph. 4:15–16)

This passage pictures the church as a maturing, ministering body and shows how God intends believers to serve Christ.

Service by the Spirit's Gifts

We are just like old pieces of rock, yet we can be sculptured by the Holy Spirit. He chips away at us until He fashions us into beautiful servants of Christ.

Elizabeth O'Connor, in her excellent book *The Eighth Day of Creation*, tells the story of a curious neighbor who one day saw Michelangelo lugging a huge rock down the street. The neighbor called out to ask why he was struggling so hard over an old piece of stone. Michelangelo replied, "Because there is an angel in that rock that wants to come out."[12] We are just like old pieces of rock, yet we can be sculptured by the Holy Spirit. He chips away at us until He fashions us into beautiful servants of Christ.

Paul uses the "body" metaphor. Obviously, a body functions, works, and serves. The New Testament uses many other figures to describe the people of God—"bride of Christ," "God's vineyard," "God's flock," "God's building," "a holy priesthood," "the new Israel," "a holy nation." But as the "body of Christ" we see the church in its working, serving role. Some important principles emerge out of this idea.

Diversity

First, just as a body has different parts with different functions, so does a local church. Members of a congregation cannot all serve in the same way. Abilities, gifts, talents, and ministries vary with each member. Paul asked:

> All are not apostles, are they? All are not prophets, are they?

> All are not teachers, are they? All are not workers of miracles, are they? All do not have gifts of healings, do they? All do not speak with tongues, do they? All do not interpret, do they? (1 Cor. 12:29–30)

The apostle also said:

> For even as the body is one and yet has many members, and all the members of the body, though they are many, are one body, so also is Christ. For by one Spirit we were all baptized into one body, whether Jews or Greeks, whether slaves or free, and we were all made to drink of one Spirit. (1 Cor. 12:12–13)

A healthy church body has a diverse membership offering many differing skills. This variety of talent must be recognized and implemented for a church to accomplish its God-given task.

Unity

Second, the metaphor of the body further suggests that in the church's diversity there will still be found a central unity. After all, our human body always functions as a single unit; if it does not we are either sick or disabled. The implication of this is that every member of a church is equal before God. It also means that every member has his or her own responsibility in the ministry of the church as a whole. John Stott reminds us, "The essential unity of the Church, originating in the call of God and illustrated in the metaphors of the Scripture, lead us to this conclusion: the responsibilities which God has entrusted to His Church He has entrusted to His *Whole Church*."[13] The commission to serve God applies to the entire body, and, in turn, the entire membership works to enhance the life and health of the whole church. God wants every member of the body of Christ to fulfill a unique task: no exemptions. That makes for a healthy unity. The Holy Spirit does not create a body with lame legs or withered arms. The church as a diversified yet unified body fulfills its purpose only when every member contributes. We are all one in service.

Laity Versus Clergy!

This raises an important question: What kind of relationship, therefore, exists between the so-called laity and clergy? They do seem divided at times. The laity are the whole people of God. Every church member is a part of the laity regardless of their role in the congregation. The clergy are distinguished from the laity by the fact that they have the privilege of overseeing, shepherding, and equipping the church for service.

Paul presents this clearly in Ephesians 4:11–12: "He gave some as apostles, and some as prophets, and some as evangelists, and some as pastors and teachers, for the equipping of the saints for the work of service, to the building up of the body of Christ." The clergy are like the coach of a ball team. The coach instructs, motivates, and directs the team. The team then fulfills its role by actually playing the game. Or again, the minister is like a filling-station attendant. The attendant fills the car with fuel and takes care of mechanical upkeep and repair. But the layman actually drives the car. It goes without saying that, in common with all Christians, the clergy must serve. The term *laity*, which in Greek is *laos*, means the people of God. That includes the clergy. They work right alongside the laity as helpers and equippers. John R. W. Stott underlined this point well when he said that if anyone belongs to anybody in the church, it is not the laity who belong to the clergy, but the clergy who belong to the laity.

The Pragmatics

How can a church become a healthy, fully functioning, unified body of Christ, ready to serve the world? Several passages from Paul give the answer. In Ephesians 4, Romans 12, and 1 Corinthians 12, Paul says that God equips the church for ministry with special abilities that the New Testament calls the "gifts of the Spirit." These grace gifts enable each member of the church to serve Christ with power and effect.

We wish to urge caution at this point. Considerable misunderstanding has grown up around the idea of the gifts of the Spirit. The single most important fact to realize is that the gifts of the Spirit are *abilities* given to believers *for ministry*. They are not personal spiritual indulgences of any kind. The Holy Spirit graciously imparts these useful gifts so believers may better serve their Savior. Now let's examine what the Bible says about these gifts.

What the Bible Says

Paul told the Ephesian church that when Christ ascended to the Father, "He led captive a host of captives, and He gave gifts to men" (Eph. 4:8). The "gifts"—distinguished from the "fruit" of the Spirit—are manifestations of the Holy Spirit through each believer to make service effectual. They are recorded in the three passages mentioned above.

First Corinthians 12:8–10 lists the following:

1. word of wisdom
2. word of knowledge
3. faith
4. healing

5. miracles
6. prophecy
7. distinguishing of spirits
8. various kinds of tongues
9. interpretation of tongues

In 1 Corinthians 12:28–29, the following are listed:

1. apostles
2. prophets
3. teachers
4. miracles
5. gifts of healing
6. helps
7. administration
8. various kinds of tongues

Romans 12:6–8 presents additions to the Corinthian passage:

1. prophecy
2. service
3. teaching
4. exhortation
5. giving
6. leading
7. mercy

If we eliminate the obvious duplications we find that Paul records nineteen gifts. The entire work of Christian service can be met by these spiritual gifts. They are worked out in the following way:

1. For proclaiming God's self-disclosure: the gift of prophecy or preaching. This gift enables us to proclaim God's truth, to challenge, to comfort, and to point people to Christ.
2. For clarifying the divine revelation: the gift of teaching. The teaching gift helps people understand God's Word better and more fully.
3. For enabling God's blessing to flow: the gift of faith. This allows believers to rest in God's promises, trusting in His power and plans, which are so far beyond our own sphere of human possibilities.
4. For revealing God's will: the gift of wisdom. This is bestowed by the Spirit so that God's purpose in His Word may be grasped by seeking people.

5. For understanding the practical application of eternal principles in daily experience: the utterance of knowledge. How the church needs this gift!

6. For guarding against evil: the gift of discernment of spirits. We find ourselves in spiritual warfare. We are vulnerable without this gift.

7. For manifesting in a practical way the love of Christ—three gifts: mercy, the Paraclete gift, and giving. The world desperately needs to see the exercise of these blessed ministries expressed in the church.

8. For maintaining order in the life and work of the church: the gift of government. This gift stresses the importance of church administration. Christ expects His church to be run well.

9. For helping in the community: the gift of serviceable ministries or "helps." Many people languish for just a bit of help. The church should rise to the occasion.

10. And finally, as special signs of God's power and presence—four gifts: miracles, healings, tongues, and interpretations of tongues.[14] How powerful a church can become in its witness when these gifts are manifest.

All this makes it quite obvious that the Holy Spirit covers every aspect of Christian ministry with these serviceable gifts. That is why Paul stressed their significance and said, "Now concerning spiritual gifts, brethren, I do not want you to be unaware" (1 Cor. 12:1).

Some Principles

We can certainly conclude that a gift apart from a believer is meaningless, and a believer who does not exercise his or her spiritual gift is an ineffectual servant.

In the Scriptures, there are times when the emphasis is not so much on the nature of the gift as on the people to whom it has been given, be it apostles, prophets, or teachers. In other instances, the stress is placed on the function itself rather than on the gifted people, for example, faith and varieties of tongues. Whichever way it is we can certainly conclude that a gift apart from a believer is meaningless, and a believer who does not exercise his or her spiritual gift is an ineffectual servant.

Gifts or Talents?

Moreover, the gifts of the Spirit should not to be confused with natural talents. Though all people have some natural abilities, the abilities that God uses in His service—spiritual gifts—are not talents *per se*. As one commentator pointed out, gifted believers have "certain powers which they had not previously possessed and which were due to the influence of the Holy Spirit."[15] Spiritual gifts are grace gifts of the Holy Spirit. It follows that these gifts must be employed under the control of the Holy Spirit. As one scholar said, "The operator . . . is always God; every one of the gifts in every person that manifests them . . . is bestowed and set in motion by him."[16] Paul wrote three chapters (1 Cor. 12–14) to direct the proper use of the gifts under the control of the Holy Spirit.

A Wonderful Truth to Realize

All believers have at least one or more spiritual gifts. Paul said, "But to each one of us grace was given according to the measure of Christ's gift" (Eph. 4:7). Alexander Hay explains:

> The Holy Spirit distributes them (the spiritual gifts) to every believer. There are no exceptions: every believer has a gift or gifts apportioned to him or her. That is, the Holy Spirit would manifest Himself through every believer in the accomplishing of some part of the work. Every believer is responsible to exercise these gifts.[17]

We are given these gifts for the development of ministry. As one writer stressed, "It is simply the Holy Spirit working through us in a given manner, at a given time he, the Spirit, chooses, for carrying out the ministry to which we have been appointed of God."[18] In that way the Holy Spirit creates a full-functioning, healthy, serving body of Christ—and the kingdom goes forward.

Of course, no single believer possesses all the gifts; that would make him or her the entire church. At the same time, to say we have no ministering gift is the same as saying we are not in the body of Christ. The conclusion? *All true Christians can—and should—serve Christ.*

How important then that we know what our gifts are. Can we discover them?

Discovering Your Gift

Perhaps the following suggestions will help. They could be called "The Ten Commandments for Discovering Your Spiritual Gifts."

1. Study the Scriptures; the answers are there.
2. Ask: How has God used me, really used me, in the past? That may give some clues.
3. Ask: What do spiritual people say? They may provide some insight. Others often understand us better than we do ourselves.

4. Ask: What do I like to do? We like to do what we do well, and we always do well when we exercise our serviceable gift.
5. Ask: What needs burden and challenge me? God may be calling through a concern.
6. Ask: What open doors lie before me? What opportunities are presenting themselves? God may be in it.
7. Do something—keep moving—be disciplined.
8. Be open to change.
9. Have confidence that you do indeed have a gift and that God will help you discover it.
10. Above all, pray for God's will to be revealed.

Responsibility

Some time ago, during a home study on the subject of spiritual gifts, one of the older ladies in the group suddenly burst out in happy realization, "Why, I have the gift of helps!" Then she overflowed, sharing all the wonderful ways she enjoyed helping others in their moments of need. For the first time in her Christian life, she had realized that her service to Christ was actually a spiritual gift. It came as a refreshing revelation to her. Discovering what our spiritual gifts are can be revolutionary. After we have discovered these gifts, however, certain responsibilities become incumbent upon us. Our gifts, for example, need to be continually developed, perhaps by study and certainly by exercising and practicing them. Receiving gifts does not mean there should be no enhancement of them. And most importantly, we have to use our gifts and serve through them.

Liberty

Discovering what our gifts are not only motivates, it liberates. When we realize we have received an ability from God Himself, it frees us from feelings of inadequacy. We know we can serve Christ with true power and effect.

When we realize we have received an ability from
God Himself, it frees us from feelings of inadequacy.
We know we can serve Christ with
true power and effect.

God does, of course, use our natural talents as well. For example, some people are musical, and God will honor this. However, there are many who feel that because they have no natural talents at all God cannot use them. This is not the way it is. Everyone has at least one spiritual gift. There is no excuse for not serving Christ. And once we have discovered our gifts and begun to *develop* them, we can then *deploy* them.

Deploying the Gifts

The word *deploy* means exercising our gift in the fellowship of our church. Elizabeth O'Connor served in a great church in Washington, D.C. That church structured its ministry on the principle of using the congregation's spiritual gifts. When people were discovered with certain gifts, programs were created accordingly. Conversely, a program would not be developed unless gifted people could be found to undertake the task. This makes sense because, in the final analysis, programs are not as important as people. After all, God primarily anoints *people*, not programs. People are always central in God's economy. Every church would do well to copy this approach to ministry.

Paul's Example

How was Paul able to go to a completely pagan mission field, spend a relatively short time there, and leave a thriving, indigenous, self-supporting, evangelizing, growing church? Simply put, he planted a new church and then encouraged each member to exercise his or her gift in its service. Soon the church was able to function whether Paul was there or not.

An insightful missionary to South America discovered that great churches grew out of the exercise of spiritual gifts and followed Paul's example to the letter. He would go into a community, lead a number of people to Christ, help them discover their gifts, get them established in the church, and then leave them in the hands of the Holy Spirit and the Word of God. Off he would go to the next community and do the same thing. He found that God could do in the twentieth century what He did in the first. If we utilize the gifts the Holy Spirit makes available we can trust the work will get done.

Evangelism

When a believer uses his or her gifts, witnessing takes on increasing power.

Evangelism naturally flows from serving the church. When a believer uses his or her gifts, witnessing takes on increasing power. And let it be remembered, witnessing itself is a command, not a gift. Christ wants *everyone* to witness. Remember, Jesus said, "You shall be My witnesses" (Acts 1:8).

An Example

A great church that geared its life on the exercise of spiritual gifts is the Peninsula Bible Church in Palo Alto, California. The pastor, Ray Stedman, whom God recently called to His presence, said in his excellent book *Body Life*:

I have had the privilege of pastoring one church for over twenty years. In all that time we have never held an evangelistic meeting in the church, but there has been a continual stream of new converts coming into the church for instruction and development in the Christian life. Evangelism has been occurring within the homes of members, and in public halls, back yards, school rooms, and wherever a hearing for the gospel could be obtained. But every meeting held in the church building has been aimed at the instruction, training, or worship of Christians together. Our entire Sunday school is set up to equip the saints, of all ages, to do the work of the ministry.[19]

One More Word of Caution

There is always a danger in thinking that some gifts, because they are more spectacular, are more important than others. Not true! All the gifts come from the Holy Spirit and all are needed. As one writer writes: "All the gifts of the Spirit are equally necessary, equally honourable and equally important. They are but different manifestations of the same Spirit and are all essential to the accomplishing of one purpose: the building up of the Body (1 Cor. 12:20–24)."[20] Ray Stedman put his finger on it when he said, "No Christian needs to be the rival of another; there is a place for all in the body and none can take another's place."[21] There is no place for competition and self-exaltation in the body of Christ. God wants His church in balance. When each believer peacefully fulfills his or her function, the church stays healthy. Remember that the "more excellent way" (1 Cor. 12:31) is love. So the work of Christ goes on among our Lord's gifted, spiritually-minded servants.

Conclusion

Quite evidently, God does intend His people to be servants of the Lord in and through His church. Love demands it; God demands it. Would you be a spiritual woman who serves, like Henrietta Mears? Then get involved in a church. Do not look back. Trust God to reveal to you your gift; develop it, deploy it, and faithfully exalt the Lord Jesus Christ in a life of service. This, too, is spirituality.

Prayer

Our Father in heaven, I pray Your will to be done on earth as it is in heaven. I know that means I must serve You, as did that dear saint Henrietta Mears. Please enable me to discover my spiritual gift and use it in Your service. May my church help me, and may I help it, so that we may work together as the true body of Christ, in whose name I pray. Amen.

10 Questions for Study and Discussion

1. How do you account for Henrietta Mears's life of service?
2. What leadership principles did Henrietta employ?
3. Why should we serve our Lord—what could motivate us?
4. What is the relationship between our service and the kingdom of God?
5. What is the nature of the church?
6. Why is the church important in God's eyes?
7. What role do spiritual gifts play in service to the church?
8. Do you know your gift or gifts? If not, how can you learn what they are?
9. How could your gifts be further developed?
10. Are you serving Christ? If not, why not? How can you serve Him better?

The Spiritual Woman Shares God

MEET VONETTE BRIGHT
A WOMAN WHO SHARES GOD

You shall be My witnesses.
(Acts 1:8)

$\mathcal{G}$reat soul winners often have unremarkable backgrounds. It is not necessary to be born into a wealthy or famous family to become a witness for Christ. Vonette came into the world in the little town of Coweta, Oklahoma, and it is unlikely that her parents ever suspected for a moment that she would one day help multitudes come to Christ. Vonette was the eldest of four children born to Mary Margaret and Roy E. Zachary. The family had a modest but secure life together. Zachary was something of an entrepreneur. He was an automobile salesman, he worked in the real estate business, and he also owned a filling station. Vonette says that the filling station probably put her through college.

Vonette's family lived next door to the local Methodist church, which they attended regularly. The Methodist pastor and his family lived close by, and the pastor's children spent a great deal of time playing with Vonette and her siblings. The Zachary home was the gathering place for Vonette's many friends. There were ice cream and watermelon socials in the summer, and hayrides in the fall. The door always stood open. The entire Zachary family tried to exemplify the Christian life. It was no surprise when each of the children came to know Christ personally.

Vonette's Hopes

Not far away the Brights' rural home, where Bill was born, was very similar. It was a place where young people would meet to relax and have fun, and it was also a place where the community would gather for worship, Bible study, and devotions.

Vonette remembers having serious thoughts about Bill while she was still in the seventh grade and Bill was a high school senior. He had been chosen to give a senior oration, and Vonette sat in the back of the auditorium listening intently. She thought at the time that Bill would be a great man someday, and just the kind of man she would like to marry.

Bill's Adventures

By the time Vonette finished her freshman year in college, Bill had moved on from little Coweta and had traveled west to establish a lucrative business in California—Bright's California Confections—marketing gourmet foods and fruits. He soon was selling to upscale establishments such as Saks Fifth Avenue and Neiman Marcus. One day, while Bill's sister was visiting over her birthday, they went to dinner at a fine restaurant to celebrate. There Bill saw a young actress, Diana Lynn, sitting at a nearby table. The beautiful woman brought Vonette to mind. He asked his sister about "the little Zachary girl," and he decided there and then to write Vonette a short letter telling her he was thinking of her, and how he had been reminded of her. Vonette, of course, felt very flattered to receive the letter, but she did not answer it for quite some time. When she did finally respond it was with a ten-page letter cheerfully telling him all that had been happening in her life since they had last met. Bill responded with a note, sent special delivery, asking if he could telephone her. Vonette agreed. Bill also asked if he could continue to write. By Christmas time Vonette was receiving a letter from Bill every day of the week.

The Courtship Grows

By this time, Vonette was being deluged, not only
with daily letters and weekly telephone calls,
but also with telegrams and flowers from Bill.
As she put it, "He totally swept me off my feet."

The courtship accelerated by mail and telephone. Bill decided to go back to Coweta for Christmas by way of Denton, Texas, where Vonette was attending Texas State College for Women (later renamed Texas Women's University). He thought he could pick her up there and they could travel the rest of the way home together. Because this was a girls' school, Vonette had to get permission from her parents to travel any more than two hundred miles in a car with a young man. As it turned out, when the time arrived, Bill's business prevented him from making the trip. It was not until late March that he finally reached Texas. By this time, Vonette was being deluged, not only with daily letters and weekly telephone calls, but also with telegrams and flowers from Bill. As she put it, "He totally swept me off my feet."

When Bill arrived in Denton that March, the couple attended a ball on campus—one of the biggest social events of the year. Then and there, on their very first formal date, Bill proposed to Vonette. He was convinced the Lord had told him that Vonette must be his wife. And that settled it. Before the end of the weekend, the young couple wrote to Vonette's parents and let them know that Bill would be coming to see them for her hand. Mrs. Zachary received the letter on April Fool's Day, and actually thought it was a joke! However, when Bill arrived at the Zachary home, it soon became obvious that this was no joke. The whole household was thrilled at the prospect. God's Spirit had surely engineered it all.

Postponed

Bill and Vonette were eager to be married right away. Their plan was that Vonette would stop attending college in Denton and study for her degree with a private tutor. That way the couple could travel together in Bill's growing international business. However, Vonette's parents were concerned that she might be too young to begin this kind of life; after all, Bill was some six or seven years older than Vonette. And they very much wanted their daughter to finish college. They finally convinced Bill, and so Vonette returned to complete her degree. She now believes it was a wise decision.

A Spiritual Journey Begins

Vonette majored in home economics and minored in chemistry. Her science courses presented certain challenges to her faith. She had grown up believing in God and sharing in family prayer when the pastor came to visit. And her parents had certainly taught her proper morals. Still the Bible played no dynamic role in her life. It just seemed something to be read for a Sunday school lesson. Vonette had "accepted Christ" as a small child, but the experience had given her no true sense of the presence of God in her life.

Bill had no such problems. He had come to faith in Christ after moving to the West Coast and was an active member of Hollywood Presbyterian, Henrietta Mears's church. It was only after he had become a Christian that he learned his mother had committed him to Christ before he was born. During her difficult pregnancy, Mrs. Bright had asked God to let her carry her baby to full term (she had lost a child previously). She told the Lord that she would dedicate her little one to Him if He would allow her to bring the child into the world. Once Bill had received the Lord, he fully and completely committed himself to service right from the very beginning. As Vonette says, "He has never wavered. He has a singleness of mind."

Vonette Struggles

She prayed but felt that her prayers went "as far as the ceiling" and stopped. It seemed as if no one was listening. When she read the Bible, she only read words on a page. There was no reality to it.

Vonette's spiritual struggle deepened. She prayed but felt that her prayers went "as far as the ceiling" and stopped. It seemed as if no one was listening. When she read the Bible, she only read words on a page. There was no reality to it. Bill would write to her, highlighting certain passages he thought would help. No matter how hard she tried she could not get the depth of meaning from the Scriptures that Bill did. Vonette began to conclude that Bill had fallen under the influence of fanatics. She loved him too much to give him up. She decided it was her duty to show him that it was all right to be Christian but you did not have to "go off the deep end," as she put it.

A Problem

Vonette and Bill planned to marry in the fall of 1948, but by June, the couple realized they had a problem. They were miles apart in their attitudes about Christ. They believed they should always agree and if they found they did not, they should work things out until they did. And so they looked hard at the matter of their faith. Bill invited Vonette to a conference in California where she could come to some idea of where he stood. She went, but only in order to spend time with Bill and, even better, to convince him that he needed to give up his "fanatical" ideas. Things did not turn out the way Vonette expected. When she arrived in California she got to know some very wonderful people, people who were walking with Christ. The way these new friends talked about the person of Jesus Christ was revolutionary to Vonette. Their enthusiasm about their faith, their stories about answered prayer, even the quality of their lives deeply moved and impressed her.

Yet she still had reservations. About three days into the conference, Vonette told Bill that she was different from these new friends. They had just found Christ whereas she had grown up in the church. "Being a Christian is just not that exciting," she said. "This is going to wear off. I have tried this. I have received Christ any number of times in my life, and it lasts for a little while, and that's it!" But Bill would not give up on her. As she puts it, "I know I am what I am because of who he is." He finally suggested that they go and talk to Henrietta.

Henrietta Wins Another

Henrietta lovingly challenged Vonette to see that she had nothing to lose, but everything in the world to gain, by giving all to Christ. The Holy Spirit used Henrietta to deeply touch the seeker.

At Bill's request, Henrietta had been praying for Vonette for months. Because Henrietta had been a chemistry teacher herself before coming to Hollywood Presbyterian Church, she could respond to the doubts and fears science had raised in Vonette's mind. Every "scientific" argument Vonette offered received a convincing answer. And then Henrietta lovingly challenged Vonette to see that she had nothing to lose, but everything in the world to gain, by giving all to Christ. The Holy Spirit used Henrietta to deeply touch the seeker. Vonette points back to this as the time when she truly turned to God and saw her life dramatically changed. From then on it became exciting to pray and read the Bible. At last Vonette felt genuine peace and the reality of God in her life.

Vonette began to make wonderful discoveries in the Word of God—and she shared them with Bill. She was learning to apply Christian principles to her daily life and found that she could now cope with things that previously had seemed impossible. She sensed God profoundly changing her personality, giving her power to cope, and making her a "far more reasonable person." Vonette and Bill began to plan a December wedding.

A New Life and a Glimpse at the Future

After Vonette and Bill were married, on December 30, 1948, Vonette began to teach in a junior high school under the Los Angeles Board of Education. She lectured on several subjects in addition to home economics. Since that time Bill and Vonette have been blessed with two sons. The eldest, Zachary, serves as a Presbyterian minister in Erwindale, California. His church is an English-speaking Spanish church. The younger son graduated from Wheaton in political science and worked in Washington for five years with Senator Armstrong and the National Republican Congressional Committee. He came to the conclusion that the world could never be changed through politics, so he joined the Campus Crusade staff. He now heads a ministry called Pinnacle Form and has moved to Scottsdale, Arizona, to work with businessmen.

The Beginnings of the Crusade

During the early years, while Vonette was teaching and working on her master's degree at the University of Southern California, she wrote a course of study for boys called *You, the High School Man,* on character and etiquette. An outline of it was published in the *Los Angeles Examiner* in a syndicated column. Eight thousand letters were written to the paper in response. However, new things on the horizon would take precedence. It was about this same time that God began to lay on Bill's heart a work that would ultimately result in Campus Crusade. The Holy Spirit was challenging the couple to reach university students for Christ and train them in personal evangelism. Little was being done in that field of ministry in the early 1950s. In particular, the campus of UCLA seemed to beckon. Bill and Vonette were unsure.

They started by establishing a twenty-four-hour prayer chain to seek God's will in their plans. Already some work had been done with sororities and fraternities, mostly consisting of inviting young people to attend the Hollywood Presbyterian Church. But they deeply felt they should begin doing more.

The Contract

They signed a "contract" that listed what they wanted to do with their lives, in what way they wished to contribute, and, above all, how they wanted God to be in full control. They determined to be "slaves of Jesus Christ."

Bill and Vonette spent a Sunday afternoon talking about their goals and how they deeply desired their lives to count for Christ. As a result, they signed a "contract" that listed what they wanted to do with their lives, in what way they wished to contribute, and above all, how they wanted God to be in full control. They determined to be "slaves of Jesus Christ." Not long after this afternoon of surrender, the Holy Spirit brought them to the realization that they had to move to the UCLA campus to work there.

Vonette felt a little frightened at the prospect, but she had committed herself to serving her Lord at any cost. Nothing was going to stop her from doing this. And so the plans went forward and Campus Crusade was born. For the next six years the Brights also stayed involved in their very successful business, but it was too much. They knew, by that time, that God had better plans. They let it go.

Several other Christian organizations at the university had Bible studies and discipling activities, but Campus Crusade took a new line. The plan was to train Christian students to become effective witnesses for Christ themselves. This new approach caught on fire.

The Work Unfolds

The Brights had rented a large house one block from the UCLA campus. One night Bill visited one of the sororities, and he saw a tremendous response for Christ. Thirty-five girls stood in line to tell Bill they had prayed with him and wanted to move forward in their Christian life. He announced that he wanted all those who were interested to meet at his home. Close to 150 students showed up. By the end of Campus Crusade's first year more than 250 students had committed their lives to Christ. The Brights sent these students right back to the sororities and fraternities to share the gospel. Over time a weekly rhythm began to appear. On Monday nights, as many as sixteen students would speak to various campus organizations. Everyone would be invited to an "open meeting"at the Brights' home on Tuesday nights. Then a breakfast and follow-up Bible study was conducted on Saturday mornings.

Teaching a Different Lesson

Vonette still taught school, but she soon found it meant far less to her than the work at Campus Crusade. By the second year Vonette had joined Bill full time. The first fifty girls she spoke to on the UCLA campus all made commitments for Christ. Vonette knew God had put her exactly where He wanted her.

Not an Easy Road

*Difficulties only made them trust God all the more. They
prayed that God would resolve any problems that arose in a
way that would bring honor to Himself alone.*

The Brights, as might be expected, did encounter many difficulties. Satan
could be counted on to raise opposition to so many finding Christ. They had
to learn to fight spiritual battles as well as deal with a fast-growing ministry,
with all the administrative details such an undertaking involved. But Vonette
learned that difficulties only made them trust God all the more. They prayed
that God would resolve any problems that arose in a way that would bring
honor to Himself alone. And God has heard that plea. He has granted continual
victory and phenomenal growth.

The Work Today

Today, after many years of fruitful ministry, Campus Crusade commands
a staff of more than two hundred thousand full-time workers and has volun-
teers in 167 countries.

On top of this is the success of the "Jesus" film. For years Bill had dreamed
of creating a film that would get people's attention. Eventually the Brights
were approached by a Jewish man, John Hayman. He had been working on
plans to make a film on the book of Luke but he needed some influential en-
dorsements. The Brights realized that a film combining Hayman's interests
and those of Campus Crusade could be an powerful evangelistic tool. In the
end a Mr. Bunker Hunt volunteered to pay for it, John Hayman made it, and
Campus Crusade produced it. And the result has been nothing short of miraculous. The film has been seen by more than one billion people around the
world. At an average showing, half the audience commit their lives to Christ.

A New Center

In 1962 Campus Crusade bought the lovely Arrowhead Springs Hotel in
Southern California. The purchase in itself was a miracle. The property was
worth two million dollars, and there was only fifteen thousand dollars available. Many, of course, thought the Brights were crazy, but they entered the
venture with faith—and God supplied. People joined with them, and all the
payments were made right on time. One person offered them $250,000 if they
could raise the balance of the capital within a certain length of time. Two minutes before midnight on the day of the deadline, all the money came in. That
experience, as Vonette put it, became a real "faith-builder." Arrowhead Springs
now encompasses a wonderful retreat center, and many have been richly
blessed through the ministry there.

A New Prayer Challenge

*Bill has said of Vonette, "I don't know
of anyone whom God has used more to call people
to fast and pray than has she."*

Prayer has always played a central role in Vonette's spiritual life. Bill has said of Vonette, "I don't know of anyone whom God has used more to call people to fast and pray than has she." Fasting and prayer precede powerful evangelism. With this truth in mind Vonette felt called to launch a women's prayer movement. She drew on other groups and together they formed a prayer base for the work of Christ worldwide, which they called the Great Commission Prayer Crusade. God has honored that work marvelously.

New Realm

Another accomplishment for Campus Crusade has been the little masterpiece they developed some years ago: *The Four Spiritual Laws*. More than two billion copies of this booklet have been printed and it has been read and used all over the world. And now Campus Crusade is entering a whole new realm. As Bill Bright put it, he and Vonette are "pulling out all the stops" to take the gospel to everyone on the planet as we begin the new millennium. They are gearing up their International Leadership University. Using CD-ROMs, they plan to train millions of people to witness for Christ. They are strategically ready to influence current culture worldwide through the information highway. This "high-tech" approach will make it possible for people to learn without having to give up their jobs and time with family. Necessary information will be available at any time. Campus Crusade has the goal of ten thousand training extensions at locations all over the globe. What a challenge!

Discipleship Training

Everyone knows Campus Crusade as an evangelistic organization, but their discipling program is just as exciting. Vonette has continually tried to train Christians in spiritual growth, trusting the Spirit to make them strong and powerful witnesses in the world. Since the beginning of their organization, Vonette and Bill have prayed that God would use them as catalysts to accelerate maturing discipleship.

Encouragement

God continually encourages Vonette. For example, she spoke at a conference in Oregon several years ago and met a woman there who was attending with her daughter. As it turns out, Vonette had won her to Christ back in 1952.

The lady came forward to thank Vonette for changing her life. Such experiences—countless in number—greatly inspire and hearten this woman of God.

Sharing the Message

And so the work goes on. Vonette is the epitome of an effective witness for Christ. She has responded wholeheartedly to the words of our Lord when He said (in a verse we have quoted almost to a fault, but which gets to the heart of it all), "You shall be My witnesses" (Acts 1:8). She has learned, as we must, that to grow and mature in the Spirit we must share the message of God. A truly spiritual woman becomes a witness for Jesus Christ. Our Christian faith finds its fullest expression in introducing a lost and dying world to the Savior we know and love.

The Mission of the Church

In recent years many churches have written what has come to be called a mission statement. This statement is usually a brief but pungent sentence or two giving the rationale for the existence of the congregation. Such a step makes sense. A mission statement can give a church direction in developing its programs. Henrietta Mears did it in her work, remember? It also enables each member of the congregation to keep a proper goal in mind. This principle has permeated the business world. Larger corporations have been writing mission statements for years. This does not meant that churches are employing worldly methods. It is a wise move for any group that needs to pull together with focus and direction.

God's Mission

It stands to reason that, when God created this vast universe, He had a distinct, definite purpose in mind, one that will be fulfilled.

Churches and businesses develop mission statements. Little wonder then that Bible scholars recognize that God Himself has a purpose for His creation. Scholars call it the *missio Dei*—God's mission. It stands to reason that, when God created this vast universe, He had a distinct, definite plan in mind, one that will be fulfilled. This mission statement has been set out in the Bible. What is it? What does it mean to us?

Given the infinite wisdom of God, words could never exhaust His purpose in creation. Yet we human beings can at least grasp our role in it, and it is this: We are to bring His wayward world to the foot of the cross. We are to extend His kingdom until that glorious day when all creation will recognize and acknowledge Jesus Christ as King of Kings and Lord of Lords.

How Does God Work?

If God's purpose is world redemption through knowledge of His Son, evangelization is the primary means to accomplish the *missio Dei*. As the Bible says, "The Lord . . . is patient . . . not wishing for any to perish but for all to come to repentance" (2 Peter 3:9). God, out of His great love and compassion, desires that all people everywhere will come to a saving, redemptive faith in His Son. Although He desires to see many things accomplished in His creation, the evangelization of the lost creation takes first place in His great heart. God's mission statement comes in the form of a glorious invitation: "Come to Me, all who are weary and heavy-laden, and I will give you rest" (Matt. 11:28).

The chief instrument God uses to bring Christ to the world is the church. Because He enlists His people to further his mission, we are affected personally. We are all commissioned to be witnesses to the needy world—as Vonette Bright learned so well.

God and His Word at Work

Christians are not expected to accomplish this task alone. The Holy Spirit speaks through our human witness, making it vibrant, dynamic, and effectual. And the gospel message contains its own power. We have quoted before what Paul said on this point, "I am not ashamed of the gospel, for it is the power of God for salvation" (Rom. 1:16). Still, it is only through the witnessing work of believers that the Holy Spirit and the power of the gospel are brought to the unbelieving and needy world.

Peter and Cornelius

The responsibility to share Christ belongs to believers. . . . It is God's people who are to fulfill His plan for world redemption.

An incident in the book of Acts brings out this principle clearly. In Acts 10 we find the intriguing tale of the conversion of Cornelius, the Roman centurion. Cornelius was a man of prayer. One day, during his time of intercession, an angel appeared and gave him a strange message, telling him to, "Send to Joppa, and have Simon, who is also called Peter, brought here; and he shall speak words to you by which you will be saved, you and all your household" (Acts 11:13–14). What is so peculiar about this account is that Cornelius desperately needed to hear about Christ, and the angel certainly knew that message. Yet the angel did not share one word of the gospel. Why? Cornelius was told to send for Simon Peter so that Peter could tell him how he might be saved. Cornelius responded, Peter came, and salvation enveloped the household. Here is the point. Evangelism is not the task of angels. The responsibility to share Christ belongs to believers like Simon Peter. It is God's people who are to fulfill His plan for world redemption.

Putting it all together: God's mission becomes our mission. Every church—and every individual Christian—should adopt a mission statement with evangelization at its heart. That alone fulfills the *missio Dei*.

The Beauty and Wonder of Personal Witnessing

Our Lord Jesus Christ repeated His command to witness many times. One of the most personal expressions of our Lord's commission is in John's gospel where He said, "As the Father has sent Me, I also send you" (John 20:21). The beauty and wonder of personal witnessing is that we are engaged in the same task as our Lord Jesus Christ during His days on earth. This means several things. First, we will certainly have His leadership. Second, God will bring people across our path who need to hear the saving message of Christ. Third, we will help God in the work of the kingdom, and what an incredible privilege that is! Finally, we will please Him. Witnessing is Christ's command, and our obedience *always* pleases Him.

Commitment

Since we know that God has commissioned each of us personally, we should make a commitment to witness for Him. Witnessing is no easy task. We must learn to face each problem as it arises and find a solution, always in the knowledge that God's power is working through our lives to bring others to Christ. Moreover, our own commitment and determination will help us overcome fear and reluctance.

Many years ago, a deeply spiritual man of God, C. G. Trumbull, wrote a little book called *Taking Men Alive*. It spoke of the principles and challenges of individual witnessing. The book's key text was our Lord's words recorded in Luke 5:10, "Do not fear, from now on you will be catching men." Trumbull stressed that a firm commitment is necessary to "catch" people for Christ. He expressed a resolve—something of a personal mission statement. It was: "Whenever I am justified in choosing my subject of conversation with another, the theme of themes shall have prominence between us, so that I may learn his need, and, if possible, meet it."[1] Trumbull lived out that commitment with remarkable dedication. He won untold numbers to the Lord Jesus Christ. We should all make a resolution of that sort. When we do make such a decision, God gives us the power to fulfill it.

Power for the Task

*He uses us in that grand work. We need have
no fear; the Spirit of God permeates
every move we make in the sharing of the gospel.
What an assurance!*

Rest assured, God fully empowers the faithful witness. We do not engage in the task alone, not by any means! The Spirit of God stands right beside us in the entire witnessing encounter. He works by preparing the heart of the lost person to receive the message. Then He takes our simple words into the heart He has prepared. He convicts the unbeliever of sin, and convinces him of the reality of judgment (John 16:7–11). He reveals Jesus Christ as the only hope of salvation. The Holy Spirit then urges and leads the lost soul to true repentance and faith. Finally, when that needy person genuinely turns to our wonderful Lord, the Spirit regenerates him, making him a child of God. And the beautiful thing is, He uses us in that grand work. We need have no fear; the Spirit of God permeates every move we make in the sharing of the gospel. What an assurance!

God not only uses us as His witnesses, He also guarantees victory in the work. This does not mean that everyone with whom we share the message of Christ will be saved immediately. Vonette Bright and Campus Crusade define successful witnessing as simply sharing the gospel of Christ in the power of the Holy Spirit. Our Lord does the winning; our part is the sharing. Of course, if we can actually lead a soul to the point of decision, we rejoice that we have had that honor. But in the life of virtually every person who comes to faith in Christ, there have been many seeds sown, and much cultivating and watering undertaken by many effective witnesses before the moment of harvest arrives. We must not be discouraged if it seems as if we are always sowing and rarely reaping. Paul said:

> So then neither the one who plants nor the one who waters is anything, but God who causes the growth. Now he who plants and he who waters are one; but each will receive his own reward according to his own labor. For we are God's fellow workers. (1 Cor. 3:7–9)

Therein lies the secret of the witnessing experience: God uses the witness, but it is by His power alone that people are saved. What a beautiful, divine-human labor witnessing can be. But how can we engage in the task with effect?

The Effective Witness

The gospel, and the gospel alone, is the "sharp, two-edged sword" that brings people face-to-face with Jesus Christ.

The gospel is the "power of God for salvation" (Rom. 1:16). If we are to lead people to Christ we must ourselves have an understanding of the centrality of the good news. How easy it is to become sidetracked into less important issues. We may speak of our fine pastor and church staff, or the wonderful fellowship and programs at our church, but that is not what people need to hear. These things are secondary for they do not lead people to Christ. The gospel, and the gospel alone, is the "sharp, two-edged sword" that brings people face to face with Jesus Christ. The gospel message was outlined fully in step one. Yet it is so important that we know the proper truths to share, it might be helpful to outline again the essence of Peter's first sermon:

1. Jesus Christ came as the incarnate Son of God; Jesus of Nazareth was a man (Acts 2:22).
2. Jesus lived an exemplary, miraculous, sinless, revealing, victorious life. Peter said Jesus was "a man attested to you by God with miracles and wonders and signs which God performed through Him in your midst" (Acts 2:22).
3. Jesus died on the cross for our sins; described as "nailed to a cross by the hands of godless men and put . . . to death" (Acts 2:23).
4. God raised Jesus from the dead. Peter stressed, "God raised Him up again, putting an end to the agony of death, since it was impossible for Him to be held in its power" (Acts 2:24).
5. We must repent and believe in response to all that Jesus is and did to save us from our sins. As Peter stated, "Repent, and let each of you be baptized in the name of Jesus Christ for the forgiveness of your sins; and you shall receive the gift of the Holy Spirit" (Acts 2:38).

These truths are the essence of the gospel. When people hear of the incarnation, life, death, resurrection, and promised return (Acts 3:19-21) of the Lord Jesus Christ, along with a call to repentance and faith, they are truly faced with the choice—eternal life or death.

A Pressing Need Today

We find ourselves living in a day, however, when certain aspects of the gospel need to be especially stressed. This may be due to the fact that they get scant mention. The biblical response to Christ and His sacrifice demands *repentance* and *faith*. Nothing short of that brings salvation.

The Meaning of Repentance

Repentance means several things. Initially, it means that people must become vividly conscious of their sin and God's judgment on that sin. Remember, sin estranges us from God and brings us under His judgment. We must see ourselves as lost, far from God, before we can expect to be found. From a broken heart and a convicted, disturbed mind, we do an about-face from sin, and honestly face God. Repentance means falling in complete contrition at His feet and making Jesus Christ our Lord and Master. That and that only is true biblical repentance. And as the Scriptures say, "Unless you repent, you will . . . likewise perish" (Luke 13:3). This really needs to be made clear to people. Telling them to ask Jesus to come into their hearts or to "merely believe" does not bring about the real brokenness that the Spirit of God needs for a person to be soundly converted. We must understand the bad news of our life before we can truly embrace the Good News of life in Christ.

True Faith

Moreover, we must exercise faith. And note: Believing in the Lord Jesus Christ means far more than having an intellectual knowledge of the gospel. The demons know that—"and shudder" (James 2:19). As stressed earlier, faith means casting ourselves utterly on the grace and mercy of God, seeking forgiveness, and *personally trusting* the Lord Jesus Christ for salvation. In relation to Christ, words like "resting," "trusting," "committing to," "relying on" get to the heart of biblical believing. It can all be brought together in Paul's well-known verse, "Whoever will call upon the name of the Lord will be saved" (Rom. 10:13). Jesus said, "If anyone wishes to come after Me, let him deny himself, and take up his cross, and follow Me. For whoever wishes to save his life shall lose it; but whoever loses his life for My sake shall find it" (Matt. 16:24–25). This is the heart of the gospel message. We need to fully understand it and then we need to make sure those we witness to understand it.

The Wise Approach

It is sometimes difficult for the witness to know how to approach people. There are hurdles to clear as we attempt to point people to Christ. In an excellent book on personal witnessing, *How to Give Away Your Faith*, Paul E. Little lays out seven action principles for winning a hearing:

1. **Contact others socially**. Jesus contacted people in the "traffic pattern" of their lives. In our everyday encounters with people there are often opportunities to share Christ. We can sometimes plant a seed in a casual encounter, but it is best to establish a relationship with people

first, at least as far as we can. The better we know others, and the better they know us, the more effective our witness can be. Because of this Christians have the obligation to establish relationships with lost people. How easy it seems to enclose ourselves in a "Christian ghetto," surrounding ourselves with Christian friends, Christian influences, and centering our social life in the church. We should break out of that mentality and befriend those who need us most. The lost are all about us—in stores, on the job, in school, and in our neighborhood. How important that we seize every encounter to share Christ.

2. **Establishing a common starting point**. The breakthrough to witnessing is never easy. How do we get started in a gospel presentation? As we begin to talk with people, we often find mutual interests. These secular subjects help us engage in positive conversation. Jesus certainly did this in His encounter with the Samaritan woman at the well. In John 4 we read, "There came a woman of Samaria to draw water. Jesus said to her, 'Give Me a drink'" (John 4:7). The common interest was water. The woman came to draw some, and Jesus was thirsty. The Lord led her from that neutral subject into spiritual matters. In that simple way, the woman came to recognize who Jesus really was and put her faith in Him as God's messianic Savior. We can follow this course of action.

3. **Arouse interest**. After Jesus had talked on a common point of interest with the Samaritan woman, He aroused her curiosity by saying that if she drank of the water He had to give, she would never be thirsty again (John 4:13–14). That moved the conversation into spiritual things. Good psychology. The message of Christ always proves intriguing when presented in a good, positive, sensible fashion. After all, it answers life's basic questions and difficulties.

4. **Do not go too far**. We must be sensitive as to how far the Holy Spirit will lead us in particular witnessing encounters. Psychologists tell us that if a person says no to a given proposition a certain number of times it becomes psychologically impossible for that person ever to say yes to that proposition. Of course, the Holy Spirit can break any resistance, but we do not want to push people to the point where they become antagonistic and build up a wall of resistance to the message of Christ. We need to know just how far to take the person and go no further. It may be only a step, or it may be five steps, or it might even lead to the point of decision. Rest assured, the Holy Spirit will direct us (Rom. 8:14).

5. **Do not condemn**. Our Lord did not condemn the woman at the well, nor the woman taken in adultery (John 8:1–11). He stood open and ready to receive, to forgive, and to grant new life to the repentant heart. From a practical perspective, this may mean beginning by

complimenting the person on something that is truly commendable. Charles Trumbull said we can always discover at least one thing to compliment. This establishes a positive relationship and will often open the mind and ultimately the heart of the listener to hear the message. This does not mean we need to gloss over the reality of sin and its damning effects. We tell the full truth. At the Samaritan well, Jesus pointed out the woman's sin and hence her need of forgiveness (John 4:16–19). But we do not condemn; we too are sinners. We point out these serious truths *in love*.

6. **Stick with the main issue**. People will often try to sidetrack us as we begin to share the gospel. The Samaritan woman changed the subject to places of worship. Jesus addressed that subject briefly and then brought her right back to the key issue—namely, her deep need. We must not be diverted. This does not mean we cannot answer honest questions. But we must be able to discern between an honest question that deserves an honest answer and one that is merely a diversion. Stick to the point.

7. **Confront him or her directly**. We cannot escape the fact that effective witnessing is confrontational. Remember, we are challenging people to make the most important decision of their lives. We must not dance around the issues of sin and salvation. We bring them face to face with their own rebellion against God. Quite naturally this can spark an emotional response. People often get irritated or angry. On the other hand they may only express indifference, unwillingness, or apathy. But still we press on lovingly. We must go as far as the Spirit of God leads us. And remember, we have *good news* to give, news of forgiveness and restoration. Sometimes the best we can elicit is a commitment to pray privately about the matter. But that is a positive step. Make no mistake; we do confront people and seek a decision. It is never easy, but it must be done.[2]

These seven principles for action do not cover every situation we might meet in attempting to share Christ. However, they do present some general guidelines and can help us get over the first hurdles in becoming effective witnesses for the Lord. In the final analysis, witnessing is far more "caught" than "taught." We learn by doing. This brings us back to the original premise that God, by His Spirit, is the One who wins. All that we have presented in this book points to the fact that Spirit-sensitive people who know God, abide in Christ, live the Spirit-filled life, and bear the precious fruit of the Spirit, will be open to His leadership in sharing their faith. In that way, witnessing becomes truly effective because we engage in the *missio Dei* with God's own Spirit. We have called this the "grand enterprise," and grand it is.

Ministering to the Whole Person

Up until now we have looked at the deep and desperate need people have for Christ and His salvation. However, people have physical and emotional needs as well as spiritual. Because of this God intends His people to minister to the whole person. Love demands it. It may well mean that we shall have to feed the hungry stomach before we can feed the hungry soul. As John R. W. Stott said, "A hungry man has no ears." People also find it hard to hear the gospel if emotional difficulties are swamping them. Maybe their marriage is crumbling, or perhaps their children are a worry. If we can do anything to alleviate those pressures, as Christians we must do it. We should step into needy lives with an encouraging word and a helping hand, bringing Christ's ministry to them. That is how our Lord did His work while on earth. He simply met needs as He found them—all kinds of needs. Only then, after we have met the most pressing requirement of people, can we endeavor to win them to Christ.

We meet needs because the love of Christ constrains us to do so. But then . . . we can often effectively communicate Christ to them.

Let it also be clear: We do not minister to the temporal wants of people just as a means or a gimmick to soften them up for the gospel. Meeting needs may well be an avenue for communicating the gospel to be sure, but the principle of Christian love demands that we touch hurting people whether we have the opportunity to share Christ with them or not. John told us in his first epistle, "Whoever has the world's goods, and beholds his brother in need and closes his heart against him, how does the love of God abide in him?" (1 John 3:17). We meet needs because the love of Christ constrains us to do so. But then, if we have had the right serving spirit toward people, motivated by our own love for the Lord, we can often effectively communicate Christ to them. When people were hungry, Jesus fed them; when they were distraught, He comforted them; when they were in need of healing, He touched them; when they needed His forgiveness and salvation, He redeemed them. We follow in our Master's footsteps. Can we do less?

Using the Right Words

One further word needs to be said in the context of effective witnessing, and that concerns using the right words. There was a time when the so-called "language of Zion" could be understood by most people. But *repentance, salvation, redemption, born again, sin, faith,* and similar terms mean little in our postmodern world. We need to be something of a spiritual dictionary to contemporary, secular society. We should use words that people understand,

and when more technical biblical and theological terms must be employed, we have to remember to explain them and the concepts that rest behind them. If we fail to do this, people will make false, shallow decisions, without a saving understanding. Our Lord Jesus Christ gave a stern warning. He said:

> Not everyone who says to Me, "Lord, Lord," will enter the kingdom of heaven; but he who does the will of My Father who is in heaven. Many will say to Me on that day, "Lord, Lord, did we not prophesy in Your name, and in Your name cast out demons, and in Your name perform many miracles?" And then I will declare to them, "I never knew you; depart from Me, you who practice lawlessness." (Matt. 7:21–23)

It is a tragedy when people nurse a superficial understanding of the gospel and think they are saved but are not. Do not forget, this was Vonette's predicament until she genuinely understood the gospel and was wonderfully and truly saved. When the "deceived" stand before God, what rude awakening that will be. But upon whose hands will their blood be found? May God help us to make the full gospel understandable and clear. May we never be found guilty of failing to communicate all the truth of Christ in an understandable fashion.

Good Resources

Many more things should probably be said about effective witnessing, but the principles we have covered will get us started. There are a multitude of books and programs available to guide us. Often churches conduct short courses. Moreover, excellent booklets on God's way of salvation have been produced for our use in evangelism. A good example is *The Four Spiritual Laws* mentioned earlier and published by Campus Crusade for Christ International. If we can do no more at the start than hand someone a booklet or tract, at least that is a beginning. We will grow in effectiveness. Perhaps the most meaningful thing to do is to give a simple testimony of our own conversion and what Christ means to us. On numerous occasions the apostle Paul shared his faith. He constantly testified, whether he stood before Jewish worshipers in their synagogue, before kings in their palaces, or before Caesar himself. Anyone can do it, and personal testimony is a powerful tool.

This now leads us to the final consideration of this step, the necessity of helping those who do come to Christ to get started in their Christian journey.

The Necessity of Discipleship Training

The new convert, the Bible says, is "born again" spiritually as a mere babe. How tragic it is in a human family to see a beautiful baby neglected. Yet this often happens in the spiritual family of God. People come to faith in Christ but do not receive care or nurture; they are never shown the way toward Christian maturity. The result is spiritual anemia. What then should we do to help people get a proper start in their spiritual lives?

Getting Them Started

A person getting started in spiritual growth must first have full assurance of salvation. Without this assurance new converts will never mature in Christ. This is one of the errors that the book of Hebrews attempts to correct. The author of Hebrews wrote:

> Therefore leaving the elementary teaching about the Christ, let us press on to maturity, not laying again a foundation of repentance from dead work and of faith toward God, of instruction about washings, and laying on of hands, and the resurrection of the dead, and eternal judgment. And this we shall do, if God permits. (6:1–3)
>
> But, beloved, we are convinced of better things concerning you, and things that accompany salvation, though we are speaking in this way. (6:9)

People begin to mature in Christ when they know they are in Him.

How to Grow

If people are not taught how to study the Bible, how to pray, how to walk in the fullness of the Spirit, how to achieve Christian victory, how to serve Christ and witness, they will never grow spiritually.

New converts must learn how to grow and mature spiritually. That is the entire focus of this book. If people are not taught how to study the Bible, how to pray, how to walk in the fullness of the Spirit, how to achieve Christian victory, how to serve Christ and witness, they will never grow spiritually. These disciplines cannot be ignored or neglected. They keep us all growing in Christ.

New converts must also get involved in the life of a church. No church is perfect, nor is any pastor or leader sinless. But in spite of the problems, the church is the body of Christ. Those new to Christ need to take part in the fellowship, worship, and outreach of a vibrant congregation.

God's Workings

Those who have come to faith in Christ need to acquire a full grasp of what God expects of His children. . . . They should be encouraged, right from the outset, to share their faith with others.

Finally, those who have come to faith in Christ need to acquire a full grasp of what God expects of His children. That is what this step is all about. They should be encouraged, right from the outset, to share their faith with others. In the early days most of their friends will still be in the world and lost. These friends will listen to them because of their preconversion relationship. New Christians have a unique opportunity for a receptive hearing that they may not have once they get involved in the church. We may think that new converts will not know what to say until they have training. This is not true. The first year after being converted may be the most fruitful year in witnessing they will ever have.

Conclusion

True spirituality leads to sharing our faith with lost people. Thus we pray with David, the sweet psalmist of Israel, "Restore to me the joy of Thy salvation, and sustain me with a willing spirit. Then I will teach transgressors Thy ways, and sinners will be converted to Thee" (Ps. 51:12–13).

Prayer

God, our Father and Savior, I do thank You for saving me through Your Son, the Lord Jesus Christ. Enable me to draw so close to You that I may find the commitment and power to share the good news with others. I pray You will make me a faithful, effective witness to Your grace and salvation. Lord, lead me to that person who needs You. In Christ I ask these blessings. Amen.

10 Questions for Study and Discussion

1. How important was the influence of Bill Bright on Vonette, and what are the implications of that for all relationships?
2. How does Vonette's life exemplify the way God leads us in ministry?
3. What is the *missio Dei*, and what does it mean to us?
4. How do we become involved in God's mission?
5. Why should we witness for Christ?
6. What is the message we must share?
7. How do we get over the first hurdles in a witnessing situation?
8. Is witnessing our only responsibility toward others? What other tasks do we have? What are we doing about it?
10. What do we need to help new converts to do so they may grow spiritually?

The Spiritual Woman Loves God

MEET ELISABETH ELLIOT GREN
A WOMAN WHO LOVES GOD

You shall love the Lord your God.
(Mark 12:30)

$\mathscr{N}$ ow abide faith, hope, and love, these three; but the greatest of these is love" (1 Cor. 13:13). The apostle Paul knew this truth so well; Elisabeth Elliot Gren lives it so well. If ever a woman of God has loved her Lord and exemplified that love, it is she. Her life has been one of dedicated faithfulness through many trials and heartaches. Her love of Jesus has shone like the sun on a bright spring morning. Through her, God has been manifested and glorified.

First Years

Elisabeth Howard was born in Brussels, Belgium, just a few days before Christmas in 1926. Spiritual life had greatly deteriorated in Western Europe since the days of the great seventeenth-century Pietistic Revival. At the time of her birth, Elisabeth's parents were serving there as missionaries.

While Elisabeth was still a toddler the family moved back to the United States and her father, Philip, became the editor of a Christian weekly magazine known as *The Sunday School Times*. This publication was the only non-denominational Christian weekly periodical published in the United States at the time. It was widely read for many decades, especially for its Sunday school lessons. The world-renowned writer and evangelist, Dr. Charles Trumbull—whom we met in a previous step—had once been its editor, and he did much to establish the work of the publication. Philip was following in worthy footsteps.

A Spiritual Heritage

Elisabeth always expressed gratitude for the blessing and influence of her godly parents. Family devotions were a regular habit in the Howard home. Twice a day, the family gathered to sing old hymns of the faith, to hear the Word of God, and to pray. Elisabeth memorized hundreds of Scripture texts during these devotional times. Her parents exercised a firm but loving Christian discipline. The children were expected to obey immediately and to share in the housework. Washing dishes, mowing the lawn, dusting the furniture, sweeping the carpets, and other such chores were a daily routine. And, of course, the family maintained a faithful commitment to the church. All this sowed a sense of responsibility and spiritual sensitivity in the lives of the children that earned rich dividends later.

*Elisabeth's parents instilled a love of good literature in
the children at an early age. Little did Elisabeth know
at that time that she would make a significant contribution
to the cause of Christ through her writings.*

Not only were discipline and church life priorities in the Howard home, the family approached school in a serious, wholesome manner. The children did their schoolwork thoroughly and honestly. They learned to use correct English and above all, to appreciate books. Elisabeth's parents instilled a love of good literature in the children at an early age. Little did Elisabeth know at that time that she would make a significant contribution to the cause of Christ through her writings.

Missions Inspiration

Missionaries were often welcomed into the Howard home, and because of this the children never lacked examples of Christian servants. Elisabeth said that as they gathered around the dinner table the whole family would thrill to the incredible stories the missionaries brought from all over the world. Nor were the children unaware of how much it cost to serve Christ. John and Betty Stam were guests in their home. Later this godly couple would be beheaded by the Chinese Communists.

Elisabeth later wrote a book called *The Shaping of a Christian Family*, in which she told the story of her home life. Out of the Howards' six children, four became foreign missionaries, and the others are faithful Christians. As parents they had great reason to rejoice.

Educating a Future Missionary

After high school, Elisabeth went to Hampden DuBose Academy in Florida. Over the years this wonderful institution has produced many fine Christian graduates who have greatly contributed to the kingdom of God around the world. Elisabeth was a shy girl, shy to a fault. She would blame herself for things over which she had no control and no responsibility. Servants of Christ cannot be proud and arrogant, but neither can they be so shy and retiring that they cannot fulfill God's purpose for them in ministry. Mrs. DuBose, the headmistress, took a personal interest in her students. Like Elisabeth's parents, she was a strict disciplinarian with a heart full of love. She was always eager to see her students reach their potential, and she determined to eliminate Elisabeth's timidity

Activities in Florida

And she did an excellent job. With Mrs. DuBose's encouragement Elisabeth tried a variety of activities. She studied singing and piano and was taught how music could be used in Christian worship and evangelism. She learned to walk onto a platform and speak forthrightly and convincingly in the name of Christ. Best of all, Hampden DuBose inspired Elisabeth to write.

Amy Carmichael's Influence

Mrs. DuBose introduced Elisabeth to the work of Amy Carmichael. Elisabeth calls it a "life-shaping gift." Amy had written more than forty books and had also been an active missionary in Japan, Ceylon (now Sri Lanka), and Dohnavur, in southern India, where she served needy children. Elisabeth was hugely influenced by the life of this woman of God and years later wrote a beautiful biography, *A Chance to Die: The Life and Legacy of Amy Carmichael*, in tribute to her. She began to feel called to the mission field herself.

Wheaton

*She was convinced of her call to the mission field,
and she also sensed that God was leading her to a part
of the world where native people did not
have the Scriptures in their own language.*

In the fall of 1944, Elisabeth traveled north to attend Wheaton College. This was an ideal place for her. Wheaton always enjoyed the reputation of being a spiritually dedicated institution, training men and women for a life of service to Jesus Christ. It is situated in a small town just west of Chicago, Illinois, and spiritual giants like Billy Graham, Ruth Bell, Bob Evans, and a host of others have had their lives shaped by its faculty, staff, and administration. Along with its strong spiritual emphasis, scholastic standards have always been kept at the highest level. Elisabeth majored in classical Greek. By this time she was convinced of her call to the mission field, and she also sensed that God was leading her to a part of the world where the native people did not have the Scriptures in their own language. She determined to work in Bible translation. She felt sure that a background in Greek would be a good start in preparing her for that field of missionary ministry.

The Wycliffe Bible translators, a faith mission society, conducted an excellent summer course on the campus of the University of Oklahoma to prepare people for the work of Bible translation. Elisabeth felt so committed to a ministry of Bible translation that she took the course in the summer of 1948. She immersed herself in the work and had high hopes of being appointed to a translating team by the Wycliffe Translators Mission Society, but that appointment never materialized. God had another route for her to follow.

A New Venture

Elisabeth never gave up her dream of Bible translation work, and eventually she found the perfect place to do it. In April of 1952, Elisabeth traveled to Quito, Ecuador, where she threw herself into studying Spanish. Once she had become proficient in the language, she was moved to the western jungle of Ecuador. There she joined two British women missionaries who were living with a remote South American tribe known as the Colorado Indians—"Colorado" because that word means "red" in Spanish, and the people had the custom of painting their bodies from head to toe in brilliant red dye.

Elisabeth felt she had found her life's work among the Colorados. The tribe had no written language, let alone a translated Bible. Transcribing an unwritten language is painstaking work. She found that her home and her time at Hampden DuBose Academy had prepared her well for the disciplined life and Herculean challenges she now faced.

No Easy Task

Elisabeth settled down with her companions into the jungle community. So much about it fascinated her. Occasionally she and her roommate, Dorothy, would travel into distant San Miguel. They would hire a horse (a horse that was far more like a pony) for ninety cents a day, pile a few things onto its back, and away they would go. It was always a beautiful trip through the forest, with its giant trees, ferns, and elephant ears crowding in on all sides.

Yet life was difficult. Later Elisabeth described those days:

> Missionary life, in my mind's eye before I went to Ecuador, comprised green jungle, thatched roof houses, and Indians. San Miguel fit the picture well, but what had I not seen in my imagination was what would be involved in putting those elements into some kind of working relationship. What was involved, I found, took up about nine-tenths of our time.[1]

Simple home life was no easy chore. There were snakes and scorpions to watch out for. The only water supply was a river some three hundred yards away. Toilet facilities called for an even longer walk down the river. Getting enough wood for fuel was a problem. Ironing had to be done with a gasoline iron and cooking on a pressure stove. The smallest tasks took so much time and effort. Elisabeth contracted scabies, not a serious malady, but very offensive to others. And always there was the work Elisabeth had come to do—getting the unwritten Colorado language down on paper so that the people could learn to read the Word of God. Days were demanding and often frustrating.

She later wrote the story in her inspiring book, *These Strange Ashes*. Among the Colorados, Elisabeth was forced to learn some very important spiritual lessons, "stunning ones," as she later wrote. Rather than give way to discouragement and fear, Elisabeth had to learn to let God work in her life. Occasionally she felt that old inclination to worry and assume burdens that God never intended her to bear. At such times the Holy Spirit would speak to her heart and say, "Trust Me." She learned to do just that, and that fully.

A Real Trial

*Elisabeth developed what she called a
"sinewy faith." That faith made her strong
for what she would face in the future.*

Elisabeth had settled down to work one night, when someone came banging on the door crying, *"Senorita, senorita!"* One of the Indians had come seeking help; his wife was giving birth and it was not going well at all. As Elisabeth ran home with the man he kept crying out, "She's dying, she's dying!" One look at the mother convinced Elisabeth that death was indeed inevitable. She leaned close to her and heard the woman say weakly, "Good-bye. Good-bye to all my friends. Good-bye to my family, whom I have loved. Good-bye to my newborn child, my son, my little one. This child whom God has given and from whom He takes the mother."[2] Then she slipped off into eternity. Elisabeth went home deeply moved. It was the first time she had seen someone die, and she had clearly seen the despair death brings to those who have no hope in Jesus Christ.

The woman's death seemed to close the door on the gospel. Had she lived, the Indians might have been more open to accepting the all-powerful God Elisabeth represented. As it was they distrusted her message. Tragically, the child died as well. Why had God not stepped in? This became one of Elisabeth's hard periods, when she felt nothing but darkness and silence. Even she wondered if God had failed.

Lessons

Another tragedy struck in January of 1953. Elisabeth had been reading *Daily Light,* a book of Scripture verses assembled for each day. The passage for that particular day read, "Think it not strange concerning the fiery trial which is to try you as though some strange thing happened unto you, but rejoice, inasmuch as you are made partakers of Christ's suffering" (1 Peter 4:12 KJV). Suddenly she heard gunshots and the scream, "They've killed Don Macario!" Macario had been Elisabeth's trusted companion and colleague. He had spoken both Spanish and the Colorado dialect with ease—the only person who could—and was key in Elisabeth's efforts to transcribe the Indians' language. This fatal night, he had fallen into dispute with a man from another tribe over a land right and had been shot point-blank in the head.

The work came to a sudden stop. Elisabeth wrote to her parents, describing it as "the most nightmarish day of my life." She interpreted it as a token of her failure. She felt both remorse and responsibility. Elisabeth would describe that tragedy as "lesson one" in the school of faith. The deaths of the Indian mother and her baby were terrible in themselves. This death was also a serious impediment to God's work. It seemed inexplicable. But by praying, reading the Bible, and remembering those who had suffered bravely, people such as John and Betty Stam, Elisabeth found the courage and strength to carry on. She remembered what Amy Carmichael had written:

> Why these strange ashes, Lord, this nothingness,
> This baffling sense of loss?
> Son, was the anguish of my stripping less
> Upon the torturing cross?

Through these experiences Elizabeth was made to realize that she could do nothing but cast herself utterly on the Lord's mercy. They were of tremendous consequence. They schooled her to hold close to Christ. And through it all, Elisabeth developed what she called a "sinewy faith." That faith made her strong for what she would face in the future.

A New Life Begins

While she was serving in South America, Elisabeth had been exchanging letters with Jim Elliot, a fellow graduate of Wheaton College. Over time the letters had become more serious. Three days after Macario's death, Elisabeth received a telegram from Jim. He was waiting for her in Quito. Elisabeth made the difficult trip to the large Ecuadorian city, and it was there he asked her to be his bride.

> *It seemed as if the days of trauma among the Colorados were coming to an end. . . . Elisabeth saw before her a joyous life of missionary service in this new location, with her beloved Jim. How bright it looked!*

Elisabeth had a difficult decision to make. If she married she would have to leave her work with the Colorado Indians. She loved Jim deeply, but she loved God above all. What did He want of her? In time God let her know and gave her peace. She felt sure that marrying Jim was His will for her. And so it seemed as if the days of trauma among the Colorados were coming to an end. Jim was a missionary under the same agency as Elisabeth. His work centered in Shandia, in the eastern jungles of Ecuador with the Quichua Indians. Elizabeth saw before her a joyous life of missionary service in this new location, with her beloved Jim. How bright it looked! Strangely, just as she was about to leave San Miguel de Los Colorados, someone stole her suitcase containing all the laborious translating work she had done in her time there. It was just one more step in understanding that "strange ashes" come from God's will.

Married Life

When Jim sought Elisabeth's hand in marriage, he gave her a challenging condition: She was to learn the Quichua language first so she could minister to that tribe with him. Elisabeth mastered it just in time for her wedding on October 8, 1953, Jim's twenty-sixth birthday. In February 1955, as they labored in Puyupungu, in eastern Ecuador, their daughter, Valerie, was born. Only one year later, Elisabeth would face the darkest trial of her life.

Through Gates of Splendor

Elisabeth's classic volume, *Through Gates of Splendor*, tells the story. As Elisabeth and Jim settled into their ministry they became burdened with the tremendous need of the Auca Indians. The Aucas were an isolated, semi-nomadic tribe in eastern Ecuador. No one knew very much about them, but through the years a little information had seeped out of the jungle. They were a people weighted down with countless demonic superstitions. Jim and four other missionaries felt an increasingly strong call to reach these needy people with the gospel.

All were aware that the first missionary to the Aucas, a Jesuit priest by the name of Pedro Suarez, had been speared to death. That had been many years before, but there was no indication that the Aucas had softened in their attitude. White men rarely came near their territory, and the few who had, had attempted to exploit them. There was little reason for the Aucas to trust any other newcomers. Nevertheless, Jim and his companions began to make plans to contact the tribe. Pete Fleming, one of the five, wrote in his diary:

> I am longing now to reach the Aucas if God gives me the honor of proclaiming the Name to them. . . . I would gladly give my life if only to see an assembly of those proud, clever, smart people gathering around a table to honor the Son— gladly, gladly, gladly! What more could be given to a life?[3]

Little did Pete know that he, Jim, Ed McCully, Roger Younderian, and Nate Saint, the missionary pilot, would soon fill that role.

Careful Plans

The men had come there with only one desire, to glorify Christ and reach the Indians with the gospel.

When all preparations were complete they boarded the aircraft that would take them deep into Auca territory. Pilot Nate Saint flew over the area and discovered a sandy beach where he felt he could land the small missionary plane. They carefully considered the next steps, how they could make contact with the people and establish a beachhead among them.

As it turned out, they encountered no initial difficulties. The Indians gave them a friendly welcome and seemed to accept them. The missionaries took one or two of them for a ride in the airplane, and things seemed to move along well. It was a false peace. The Aucas sent one of their young women over, thinking the missionaries would like to have a woman for what any Christian would see as immoral. The offer was refused, and this was taken as an insult. Things went from bad to worse. The Indians became convinced that these five men were actually dangerous cannibals. Without a word of warning, the tribe descended on the missionaries, spears in hand, and slaughtered all five within a matter of minutes.

The men had come there with only one desire, to glorify Christ and reach the Indians with the gospel. What began as a noble task had ended in tragedy—tragedy in the world's eyes. But what a sacrifice of love.

Faith Prevails

The families understood and took the heartbreak with stalwart faith. Even the children were able to put it in perspective. Stevie McCully heard about his father's tragic death and said, "I know my Daddy is with Jesus, but I miss him, and I wish he would just come down and play with me once in a while." Several weeks later, back in the States, Stevie's little brother, Matthew, was born. One day the baby was crying and Stevie was heard to say, "Never you mind; when I get to heaven I'll show you which one is our Daddy."

God powerfully used this trying event in many lives. For example, an eighteen-year-old young man in Des Moines, Iowa, prayed for a week in his room. Then he announced to his parents, "I am turning my life over completely to the Lord. I want to take the place of one of those five." The missionary martyrs remain an inspiration around the world to this day.

Elisabeth had gone through traumatic times in South America before her marriage to Jim. And now that man of God, along with four close friends, was torn from her side. She immediately sought the Lord. She wrote:

> When the men were killed, I had prayed what seemed to be
> an unlikely prayer: "Lord, if there is anything you want me
> to do about those Aucas, show me"—never supposing that
> there could be any such thing. But there was. In the fall of
> 1957 I was given the privilege of meeting two Auca women
> who came to live with me for nearly a year. Of course I could
> not speak a syllable of their language, but over the months
> gradually came to understand that they were inviting me to
> go home with them.

A Fantastic Turn of Events

What a miraculous turn of events! Here were the very people who had murdered her husband wanting her to go home with them! Most men and women would have recoiled from the very idea. But not Elisabeth. Her love for Christ constrained her. In the fall of 1958, with her little daughter Valerie, she moved back with the two Auca women to their settlement. Rachel Saint, the sister of the pilot Nate Saint, went with her. They did not go for a visit. They went to establish a mission station from which to declare Christ—there, amidst the very tribe that had killed their loved ones. By God's grace they soon mastered the Auca language and began to proclaim the gospel in that place.

Elisabeth spent a year sharing the love of Christ with the Aucas. She met men who had taken part in the murder of the missionaries, and she won several of them to Christ. After a year's work she went home on furlough, where she wrote another of her excellent books, *The Savage My Kinsman.* After a year of rest she returned to the Aucas with her daughter. Again she gave herself to evangelizing the Aucas and saw many more come to the Lord. The Indian who had killed her husband had come to a saving faith in Christ, and God used him powerfully as a proclaimer of the gospel. In one of the beautiful twists of the grace and providence of God, when Elisabeth's daughter Valerie came to salvation in the Lord, it was this man, the very man who had killed her father, who baptized her.

What a wonderful sequel to what had seemed such a tragic event. There are no tragedies or mistakes in the economy of God. The Bible tells us in the book of Revelation that a host of martyrs for Jesus will receive a special crown of glory that shall last for eternity (Rev. 6:9–11). And remember that Paul declared, "For I consider that the sufferings of this present time are not worthy to be compared with the glory that is to be revealed to us" (Rom. 8:18).

A New Ministry—and Sorrow

Elisabeth continued to work with the Aucas until September of 1963, when she returned to the States for good. She settled down in Franconia, New Hampshire, to take up her writing. She also began an itinerant speaking ministry that continues to the present time. In January of 1969, she married a widower, Addison H. Leitch. They moved to Massachusetts, where Dr. Leitch was a professor of philosophy and theology at Gordon-Conwell Seminary in South Hamilton. But once again Elisabeth had to face a time of deep sorrow. In 1973, four short years later, Addison died of cancer. Elisabeth had long since learned how to love God and leave all things in His hands.

The Ministry Grows

In 1977, Elisabeth met and married Lars Gren, a dedicated layman. Lars had spent the first ten years of his life in Norway, then had moved to Mississippi and later, Georgia. Though he had become a successful businessman he later felt called to the ministry. He attended Gordon-Conwell Seminary and, upon graduating, became a hospital chaplain. Meanwhile Elisabeth's writing and speaking ministry expanded to the point where she needed help. Lars stepped in to manage the business side of her work for her. He handled her travel arrangements, the sale of her books and tapes, and all dealings with her publishers. A deeply devout and loving man of God, Lars described his role as the ministry that God had given him. All this freed up Elisabeth to do what she did best for her Lord. Together, in complementary roles, they carried on a dynamic service for Jesus Christ.

A Happy Life and Pilgrimage

Her life is a powerful testimony to the spiritual imperative that we must love the Lord God with all of our heart, soul, strength, and mind (Matt. 22:37).

Elisabeth's life can be seen as a pilgrimage. In it she faced the most severe trials and heartaches possible, yet she always kept her sweet, loving spirit through it all. Clearly, her life is a powerful testimony to the spiritual imperative that we must love the Lord God with all of our heart, soul, strength, and mind (Matt. 22:37). In the final analysis, everything that has been presented in this book culminates in that. This final step in our quest to develop spirituality is a "love step," and in many ways it is really just a recapitulation and summary of all that has gone before.

The Spiritual Woman Is Not Materialistic

Spirit-led people are not materialistic. This does not mean that material matters have no meaning, but their role must always be secondary. For the woman who loves God, spiritual realities come first. We have seen the wisdom of setting before ourselves a mission statement predicated on God's great purpose in creation. The spiritual woman, therefore, must set a proper "love goal." Whether we recognize it or not, we all have goals. These goals govern our daily actions and decision making. For us, as believers, there is really only one end: to love our Lord Jesus Christ unreservedly. Our life must arrange itself around Him, not the other way around. We remember the words of the apostle Paul when he talked about his primary purpose in life: "One thing I do: forgetting what lies behind and reaching forward to what lies ahead, I press on toward the goal for the prize of the upward call of God in

Christ Jesus" (Phil. 3:13–14). We fix our eyes on the Lord Jesus Christ, and make decisions in the light of our relationship with Him. We attempt to follow "in His steps," and those "steps" are the pathway of love. As the apostle further expressed to the Philippians, "For to me to live is Christ" (Phil. 1:21). That is love.

The Principle to Move Us to Loving Spirituality

We love to have role models to emulate.
But for the Spirit-led believer, there is only one Hero on
whom we can pattern our lives. We know well
who that is: the Lord Jesus Christ.

We live in a day of hero worship. We love to have role models to emulate. But for the Spirit-led believer, there is only one Hero on whom we can pattern our lives. We know well who that is: the Lord Jesus Christ. In all the struggles of life, in all the petty distractions that surround us, we remain pure by seeking only the honor of our Lord Jesus. He alone is worthy. Paul said, "May it never be that I should boast, except in the cross of our Lord Jesus Christ" (Gal. 6:14). In seeking to pursue the spiritual life our confession must always be "Jesus [Christ is] Lord" (Rom. 10:9). Out of our love for Christ, we *obey Him*. As Elisabeth Elliot Gren put it, "For one who has made thanksgiving the habit of his life, the morning prayer will be, 'Lord, what will you give me today to offer back to you?'"[4] And all that to glorify our lovely Lord.

Sacrifice

God never promised the spiritual life would be one of ease. On the contrary, a dedicated Christian life will probably entail great sacrifices, because it grows out of commitment and surrender to Christ's lordship. This means different things to different people. It may mean giving up something that we cherish very dearly, an ambition perhaps that prevents us from serving God as our primary goal. At the very least it means giving up worldly and sinful habits, actions, and desires.

We had the opportunity of working in Eastern Europe before the Iron Curtain came down. God's people there endured terrible hardship in the Communist years. Some of our friends were jailed, others were ostracized, many were cruelly treated. All forfeited the "good life" for the sake of Christ. Yet we never heard a single word of complaint. The people loved God and placed their lives in His hands. To them sacrifice was an expression of this love.

On one occasion we ministered in a small community in old Yugoslavia. The little church where we were sharing the gospel filled up until it was jammed with people. People stood throughout the service, in the aisles, at the back, and in the yard outside. They strained to hear and to participate in the worship. When the final benediction was pronounced and everyone dispersed, we were told that some of the folk had walked as far as twenty kilometers—twelve miles—simply to attend that service, and then had walked the twelve miles back home. They had sacrificed in order to worship God. We must expect to do the same. The old hymn writer had it right when he wrote:

> Must I be carried to the sky
> On flowery beds of ease;
> While others fought to win the prize
> And sail through bloody seas?

No price is too dear if it is the price God demands. For some it may even mean death. More Christians suffered martyrdom in the twentieth century than in the rest of the history of the church put together. Dark days still exist. We are all called to a life of sacrifice of one kind or another. Remember the testimony of Paul:

> And now, behold, bound in spirit, I am on my way to Jerusalem, not knowing what will happen to me there, except that the Holy Spirit solemnly testifies to me in every city, saying that bonds and afflictions await me. But I do not consider my life of any account as dear to myself, in order that I may finish my course, and the ministry which I received from the Lord Jesus, to testify solemnly of the gospel of the grace of God. (Acts 20:22–24)

Jesus Christ, in love, gave His all for us. Can we love less? Being a Christian, bonded to the indwelling Christ, means dedicating our lives to pleasing Him regardless of the cost.

That is the right spirit of love. We see in Paul a desire to sacrifice anything, including his life, to accomplish the will and purpose of God. That willingness to forgo indicates a healthy spiritual life. Only that attitude will bring true glory to our Lord. We may feel that such sacrifice is demanding too much. This is not so. Jesus Christ, in love, gave His all for us. Can we love less? Being a Christian, bonded to the indwelling Christ, means dedicating our lives to pleasing Him regardless of the cost.

It can be summed up in one simple statement: *Christ comes first in all things.* That is the substance of spirituality. Spirituality is loving Christ; spirituality is following Christ; spirituality is paying any price to experience the fellowship of Christ; spirituality is obedience to Christ; spirituality is glorifying Christ. A big demand? To be sure! But how unfathomable are the rewards.

The Spirit-Led Woman Is Spiritually Rewarded

It is impossible to enumerate all the wonderful blessings of the spiritual life. God's touch of grace and love moves through every vestige of our being when we dedicate ourselves to Him. We are propelled into the realm of eternity. Just mentioning a few of these blessings can to stir us up! (2 Peter 3:1).

A Walk with God

First, we have the privilege of walking with God. Think of the beauty of it—yes, and the glory of it. We have tried to paint a portrait of God the best way we can with our limited human language. Our God is infinitely glorious. He is perfect in power and infinite in knowledge. He is always present, always loving, always holy. Yet we can walk in fellowship with Him. Recall the words from 1 John: "What we have seen and heard we proclaim to you also, that you also may have fellowship with us; and indeed our fellowship is with the Father, and with His Son Jesus Christ" (1:3). It can be rightly said that nothing excels this walk with God and the joy it brings (1:4).

A Life That Counts

How foolish, therefore, to seek temporal, earthly attainments that fade, when eternal rewards await the spiritual Christian.

Second, we can live lives that count. We need never fear that our days are meaningless when we live in spiritual fellowship with our Lord. In Christ's hands they have purpose beyond our wildest dreams. We are co-laborers with God—regardless of our circumstances and our seeming failures (2 Cor. 6:1). God will remember even our smallest labors of love. Our Lord said through the writer of Hebrews: "For God is not unjust so as to forget your work and the love which you have shown toward His name, in having ministered and in still ministering to the saints" (Heb. 6:10). We know that all of our loving efforts will be richly and eternally rewarded, even if what we have done here on earth goes unrecognized. How foolish, therefore, to seek temporal, earthly achievements that fade, when eternal rewards await the spiritual Christian.

We Touch Others

And finally, we touch other people, infecting them with Christ's love. There is a double satisfaction in this. Not only do we know we are being used by Christ, but also we can help others along life's rocky road. And as these others come closer to the Lord Jesus Christ, they too will discover the peace and satisfaction of serving Him. How grateful we should be. As C. H. Spurgeon said, "The heart must be alive with gracious gratitude, or the leaf cannot long be green with living holiness."

Conclusion

When we love God in time and eternity we are fulfilling His whole purpose in creating us. Our great God deserves all the glory that we, His redeemed people, can bring to Him. The hour is coming when we shall be mightily resurrected. The hour is coming when God will transform the entire universe. It is coming, and coming soon. The Lord is not slack concerning His promise (2 Peter 3:9). One day we shall see the King in all His splendor and glory, and stand before Him with those who have given Christ their all, in deep love for Him.

May God grant us grace to continue the glorious journey of the spiritual life until Jesus comes.

Prayer

Loving Father, glorious Lord Jesus, ever-present Holy Spirit; I want to love You. Yes, Lord, I want to love You with all my heart, mind, strength, and body—and my neighbor as myself. I give myself to You. Fulfill my quest. Make me alive to Your love and fashion me into a truly spiritual believer, through Christ our Lord in whose name I pray. Amen.

10 Final Questions for Study and Discussion

1. Elisabeth overcame timidity and guilt feelings. How can we do the same?
2. How did Elisabeth find strength to endure the trials of her life? What does that tell us?
3. Why does God's permissive will seem so difficult to understand?
4. Does sacrifice really help us and others? How?
5. What does it mean to walk with God? How should this make us behave?
6. What is the correlation between love and obedience?
7. How do we learn to love?
8. How do we maintain an obedient lifestyle?
9. What are the rewards of the spiritual woman?
10. What do you intend to do about all the truths we have shared in this book?

Epilogue

 uring the 1740s a tremendous movement of the Holy Spirit took place in New England. It became known as America's First Great Awakening. Through the inspired leadership of William and Gilbert Tennent, George Whitefield, and above all, Jonathan Edwards, the early American colonies were transformed. Those days can never be forgotten; they set a pattern for personal holiness that desperately needs to be emulated today.

Jonathan Edwards composed a covenant that the revived Christian people of his church agreed to and gladly signed. One part of that covenant is particularly relevant to all we have tried to say in this book. It is a fitting epilogue to our journey together and it reads as follows:

> We now appear before God, depending on Divine grace as assistance, solemnly to devote our whole lives, to be laboriously spent in the business of religion; ever making it our greatest business, without backsliding from such a way of living, not hearkening to the solicitations of our sloth, and other corrupt inclinations, or the temptations of the world, that tend to draw us off from it; and particularly that we will not abuse a hope or opinion that any of us may have, of our being interested in Christ, to indulge ourselves in sloth, or the more easily to yield to the solicitations of any sinful inclinations; but will run with perseverance the race that is set before us, and work out our own salvation with fear and trembling.
>
> And because we are sensible that the keeping of these solemn vows may hereafter, in many cases, be very contrary to our corrupt inclinations and carnal interests, we do now therefore appear before God to make a surrender of all to him, and

to make a sacrifice of every carnal inclination and interest, to the great business of religion and the interest of our souls.

And being sensible of our weakness and the deceitfulness of our own hearts, and our proneness to forget our most solemn vows and lose our resolutions, we promise to be often strictly examining ourselves by these promises, especially before the sacrament of the Lord's supper; and beg of God that he would, for Christ's sake, keep us from wickedly dissembling in these our solemn vows; and that he who searches our hearts, and ponders the path of our feet, would, from time to time, help us in trying ourselves by this covenant, and help us to keep covenant with him.

Edwards's words speak to us down through the centuries. The final challenge of this book is to ask you in honesty, humility, and sincerity to sign it for God's glory, to seal your spiritual walk with our blessed Savior, the Lord Jesus Christ.

Signed_____

Endnotes

Step One

1. Jill Briscoe, *There's a Snake in My Garden* (Wheaton, Ill.: Harold Shaw, 1975), 13.
2. Ibid.
3. Ibid., 14.
4. Ibid., 15.
5. Ibid., 17.
6. Ibid.
7. Ibid., 20.
8. Ibid.
9. Ibid., 22.
10. Andrew Murray, *The Holiest of All* (repr. ed., Springdale, Pa.: Whitaker House, 1996), 41.
11. Ibid., 25.
12. *Moody Magazine,* January 1998.
13. *Discipleship Magazine,* 3 October 1994.
14. Ibid.
15. Ibid.
16. Briscoe, *There's a Snake in My Garden,* 37.
17. Ibid., 38.
18. Ibid., 39.
19. Ibid., 68.
20. Ibid., 151–52.
21. Ibid., 192–93.
22. Stuart and Jill Briscoe, *Marriage Matters!* (Wheaton, Ill.: Harold Shaw, 1994), 218–20.
23. Ibid., 87.
24. Ibid., 89–90.

25. Ibid., 145.
26. J. I. Packer, *Knowing God* (Downers Grove, Ill.: InterVarsity, 1993), 20.
27. Watchman Nee, *Christ the Sum of All Spiritual Things* (New York: Christian Fellowship, n.d.).
28. Edgar Young Mullins, *The Christian Religion in Its Doctrinal Expression* (Valley Forge, Pa.: Judson, 1917), 239.
29. Augustus Hopkins Strong, *Systematic Theology* (Philadelphia: Judson, 1907), 248.
30. Andrew Murray, *The Holiest of All* (repr. ed., Springdale, Pa.: Whitaker House, 1996), 461.
31. Nee, *Christ the Sum.*
32. Murray, *Holiest of All*, 42.

Step Two

1. Amanda Smith, *The King's Daughter* (Yanceyville, N.C.: Harvey & Tait, 1977), 7.
2. Ibid., 14.
3. Ibid., 15.
4. Ibid., 16.
5. Ibid., 16–17.
6. Ibid., 24.
7. Ibid., 25.
8. Ibid.
9. Ibid., 26.
10. Ibid., 27–28.
11. Ibid., 140–43.
12. Helmut Thielicke, *How the World Began* (Philadelphia: Fortress, 1961), 13–14.
13. Ibid., 72.
14. Martin Luther, *Luther's Commentary on Genesis* (Grand Rapids: Zondervan, 1958), 28.
15. J. I. Packer, *Knowing God* (Downer's Grove, Ill.: InterVarsity, 1973), 17–18.
16. Andrew Murray, *The Holiest of All* (repr. ed., Springdale, Pa.: Whitaker House, 1996), 469.
17. Ibid., 387.

Step Three

1. *Ladies Home Journal* 115, no. 4 (April 1998), 42.
2. Billy Graham, *Just As I Am* (San Francisco: Harper Collins/Zondervan 1997), 576.

3. Michael Green, *I Believe in the Holy Spirit* (Grand Rapids: Eerdmans, 1975), 153.

4. Andrew Murray, *The Holiest of All* (repr. ed., Springdale, Pa.: Whitaker House, 1996), 190.

5. Ibid., 138.

6. Jonathan Edwards, *An Humble Attempt* from "The Works of Jonathan Edwards," vol. 2 (Carlisle, Pa.: Banner of Truth Trust), 290.

Step Four

1. J. C. Metcalfe, *Molded by the Cross* (Fort Washington, Pa.: Christian Literature Crusade, 1997), 141.

2. Ibid., 9.

3. Ibid., 14–15.

4. Ibid., 18–19.

5. Ibid., 28.

6. Ibid., 33.

7. Ibid., 39.

8. Ibid., 40–41.

9. Reginald Wallis, "What Is the Deeper Meaning of the Cross?" in *The New Life* (London: Pickering & Inglis, n.d.), 45.

10. Stephen Olford, *Not I, but Christ* (Wheaton, Ill.: Crossway, 1995), 49–51.

11. Metcalfe, *Molded by the Cross*, 45.

12. Ibid., 60.

13. Ibid., 63.

14. Ibid., 66.

15. Ibid., 73.

16. Ibid., 87.

17. Ibid., 104.

18. Joseph Henry Thayer, *A Greek-English Lexicon of the New Testament* (New York: American Book, 1886), 352.

19. Steven Barabas, *So Great Salvation* (New York: Revell, n.d.), 88–89.

20. Olford, *Not I, but Christ*, 50–51.

21. Allister Smith, *Revival Before Our Lord's Return* (London: Keswick Week, Marshall, Morgan, and Scott, 1947).

22. Andrew Murray, *The Holiest of All* (repr. ed., Springdale, Pa.: Whitaker House, 1996), 112.

Step Five

1. J. Donald McManus, *Martha Franks: One Link in God's Chain* (Wake Forest, N.C.: Stevens Book, 1990), 22.

2. Ibid., 27.

3. Ibid., 33.

4. Ibid., 57.
5. Ibid., 95.
6. Ibid., 123.
7. Ibid., 169–70.
8. Ibid., 221–22.
9. Ibid., 225.
10. Andrew Murray, *The Holiest of All* (repr. ed., Springdale, Pa.: Whitaker House, 1996), 92.
11. R. C. L. Lenski, *The Interpretation of St. John's Gospel* (Minneapolis: Augsburg, 1963), 960.
12. Ibid., 48.
13. Murray, *The Holiest of All*, 488.
14. F. B. Meyer, *Peace, Perfect Peace* (New York: Revell, 1897), 7–8.
15. Murray, *The Holiest of All*, 394.
16. Miles Stanford, *Principles of Spiritual Growth* (Lincoln, Neb.: Back to the Bible, 1969), 62–63.

Step Six

1. Walter B. Knight, *Three Thousand Illustrations for Christian Service* (Grand Rapids: Eerdmans, 1952), 43.
2. Ibid., 42.
3. Ibid.
4. Ibid.
5. Henrietta C. Mears, *What the Bible Is All About* (Worldwide, 1953), 1.
6. William Temple, in J. I. Packer, *God Has Spoken* (Downers Grove, Ill.: InterVarsity, 1979), 77.
7. The following is an adaptation from *The Word of the Cross* by Lewis A. Drummond.
8. Packer, *God Has Spoken*, 52. Much of the argumentation is found in Packer's discussion of these issues. His work is most helpful and should be read in full.
9. Ibid., 158.
10. Ibid., 351.
11. Dewey M. Beegle, *Scripture, Tradition, and Infallibility* (Grand Rapids: Eerdmans, 1973).
12. Mears, foreword, in *What the Bible Is All About*.
13. David S. Dockery, *The Doctrine of the Bible* (Nashville: Convention Press, 1991), 81.
14. Beegle, *Scripture, Tradition, and Infallibility*, 301–302.
15. Ibid., 66–67.
16. J. I. Packer, *Keep in Step with the Spirit* (Old Tappan, N.J.: Revell, 1984), 238.

17. Andrew Murray, *The Holiest of All* (repr. ed., Springdale, Pa.: Whitaker House, 1996), 50.
18. Ibid., 49.

Step Seven
1. Evelyn Christenson, *What Happens When Women Pray* (Wheaton, Ill.: Victor, 1975), 113.
2. Andrew Murray, *The Prayer-Life* (Chicago: Moody), 17.
3. Walter B. Knight, *Three Thousand Illustrations for Christian Service* (Grand Rapids: Eerdmans, 1952), 506.
4. Ibid., 128.
5. Samuel Chadwick as quoted by Leonard Ravenhill, *Revival Praying* (Minneapolis: Bethany Fellowship, 1962), 440.
6. Andrew Murray, *In Christ in the School of Prayer* (Chicago: M. A. Donohue & Co.), 12–13.
7. O. Hallesby, *Prayer* (Minneapolis: Augsburg, 1931), 89.
8. Ibid., 29-30.
9. Ibid., 86.

Step Eight
1. Earl O. Roe, ed., introduction, in *Dream Big: The Henrietta Mears Story* (Ventura, Calif.: Regal, 1990).
2. Barbara Hudson Powers, *The Henrietta Mears Story* (Old Tappan, N.J.: Revell, 1957), 82.
3. Roe, 72.
4. Ibid., 74.
5. Ibid., 81.
6. Ibid., 89.
7. Ibid., 115.
8. Ibid., 133.
9. Ibid., 149.
10. Ibid., 152.
11. Ibid., 250.
12. Elisabeth O'Connor, *The Eighth Day of Creation* (Waco, Tex.: Word, 1971), 13.
13. John R. W. Stott, *One People* (London: Falcon, 1969), 24.
14. Ibid., 186.
15. Marcus Dods, *The First Epistle to the Corinthians, The Expositor's Bible* (London: Hodder and Stoughton, 1891), 276.
16. Archibald Robertson and Alfred Plummer, *A Critical and Exegetical Commentary on the First Epistle of St. Paul to the Corinthians, The International Critical Commentary* (Edinburgh: T & T Clark, 1953), 264.

17. Alexander Rattray Hay, *The New Testament Order for Church and Missionary* (New Testament Missionary Union, 1947), 177.
18. Ibid.
19. Ray C. Stedman, *Body Life* (Glendale, Calif.: Regal, 1972), 86.
20. Hay, *New Testament Order*, 178.
21. Stedman, *Body Life*, 57.

Step Nine
1. Charles Gallaudet Trumbull, *Taking Men Alive* (New York: Revell, 1938), 69.
2. Paul E. Little, *How to Give Away Your Faith* (Downers Grove, Ill.: InterVarsity, 1966), 26–45 *passim*.

Step Ten
1. Elisabeth Elliot, *These Strange Ashes* (San Francisco: Harper and Row 1979), 39.
2. Ibid., 81–82.
3. Elisabeth Elliot, *Through Gates of Splendor* (New York: Harper and Brothers, 1957), 26.
4. Quoted in "Love Has a Price Tag," *Decision Magazine*, 1997.